Praise for Brian Joiner's *Fourth Generation Management*:

I have just read Brian Joiner's book and find it to be an excellent guide to better management in today's world. It hits on the key elements of business, customers, employees, process, and most importantly, "boundary-lessness." I particularly like the examples given on things that have worked and things that haven't.

Brian Rowe
Chairman, GE Aircraft Engines

If you want to improve profits and assure a vibrant future while enhancing job satisfaction—yours and your associates—read and apply the principles of *Fourth Generation Management*. Brian Joiner, one of quality's giants, uses lively examples to illuminate elegant theory that will transform the way we lead organizations. If I were to start a business school today, Brian's book would be a centerpiece of the core curriculum.

John O. Whitney
Author of The Trust Factor and
Professor and Executive Director of the
W. Edwards Deming Center at the
Columbia Business School

Fourth Generation Management is a pragmatic, streamlined, and theoretically disciplined explanation of what today's leaders must do to assure the fastest possible rate of improvement. Brian Joiner explains the best of modern quality methods with vivid vignettes and a minimum of jargon.

Don Berwick, M.D., President
Institute for Healthcare Improvement
Boston, Massachusetts

Fourth Generation Management: The New Business Consciousness is a book filled with the lessons learned over a lifetime of experience in the study of management. Its message is so strong that it should be read by even the most experienced practitioners of quality management.

John Hudiburg
Former Chairman and CEO of
Florida Power and Light and
Author of Winning With Quality

Brian Joiner has done a masterful job of explaining variation in simple understandable English. For many managers, Brian's examples will be real eye openers.

A. Blanton Godfrey
Chairman and CEO
Juran Institute, Inc.

Organizations disappointed that their quality initiatives have not produced the expected benefits will find they are not practicing management as defined by Brian Joiner. Based upon my experience at Xerox, supplemented by benchmarking the best companies in the world, and the beneficial learning experience gained as a judge for the Malcolm Baldrige National Quality Award for five years, I believe any company that believes and practices the "Joiner Triangle" will achieve the level of benefits they expect. Dr. Joiner's book not only advises *what* should be done but also is filled with dozens of practical examples of *how* it should be done.

Frank J. Pipp, Consultant
Former Group Vice-President
Xerox Corporation

This is a well-written, informative book chock full of helpful, enlightening examples that bring the book to life. It transforms theory into practical experience that makes it a must for today's and tomorrow's managers to read.

Dr. H. James Harrington
Principal, Ernst & Young
President, International Academy for Quality

Brian has done an excellent job of pulling together everything he has learned over the last three decades and delivering it in a very readable fashion.

Ronald D. Schmidt
Chairman, President, and CEO
Zytec Corporation
Baldrige Award Winner, 1991

It has been said that quality management without statistics is smoke and mirrors. Brian Joiner has united statistical thinking with management thinking and has done so with a clarity and lucidity that will be appreciated by all managers regardless of technical background.

Harry V. Roberts
Co-Author of Quality is Personal *and*
Sigmund E. Edelstone Professor Statistics and
Quality Management,
Graduate School of Business, University of Chicago

Brian Joiner has captured the essence of the skills and understanding needed to lead our organizations into the next century. *Fourth Generation Management* should be on the desk or nightstand of anyone who believes that management practices which worked in the past will no longer suffice.

Dr. David Ward, Chancellor
University of Wisconsin, Madison

FOURTH GENERATION MANAGEMENT

THE NEW BUSINESS CONSCIOUSNESS

BRIAN L. JOINER

In collaboration with Sue Reynard

With contributions from
Yukihiro Ando, Paul Drewek, Robert Ferguson, Lynda Finn,
Patricia Fulgoni, George Hettich, Laurel Joiner, G. Thomas Jones,
Nick Kaufmann, Kevin Kelleher, William Lawton, Kevin Little,
Ralph Rosati, Peter Scholtes, Joel Smith, Ronald Snee,
Wm. Steinberg, Robert Stiratelli, Edward Sylvestre

MCGRAW-HILL, INC.

New York San Francisco Washington, D.C. Auckland Bogotá
Caracas Lisbon London Madrid Mexico City Milan
Montreal New Delhi San Juan Singapore Sydney Tokyo Toronto

Library of Congress Cataloging-in-Publication Data
Joiner, Brian L.
    Fourth generation management : the new business consciousness /
Brian L. Joiner in collaboration with Sue Reynard : with
contributions from Yukihiro Ando ... [et al.].
      p.   cm.
    Includes index.
    ISBN 0-07-032715-7
    1. Total quality management. 2. Organizational change.
3. Strategic planning. I. Reynard, Sue. II. Ando, Yukihiro.
III. Title.
HD62. 15.J65 1994
658.4—dc20   9340042

   3 4 5 6 7 8 9 0   DOC/DOC   9 9 8 7 6 5 4

ISBN 0-07-032715-7

The sponsoring editor for this book was James H. Bessent, Jr., and the production supervisor was Donald F. Schmit. It was composed by Impressions, a division of Edwards Brothers, Inc.

Printed and bound by R.R. Donnelley & Sons Company.

This book is printed on recycled, acid-free paper containing a minimum of 50% recycled de-inked fiber.

To my teachers and mentors,
  especially
    Dr. W. Edwards Deming

  To my families, those
    of my childhood
    of my adulthood
      especially my wife and business partner,
      Laurel W. Joiner

CONTENTS

Foreword

This book, by Dr. Brian L. Joiner, describes principles for 4th Generation Management. It explores the necessity to distinguish between costs and causes of cost. Costs are not causes: they come from causes. It is easy but fatal in management to confuse coincidence with cause and effect. It is wrong to suppose that if you can't measure it, you can't manage it. Most of the heavy losses caused by management today cannot be measured, yet they must be managed. Thus, management may spend $20,000 to train six people in a skill. This $20,000 is an investment. Its magnitude is known, $20,000. The future benefit (return on investment), however, will never be known, cannot be measured. Management's action is based on theory, prediction that the investment will in time pay off handsomely. Knowledge is theory. We should be thankful if action of management is based on theory. Knowledge has temporal spread. Information is not knowledge. The world is drowning in information but is slow in acquisition of knowledge. There is no substitute for knowledge.

W. Edwards Deming
12 September 1993

Preface

Ever since I was a little kid, I've loved finding better ways to do things—and hated waste and inefficiency. There was always a better way to cut and stack wood, or to carry water to the men in the field. Early on, I also learned the importance of teamwork. One day, I borrowed my cousin's new baseball to take to school. He made me promise not to let the other kids play with it. I lived up to the promise, but the other kids didn't make it easy—they wanted to use it, and for the following week, I was frozen out of their baseball games, which were played with an old beaten-up ball. And they were right: I hadn't been a team player. At the time, the lesson hurt, but I've since come to see it as a key lesson relatively easily learned.

In college, I studied industrial engineering and accounting so I could help companies improve. But then I worked as a beginning industrial engineer in the pea harvest and learned two more key lessons. The workers in the cannery did not like my time and motion studies! They "knew" I was there to make their lives harder. Clearly, we were not on the same team. That wasn't my idea of how improvement should feel! I also learned about data and experiments; mostly I learned that what I was asked to do was a wasteful and largely ineffective way to learn. But I also saw how important data were to making improvements that really worked.

I had heard that statistics offered better ways to use data to learn, so after that summer I began studying statistics. Over the final years of my studies and the beginning of my professional career, I discovered that statistics could do wonderful things. It could help people distinguish causes from symptoms, help them clearly find solutions where others saw only haze. But none of what I had learned could make managers want to improve, it couldn't make them work together with employees, it couldn't crack the walls between departments, it couldn't get customer information out of people who saw information as power.

I could see that when any of the stakeholders—customers, employees, investors, suppliers, or the community—was left out, they would find a way to freeze the others out later on. And no one would win, perhaps a key reason why quick hits always seemed to boomerang.

I knew that it was important to find better ways to do things and to eliminate waste and inefficiencies; that data could shed light on murky situations; that people needed to work together. But it took another 20 years working with large companies and small, with government, service, and manufacturing organizations, with top managers, with operators on the shop floor, before I had a good understanding of how all these pieces fit into a system of management that brings rapid learning and rapid improvement. It's a system I've come to call 4th Generation Management.

Acknowledgments

This book reflects things that I have learned from many people over a period of 55 years.

Important lessons were learned in childhood from my parents, Mr. and Mrs. R. L. Joiner, and from my aunts and uncles, Mr. and Mrs. J. L. Campbell and Mr. and Mrs. J. B. Lincoln, with whom I lived during parts of my childhood. The values, the principles, the thirst for knowledge, the zest for life that they provided shapes what is in this book, and, indeed, everything I do.

In my adulthood, my wife, business partner, and friend, Laurel W. Joiner, has been a constant source of inspiration and growth. My three children, David, Kevin, and Kristen, have also taught me much about life and caring.

In my professional life, I've had the opportunity to work with and learn from some of the very best. David S. Chambers, who kept the quality message alive through the dark years of the '50s, '60s, and '70s, was an early teacher and mentor at the University of Tennessee. Ellis R. Ott, who had a vision to establish a national center for statistics and quality improvement, guided my graduate studies at Rutgers University.

For eight years, I worked at the U.S. National Bureau of Standards (now the National Institute for Standards and Technology) under the wing of the finest statistical consulting organization in the world. Joe Cameron, Churchill Eisenhart, Jack Youden, Harry Ku, Joan Rosenblatt, Mary Natrella, and John Mandel all taught me a lot during my formative working years.

Lola Deming and I once shared an office—providing me with the opportunity in 1963 to meet her husband, W. Edwards Deming, with whom I've had the opportunity to work and learn. Many ideas in this book either originated from interactions with Dr. Deming or were greatly stimulated by those interactions. His impact on this work will be obvious to any student of the field.

For ten years at the University of Wisconsin–Madison, I had the opportunity to work with George E. P. Box and William G. Hunter, two other leaders in the development and application of effective statistical principles for improvement. And, for the past five years, I've had the opportunity to meet with and learn from Professor Noriaki Kano, one of the leading Japanese counselors in quality.

Many other people have also contributed importantly to shaping my thinking and thus to the ideas in this book: Tony Aldridge, Bill Armstrong, Charles Ashing, Ed Baker, Tim Ball, Gale Bryce, Cindy Butler-Phelps, Gary Cowger, Keiron Dey, Dan Doulet, John Dowd, Bob Galvin, Heero Hacquebord, Harold Haller, Jon and Jeff Heslop, Chuck Holland, Tracey Homburg, Lee Hunter, Taylor Huskins, Yoshinori Iizuka, Dennis Little, David Luther, Ron Moen, Hiroshi Osada, Frank Pipp, Gipsie Ranney, Brian Rowe, Bill Scherkenbach, Lou Schultz, Jerry Senturia, Dexter Squibb, Kent Sterrett, Takenori Takahashi, Myron Tribus, John Tukey, Ray Wachniak, Martin Wilk, and many more.

And finally, special appreciation goes to John Woods, who contributed a number of helpful ideas and served as project manager for this book, and to the following friends and colleagues who made very helpful comments on early drafts of the manuscript: Don Berwick, Jerry Brock, Jim Cortada, Roly Coates, John Dorsey, Liz Freeman, Tim Fuller, Conrad Fung, Lee Meadow, David Mergen, Jim Nelson, Tom and Patrick Nolan, Terri Potter, Harry Roberts, Dick Steele.

As always, I must say that none of these people are responsible for any shortcomings in the book—those are all "in the system."

Part One

Getting Better Faster

PROLOGUE

Jack walked through the door labeled Vice President of Marketing. Anna was just hanging up the phone.

"Well, Jack," said Anna, "that was Morrison I was just talking to. He told me we aren't going to be getting the Franklin business next year."

Jack grunted slightly. "Can't say I'm surprised," he said. "All my people over in Finance have been telling me for months that this was coming. . . . But I'm glad I'm not in your shoes! J.B.'s not going to want to hear the news."

"Yeah. Everyone knows how much he's been counting on launching our new product at Franklin. With their reputation in the business . . . if they bought from us, all the rest would jump in line."

"Did Morrison say why they were backing out?" asked Jack.

"Oh, he mumbled a bunch of things," Anna answered. "But everybody knows—though no one comes out and says it—that their new VP has had it in for us ever since we got him in trouble when he was an account rep."

"What reasons did Morrison say, though?"

"He said that they finally gave up on our being able to deliver our new model on time. He pointed out that the 15-month timeline we had initially promised has now stretched to over 18 months. He said they had to make a decision, and they just couldn't wait any longer. . . . What gets me mad is that no one over there really acknowledges their part in the delays . . . I don't know what we're going to do. But I'd better go tell Ed before he hears it from someone else."

Imagine you're in Anna's shoes, about to tell your boss—who in turn has to tell your CEO—that you have just lost a major customer, the flagship for the industry, one whose lead other companies readily follow. What would you do? Recommend firing the product development manager? Ignore this troublesome customer and look for business elsewhere? Write this off as a particularly difficult situation and

3

move on to the next project? Assign a task force to investigate this situation and come up with some recommendations? Do nothing?

This kind of difficult situation may sound familiar to anyone who's been in business for any length of time. What we do when faced with such situations, or better yet, what we do to prevent being in such situations, has a great deal to do with how successful we'll be. For many years, the approaches named above have been common responses to problems like these. All of them were among the instinctive reactions of the company that experienced the actual situation described.

But these executives, two years into their transition to 4th Generation Management, had second reactions that took them in different directions. They didn't ignore the problem. They stopped blaming the customer. They didn't fire people or assign a task force to investigate the situation. Instead, they rolled up their sleeves and worked together with their staff to expose the deep problems that led to this crucial failure. They discovered that the design process was not well-defined: almost every key player had a different version of how the process did (or should) work. The system was plagued by many problems: confusion, rework, equipment failures, errors in design specifications, miscommunication . . . the list went on.

How could it be that so many problems existed? In searching for explanations, the managers came to realize that all the major problems in this project were common to many projects—and, in fact, were linked to many seemingly unrelated problems throughout their organization. The roots ran deep. And thus the solutions they developed had widespread ramifications, solving many problems, not just those in product development.

These managers adopted a fundamentally different view of what their role could and should be. They still cared greatly about results. But now, they became involved in helping to develop better methods to achieve better results: achieving higher quality with lower waste. The mindsets they adopted represent a new management consciousness that is fundamental to business success today. The ingredients carry many names: Total Quality, TQM, Continuous Improvement, a passion for delighting customers, systems thinking, reengineering, business process redesign, just-in-time production, continuous flow manufacturing, lean production, supply chain management, employee empowerment, visionary leadership.

The many principles and techniques that concern managing for high quality with low waste have now begun to gel into a management

4

framework that I've come to call 4th Generation Management. Much of the synthesis of this new approach to management is the product of W. Edwards Deming, who is well known for his work both in the United States and in Japan (beginning in 1950). Other major contributors to this new consciousness include Russell Ackoff, Peter F. Drucker, Albert Einstein, Kaoru Ishikawa, Joseph M. Juran, Kurt Lewin, Taiichi Ohno, Peter Senge, Walter Shewhart, and Frederick W. Taylor.

Though many organizations are applying some of the pieces, few understand what it takes to pull these ingredients together to create an organization that functions as a single system to serve its customers, benefiting *all* stakeholders: customers, employees, shareholders, suppliers, and the community. The first part of this book provides an overview of the elements of this new framework and discusses underlying principles that tie them together. Subsequent sections describe each of the basic elements in more depth and present examples of how these principles are being used to create stronger, more successful organizations.

1
CHANGING THE WAY WE MANAGE

Years ago, I visited the headquarters and largest facility of a major midwestern corporation. Everywhere I went, the people told me how great this company was, how well they were doing, and how they were getting better every year. Having worked with companies that were making real progress, I could see this company was not as good as it thought it was. Where they saw improvement, I saw inefficiency. Where they saw gains, I saw a lack of real interest and concern for customers. Where they saw effective action, I saw managers unintentionally making matters worse. But I couldn't convince them they were in trouble. All they could see was that they were improving, getting better year in and year out.

At the time, I didn't know what to say to this company's managers to help them see they were in trouble. After all, they could point to at least some gain in many aspects of their operations. It wasn't until later that I figured out how I might have gotten through to them. The realization struck me that the important question was not "Are you improving?"—the important question was, "Are you improving *fast enough*?"

Take Company A in the figure on the next page. It started out ahead and its performance improved year after year. But what did it get for its efforts? It fell further and further behind.

How can that happen? How can you fall further and further behind while getting better and better? Answer: By having someone else get better *faster*, like Company B in the figure. How do the Company Bs of the world pass by the Company As? The key ingredi-

GETTING BETTER FASTER

ents are in learning about customer needs and translating those needs into high-quality products and services that flourish in the marketplace.

Think of the many industries you know where this has happened, where companies you once thought of as world leaders are now struggling. Automobiles, consumer electronics, steel, machine tools, computers, hotels, packaged foods, cameras. There is a long list when you start looking at it; companies in lots of industries have been in the position of Company A.

Many managers realize the importance of this chart: if they don't find ways to get better faster at things that count, they'll soon be outstripped by companies that do. How are we going to do that? How are we going to get better faster and faster, year after year?

The answer lies in 4th Generation Management.

THE FIRST THREE GENERATIONS

Let's begin by taking a quick look at three previously best-known ways to get work done.

1st Generation: Management by Doing—This is the first, simplest, most primitive approach: Just do it yourself. We still use it. "I'll take care of that, Frank." It's an effective way to get something done, but its capacity is limited.

2nd Generation: Management by Directing—People found that they could expand their capacity by telling others exactly what to do and how to do it: a master craftsman giving detailed directions to apprentices. This approach allows an expert to leverage his or her time by getting others to do some of the work, and it maintains strict compliance to the expert's standards.

3rd Generation: Management by Results—People get sick and tired of you telling them every detail of how to do their jobs and say, "Just tell me what you want by when, and leave it up to me to figure out how to do it." So you say, "OK. Reduce inventories by 20% this year. I'll reward you or punish you based on how well you do. Good luck."

All three of these approaches can be found in any organization today. Sometimes appropriately. Often not. There are times when we should do the work ourselves, 1st Generation Management. There are other times when new or inexperienced employees need close supervision and detailed directions: 2nd Generation Management. But look around your organization. Are managers using these strategies because they are appropriate? Because they think these approaches are effective? . . . or because they just don't know a better way?

And what about 3rd Generation Management: Management by Results? Doesn't it make a lot of sense to tell people what you want from them, then let them figure out how to do it? Surely this is better than treating employees like apprentices, telling them in detail exactly what they should do.

Third Generation Management sounds logical. It's an approach that is widely taught and used today, and it may be appropriate for objectives that have little interaction with other parts of the organization. But it also has serious, largely unrecognized flaws and inefficiencies that we can no longer afford. For example, we all want better figures: higher sales, lower costs, faster cycle times, lower absenteeism, lower inventory. There are three ways to get better figures:

1. **Improve the system.** Make fundamental changes that improve quality, prevent errors, and reduce waste. Example: reducing in-process inventory by increasing the reliability of operations.

2. **Distort the system.** Get the demanded results at the expense of other results. "You want lower inventories? No problem!" Inventories miraculously disappear . . . but at what cost elsewhere?!

3. **Distort the figures.** Use creative accounting. "Oh, we don't count those as inventory any more. . . . They're on our supplier's books."

Which of these options would you most want people to use? The first, of course: Improve the system. But most managers confess that they see a lot of distortion going on—distortion of systems, distortion of figures. Why? Because under 3rd Generation Management, the focus is on judging and rewarding people on *outcomes*. They are seldom provided with the knowledge or skills needed to achieve the first option; they are often poorly coached or trained how to *improve* a system; and they are usually only reviewed based on results, not improvements. So, to meet the demanded results, they resort to distorted systems and distorted figures.

4TH GENERATION MANAGEMENT

Nearly a decade ago, managers began asking me, "If you're saying that 3rd Generation Management is not getting us where we want to be, what's the alternative? Are you saying we should go back to doing everything ourselves or telling our employees every detail of how they should do their work? I can't see how that would help!" These managers were, of course, right. Going back to the older methods would not bring rapid, sustained improvement. The changing marketplace demands a move *forward*, to a new generation of management.

Fourth Generation Management recognizes the basic problems with the first three generations and incorporates methods for overcoming them. It avoids the limited capacity of 1st Generation, the micromanagement of 2nd Generation, and the distorted systems and figures of 3rd Generation. Fourth Generation managers care greatly about results but know that better results can reliably be obtained only through fundamental improvement. They become the champions of customer needs, the drivers of real improvement. They work together with other employees as partners to help develop better and better methods to get better and better results.

The Joiner Triangle

Over the years, I've searched for a way to describe the essence of 4th Generation Management. A sketch I developed many years ago with Laurie Joiner, my wife and business partner, is the only summary that has stood the test of time. We use it so often that it's now referred to as the Joiner Triangle:

The three corners of this triangle are:

THE JOINER TRIANGLE

- **Quality**—Understanding that quality is defined by the customer; developing an obsession for delighting customers—not being satisfied with merely getting rid of what annoys them but going beyond to understand their current and future needs deeply, to surprise them with products and services they didn't even know were possible. This understanding is no longer the domain of special groups within an organization; rather, it is shared with and further developed by every employee.
- **Scientific Approach**—Learning to manage the organization as a system, developing process thinking, basing decisions on data, and understanding variation.
- **All One Team**—Believing in people; treating everyone in the organization with dignity, trust, and respect; working toward win-win instead of win-lose for all stakeholders (customers, employees, shareholders, suppliers, the communities in which we live).

This model is simple, which I believe is one of its strengths. Anyone can quickly sketch it on a notepad or flipchart as a quick reminder of the core elements of 4th Generation Management. Without a simple model like this, it's easy to forget key elements. When faced with a difficult problem, managers can work their way around the triangle, looking for a critical point they may have forgotten: "Have we considered the customer's viewpoint? Do we know what the process is? Do we have any data? Are we acting as if we believe in people?"

Using a triangle reinforces the notion that the elements are interdependent: taken separately, they are not as powerful as when used together. The failure to recognize the interdependency of the elements is why so many other management initiatives have ultimately failed in the workplace. When you look closely at companies that really drove "teams" and "teamwork" in the 1980s, for instance, you find that many efforts produced mediocre results at best because the efforts were not directed toward customer-defined issues, and employees lacked the knowledge and training to use data effectively. Their efforts thus had little perceptible effect in the eyes of customers. A surge in "the customer is #1" rhetoric also seldom led to recognizable improvements because the efforts were not driven by data or an understanding of processes; decisions were based on opinion or presumed knowledge; and improvements that were identified were never captured or preserved as *methods* that would reliably achieve the needed results.

Seeing these failures time and time again was what inspired creation of the triangle. We saw that the companies making the most progress focused on quality as defined by the customer, used and understood data, processes, and variation, and built cooperation rather than competition. They were expanding markets, delighting more customers, streamlining their systems, sharply reducing wasted effort, and increasing revenue while reducing costs.

Here's an example that illustrates some key points about this triangle.

> *Herb and Ricardo were senior managers in a company that creates and produces specialty chemical products for its customers. One day, Herb asked Ricardo what he thought the key selling features were for the company's products.*
>
> *Ricardo, who had been in the business for years, said promptly, "Well . . . our products are a cut above the competition and I think we're doing a better job than we used to at shortening the delivery cycle. And, when a customer calls, we've got a great group of people who really know their stuff answering the phones . . . and the shipment almost always goes out that same week."*
>
> *"So you'd say we've got a high-quality product, friendly, competent service, and reliable delivery, right?"*
>
> *"Yeah. I don't think anyone could argue with that."*

"Don't be too sure," said Herb. "I just got the results of the market survey we commissioned a few months ago. Apparently our customers rated us behind our two main competitors in areas like 'friendliness of service' and 'reliability.' What would you say to that?"

"I don't believe it," replied Ricardo. "I talked to several customers just this week who raved about how great our technical service people are. And I know that our lab tests on reliability show we lead all our competitor's products. I don't get it."

Let me put you in the hot seat. If you were these managers, what would you do? Would you have another survey done to see if the results of this one were wrong? Would you talk to your technical staff and tell them they'd better shape up and start being friendlier to customers? Would you set out to improve reliability?

Herb and Ricardo realized that perhaps they didn't really understand how their customers defined quality. So they had their technical support and product development staff go out with the salespeople to talk with customers face-to-face, gathering data that reflected customers' attitudes. They soon came to understand that their customers' definitions of quality weren't the same as their own.

Many customers even had fundamentally different views of basic industry terms such as "reliability." The company defined it as the length of time a product could be used without failure under standard operating conditions. Many customers interpreted it as having a product work no matter what the environmental conditions were. Still others thought of reliability as having phone calls returned promptly from technical support staff. Only a small fraction of customers interpreted reliability the same way the company did. In short, *any time and money spent improving "reliability" using the company's definition would have been largely wasted because few of their customers would have noticed.*

By arming themselves with an understanding of its customers' perceptions, this company was able to make improvements in "reliability" that customers noticed and appreciated. This new understanding of customer needs also allowed the sales and technical staff to point out advantages of their products that their customers had previously overlooked. Simply being able to talk the customer's language had immediate benefits: customers began reporting much higher satisfaction with the service received from both the sales and technical support staffs.

The result: substantially increased sales and happier customers, with no increase in their costs. That's focusing on the right things in the right way.

The approach used by this company reflects the essential elements of 4th Generation Management:

- **Quality**: This company didn't ignore the survey results or repeat the survey hoping the results would come out differently. Instead, they dealt directly with customers: "Can you tell me a little more about what you mean by 'reliability'? . . . Can you give me an example of a reliability problem you've had? . . . Can you show me how you use our product?" The answers to these questions allowed them to focus on issues that would be noticed by their customers.

- **Scientific Approach:** The employees involved in this effort adopted the mindset that they had to back up their opinions with data (collected from customers). These data led them to understand how important it was for the product to work in a variety of environments. Minor changes in product design accommodated these environments.

- **All One Team**: The managers in this company didn't blame their employees for the survey results. They didn't merely exhort them to "try harder" or "be friendlier." Instead, the employees were involved in the improvement effort, trusted to make intelligent decisions on behalf of the company and its customers.

By finding out what was important to customers and spending resources wisely, everyone came out a winner: customers got better products and services, the company got increased sales, employees had more secure jobs . . . and the shareholders got greater profit.

These elements of the Joiner Triangle seem obvious at first glance. And, indeed, there's nothing particularly complicated about the individual pieces. But in years of working with managers, I've yet to meet a manager, myself included, who does *all* of these things naturally. Many of the ideas and methods of 4th Generation Management go against the grain of our natural instincts or against how we've been taught to manage our organizations. On the other hand, I've not yet met a manager who, having come to understand and develop even moderate skill in 4th Generation principles and methods, wants to go back to the old ways of doing business.

Later parts of this book explore the corners of the triangle in more depth, discussing current practices, showing why they are less effective than we need, and presenting alternatives that allow us to increase customer satisfaction, reduce waste, and thus increase profitability. These alternative methods are based on three recurring themes:

- Quality and productivity are two sides of the same coin, not opposing forces.
- Viewing our organizations as systems helps us achieve a customer focus and reduce waste and inefficiency.
- Rapid improvement requires rapid learning.

The next chapters explore each of these themes and explain why they are fundamental to business success.

2
QUALITY VS. PRODUCTIVITY?

One of the secrets behind the success of 4th Generation Management is not much of a secret any more. For decades, we were taught that if we wanted to improve productivity, we'd have to sacrifice quality, and vice versa. For some approaches, such as increased inspection, it is true that higher quality costs more. But we now know that in many, many cases, higher quality leads to lower costs.

COMPLEXITY

A beautifully simple example of the link between quality and productivity comes from Tim Fuller, who managed a large department that assembled electronic devices.

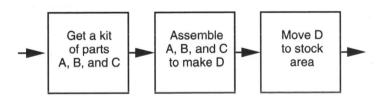

THE WAY IT WAS SUPPOSED TO WORK

The diagram above shows how the assembly operation was supposed to work: get a kit of parts, put them together, then move the assembled product to the stock area. (The real assembly had 100 parts, not 3 as shown, but the diagram gives an idea of what was involved.)

Tim knew that each of the 100 parts had a 98% chance of being there when needed. That sounds pretty good, doesn't it? Well, as Tim found out, at least 75% of the time one or more parts would be missing; in other words, 75% of the kits were incomplete when the employees began the assembly operation. So the work actually went like this:

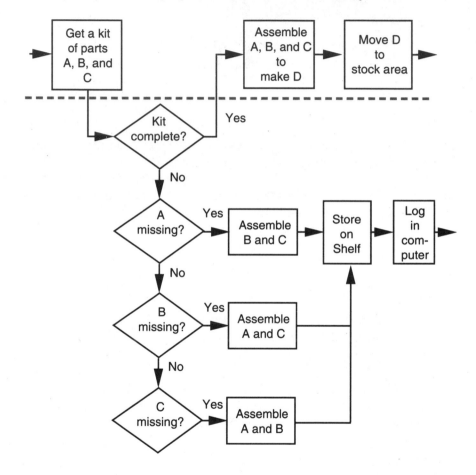

THE WAY IT REALLY WORKED

Employees would use what parts they had, complete a partial assembly, log it into the computer, and then store it on a shelf. When a part arrived, they'd go to the computer, find all the partial assemblies that were missing that component, retrieve them from the shelves, and complete the assemblies—or return them to the shelves if other parts were still missing.

In the diagram, steps above the dashed line are what Tim called the **real work**. They are the only steps that are necessary when everything works perfectly. Tim came to see all the steps below the dashed line as **complexity**, work that would never have to be done if complete kits were always available. That led Tim to a radical idea: He asked his employees to pretend there was a curtain between the beginning of their assembly operation and everything that came before it. They were not to take any kits past that curtain, into the assembly process, until they were complete.

What do you think happened to the quality of the outgoing products from that area? Quality went up because the employees could do the job in a consistent way every time—they didn't have to repeatedly adapt their procedures depending on which parts were missing. There was also less handling damage and obsolescence.

What do you think happened to productivity? You might think that having people wait around for a complete kit would waste time. Indeed, the initial productivity figures plummeted. That is why the final results were so shocking: after the initial shakedown, productivity doubled. Tim's people could do the same amount of work in half the time.

And there were more gains:

- Inventories went down dramatically because there were no partial assemblies to store all over the place, which also meant the need for complex computer systems to track partial assemblies disappeared.
- Reduced inventory freed up large amounts of space and made the work flow cleaner and simpler.
- Cycle time, the time from initiation to completion of assembly, was also reduced dramatically and became much more predictable. The time went down from 16.5 days with lots of variation to a dependable 5.5 days. In a few months, they brought it down even further, to 2 days.

Think about what these gains did for Tim's ability to do his job: to plan, to schedule, to manage. Also consider the effect that reducing complexity had on the ability of this group to make future improvements: there was now a much cleaner workflow, making it much easier to track down and eliminate other problems and to maintain the gains. Think about the opportunities for such improvement in your own area.

Cycle time reduction drives improvement

Was Tim focusing on quality? productivity? cycle time? The answer: all three. Improving the quality of the process (by eliminating the causes of complexity) improved the quality of the product, improved productivity, and reduced cycle time. These connections are so close that any one of them is a lever into improving the other two. In some cases, particularly where quality measures may be hard to define, focusing first on cycle time drives quality and productivity improvement. Any operation, no matter how faulty, can meet customer needs quickly once or twice . . . at a cost. But to do it day after day, and continuously reduce cycle time and total cost, is impossible unless we eliminate quality problems, trim slack, and reduce waste. A focus on cycle-time reduction thus drives a process focus and exposes complexity (rework and waste), just as does eliminating quality problems.

THE EFFECT ON PEOPLE

Tim's experience creates a pretty rosy picture, doesn't it? Well, stop a moment and think about how these changes affected people in Tim's group: the supervisors, assemblers, and other staff. What do you think happened to their jobs when quality problems largely disappeared, productivity doubled, and cycle time dropped from 16.5 days to 2 days?

The Supervisors' Job

Let's look first at the supervisors' job, shown on the next page. Their original job duties included expediting parts, retrieving partial assemblies, interrupting employees with instructions . . .

What do you call this work? Some people call it busy work, firefighting. I call it **whack-a-mole:** In many carnival arcades, you'll find a game where you take a big mallet and whack the moles as they pop out of their holes. Every time you whack one down, another one pops up somewhere else. The more moles you hit, the better your score. Isn't that what most of us do all day? Take care of one mole only to have another pop up somewhere else. Isn't that whack-a-mole? The difference, of course, is that when you go to a carnival, you have to pay them to play whack-a-mole. When you come to work, your company pays you to play!

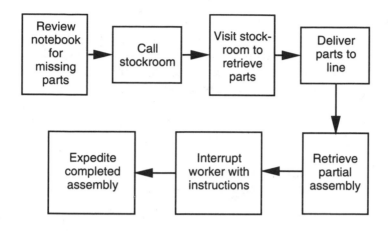

SUPERVISORS' OLD JOB

When Tim got rid of the complexity, he eliminated the need for much of the fire-fighting the supervisors had been doing. How do you think the supervisors felt when they showed up for work and all the whack-a-mole games had been taken away? How would you feel? Apprehensive? Threatened? Scared? Would you think, "What will happen to me?"

It's a common complaint that supervisors and middle managers are reluctant to try these new ideas. Can you understand why? With 4th Generation Management, their jobs will change drastically. There will be much less expediting, fire-fighting, playing whack-a-mole...instead, more gathering of appropriate data, finding out about customers, understanding processes, coaching and training. How many will think, "What'll happen to me? Will I be good at these things?" How many will consciously or unconsciously drag their feet? Our challenge is to create an environment where they can come out winners because of these changes.

The Employees' Jobs

Now consider the employees in Tim's area. They can now get the work done in half the time. What should we do now? The first part is simple: withdraw half the people from the area. We don't get the benefit of improvement until we take away most of the excess staff. But what comes after that? Do we help these people that we "take away" be successful somewhere else in the company?

21

Or do we lay them off? If we don't put them on the streets, how can we show gains on the bottom line? . . . But that isn't All One Team. It isn't win-win. It might seem like win-lose at first; that is, the company wins with quick gains and its employees lose their jobs. But such lay-offs are really "lose-lose." The quick gains rapidly disappear, and the company ends up losing the knowledge of the employees who are forced to leave and the trust of those who remain (most of whom will start spending more time politicking or trying to look good so they'll retain *their* jobs).

The solutions are not easy. Management's job, however, is to work through these challenges with a win-win mentality.

THE LEVERAGE IN IMPROVEMENT

Tim Fuller found huge leverage—gains in product and service quality, in productivity, in inventory reduction—from eliminating **complexity,** the unnecessary work caused by quality problems (in this case, incomplete kits). Such complexity, waste, and rework are prevalent in every organization.

Here's another quick example:

> At Joiner Associates a few years back we made an error in one person's paycheck, which affected the way taxes got withheld and paid. It happened at the end of a quarter, which meant our tax filings were affected. It was a simple mistake. It took five minutes to make, but several person-days to correct: phone calls back and forth, forms to file and refile, and so on.

The multipliers are colossal. Focused improvement efforts, here and there, can have an often unpredictably big impact on the effectiveness of an entire process. One organization improved its inventory practices and unexpectedly found its "book inventory" was so accurate it no longer needed to perform physical counts. This eliminated a costly step. Another company used two steps in a production process: punching the materials, then reaming them to get the right dimension. Improvements in the punch step made it so accurate that there was no need to ream. Similar gains occur when quality gets so good that inspection and rework become passé.

Because of leverage like this, organizations can often eliminate fully half of the work that is currently going on—work that does not have to be done when everything goes smoothly the first time.

The Deming Chain Reaction

The tremendous leverage from getting rid of complexity by improving the quality of what we do and how we do it is not new. Dr. Deming drew his famous chain reaction on the blackboard in Japan when he lectured there to top executives in 1950.

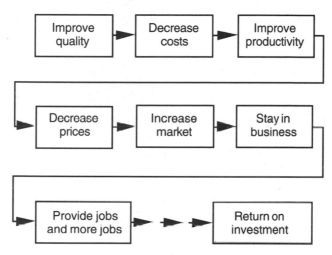

DEMING CHAIN REACTION

Dr. Deming said to work on quality. As we work on quality, we will be able to decrease costs and increase productivity. This allows us to decrease prices. If we have better quality and lower prices, we can expand our markets, stay in business, and provide jobs and more jobs. With his permission, we've added a final step to this chain: provide better return to investors.

With higher quality and lower costs, we have more flexibility to respond to the market; we gain the option of decreasing prices. And all of this enhances our profitability, which allows us to provide better return on investment to our shareholders. And producing more with the same resources raises our standard of living.

What if we try to enter the Deming Chain Reaction at "Decrease costs"? Or at "Return on investment"? Many companies have taken this route . . . but it is doomed to failure. By starting at "Decrease costs" instead of "Improve quality," they don't eliminate the *causes* of the costs. One cost-cutting drive therefore leads to further problems, which leads to yet another cost-cutting drive. The situation spirals downward. The list of the nationally recognized companies that are in this spiral is enough to scare anybody.

Real benefits come when managers begin to understand the profound difference between "cost cutting" and "eliminating the causes of costs." Think back to the assembly example in which there was a great deal of complexity, work that would have been unnecessary if all aspects of the process had worked correctly. Suppose we had tried to reduce costs by imposing a head count reduction target or overtime reduction target. What would that have done? All the complexity would have remained because none of its *causes* would have been removed. In fact, complexity and waste may have even increased as people distorted systems and distorted figures to meet their targets. Traditional measures of productivity would have improved with fewer people to do the work or without overtime to get all the work done. But the staff in this area would have had to take shortcuts. The problems might have lain hidden for a short period but would have eventually shown up in field failures or some other far more costly context and the downward spiral would have been set in motion.

A manager once gave me a knowing look and said, "Our slogan is 'we will save, no matter what the cost.'" Another manager elsewhere echoed those sentiments: "We've had any number of costly reductions!" Actions aimed at the middle or tail end of the Deming Chain Reaction lead to phantom gains . . . but very real losses.

As long as managers cling to the outdated belief that quality and productivity are opposites, they will be unable to accept the principles that underlie 4th Generation Management. By working together, using a scientific approach, and understanding the organization as a system, we can delight all of our key stakeholders with improved quality, lower costs, reduced waste, and improved productivity.

3
THE ORGANIZATION
AS A SYSTEM

An electronics company that produced instruments found itself edging more and more into the computer business. Customers who bought its computer components, however, were disappointed. The computers, produced by one division, would not work with the printers, which came from another division. To make matters worse, software developed in a third division was incompatible with both. The printer was great, the computer was great, the software was great—independently. Only one problem: they wouldn't work as a system, which is what the customer wanted.

This company, like far too many others, seriously damaged its market position by trying to make each separate piece of the organization as good as it could be rather than managing the organization as a *system of interrelated pieces*. The principle holds true for any collection of people or processes that we want to have function as a system. To manage our organizations more effectively, we must begin to think more in terms of *relationships* than of independent components.

One view of these relationships is depicted in Dr. Deming's 1950 representation of an organization as a system, as shown on the next page. There are inputs provided by suppliers, steps and processes by which work is done, and consumers who receive those outputs. From them we seek feedback to use for the design and redesign of our products and services.

This diagram captures lessons that are lost in the traditional, hierarchical view of an organization. It reminds us to consider the flow of work between functions and departments, and to remember that customers are the reason we exist. The impact of this view is profound.

25

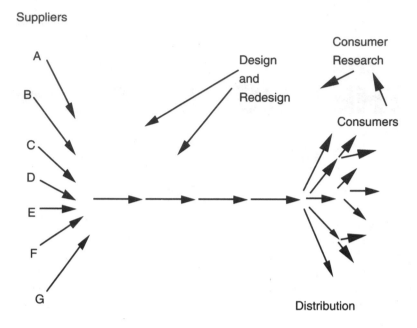

THE ORGANIZATION AS A SYSTEM

OPTIMIZING A SYSTEM

Stroll along the shoreline of the University of Wisconsin–Madison any spring morning and you're likely to see the crew teams out on the lake, working to perfect their synchronization. Their oars slice the water in unison; the sculls slice gracefully and quickly through the water. A beautiful sight.

A crew team is a finely honed system: it has individual elements all striving to reach a common goal. Destroying this system is amazingly easy. All we'd need to do is pit crew member against crew member. We could, for instance, create a forced distribution of grades where only one rower per team would receive an A, several would get Bs, Cs, or Ds, and at least one would get an F. Or we could post a list of names on the training room door with the names of the fastest rowers in green at the top and the slowest rowers in red at the bottom. Each rower would now be out to prove that he or she was the best on the "team," the person most deserving of the top grade, most deserving to be at the top of the list. That simple change would cause each rower to be more concerned with performing at his or her maximum speed than in working together for the benefit of the entire team.

The consequences of changing from a team-centered to an individual-centered focus was filmed for a video program on 4th Generation Management. When each crew member rowed at his or her individual best, the result was chaos. The scull moved forward erratically, veering in one direction then another. Crew members had trouble rowing effectively: an oar got pulled from a rower's grasp, other rowers floundered, none developed an effective stroke or efficient rhythm. Speed was minimal.

The racing scull as a system performed poorly when its components tried to maximize their individual performance; it had much better performance when crew members paced themselves to find the best fit with their fellow rowers. It is that pacing that allows the team to achieve maximum speed and accurate directional control. This lesson translates into a guiding principle of 4th Generation Management: **We need to work together to optimize the system as a whole, not seek to optimize separate pieces.**

> *Al had come to his manager's office to report on his engineering group's new design breakthrough.*
>
> *"This is great stuff, Harry. We'll be able to save over $100 per assembly with this new configuration. What do you think?"*
>
> *Harry glanced over the figures and nodded encouragement. "This sure sounds promising.... What will it take to get the equipment retooled?" he asked.*
>
> *"The retooling costs are minimal," answered Al. "But we think the production cost in our area will go up about $20 per assembly."*
>
> *"And where will the overall savings be realized?" asked Harry.*
>
> *"The changes won't have much effect on the work in our area. The real savings in time and money show up in final assembly," Al said. "I'd guess they'd be reflected in Randy's budget."*
>
> *"But we'll have to absorb the increased costs in our budget?" Harry asked.*
>
> *"Yeah, I guess so," said Al.*
>
> *"Well, uh, let me think about this for a while. It's a pretty tight year, you know. I'll get back to you."*

*Al was surprised by Harry's lack of enthusiasm. Surely the
company wouldn't let this opportunity slip by ... but perhaps
he'd better not press the issue.*

The design changes Al's team recommended never got implement-
ed. Though Harry's first reaction was to go for the savings, his self-
preservation instinct soon kicked in. Going with Al's recommendation
would mean he'd have to come in over budget while some other manager would be able to show significant savings. With his area under
tremendous pressure to reduce costs, he didn't want to jeopardize his
career. He kept mulling over the opportunity but never made the final
decision to go with the recommendation. As a result, his company lost
the chance to save hundreds of thousands of dollars each year—savings it might have been able to share with customers in terms of steady
or lower prices, something that would have given them an advantage
in the marketplace.

**Optimizing separate pieces destroys the effectiveness of the
whole.** For the organization to work well as whole, the components
must work together.

Cooperation and Win-Win

Harry knew that his chances of getting a raise, promotion, or
bonus depended on whether he met his numbers: reduced inventory,
lower costs. Under the current system, Harry would pay a stiff price for
cooperating with other managers. For customers and the company to
win, Harry would have to lose. Should we blame Harry for not putting
himself on the wrong end of a win-lose situation?

For a systems view to prevail, companies must find new approaches that create win-win outcomes for all players. Some companies, for instance, get managers together monthly to discuss ways to
reduce *total* costs. The group of managers as a whole shares the recognition for continuously improving the system's overall effectiveness.
That kind of win-win, All One Team environment would have encouraged Harry and his engineers to share their breakthrough ideas, and
the company would have realized significant savings.

We can optimize a system only when we accept some less-than-
optimum functioning of the pieces to optimize the system as a whole.
The common sense of this approach is intuitive, at least when people
are dealing with relatively small-scale efforts. The irony is that it is

devalued when it's needed most, where it could most benefit the entire organization:

> *A company had a number of divisions that sold various food ingredients to bakeries and other food preparation companies. Like most businesses, each division gave its major customers special care and attention. Yet, in this case, some customers who were critically important to one division were minor customers to another division. And minor customers often received second-class treatment. The customers, of course, made no such distinction: they just knew they got great treatment one day from this company and lousy treatment another day.*
>
> *Had these divisions been acting as independent suppliers, the differential treatment would have been bad enough. But in some ways this was worse: they were* competing *internally. Divisions with higher profits got larger executive compensation. As a result, the executives of these divisions did not go out of their way, to put it mildly, to help each other.*
>
> *Then this company got a new chief executive officer, one inclined toward 4th Generation principles. He was quite startled to be told privately by each business head, "I'm your friend and doing good things, but be careful of those other guys." He began to imagine the huge losses that ensued from this form of win-lose, optimize-the-separate-pieces thinking. Changes had to be made, and soon.*

This new CEO changed the executive compensation system so that the overwhelming share was based on companywide profitability. He put in place a system of meetings so his business unit heads met regularly to talk about common issues. He created a clear aim for the company: to be the leading food ingredient supplier in North America. And he made other important changes. Result: a substantially stronger, more profitable company with loyal customers.

Many companies fall into the trap of treating separate units as somehow independent of each other. They throw loops around each functional area or each business unit and try to optimize those pieces separately.

> *One executive was shocked to find that his organization had 132 "profit" centers (most of which never had any revenues), each trying to optimize its own profit. It's hard to imagine the*

29

destructive forces that were loose: time spent arguing about transfer prices, games played moving inventory. . . . He changed to one profit center so they could all work together.

Looking at a system as a whole is not easy. Often times the *interactions* among the parts are obscure:

A newspaper set out to reduce the amount of scrap newsprint and achieved impressive results. But some time later they noticed the number of customer complaints about wrinkled paper and ink rubbing off the pages had skyrocketed. No one saw the connection until an outsider pointed out that the increased complaints were linked to the fact that the company had only changed its rules on what *to scrap; it hadn't changed the* need *to scrap.*

The interdependencies within any system are often exceedingly complex and widely separated in time and space. A change in one area frequently has major unpredicted consequences in some other area, days, weeks, months, or even years later—interactions that are often overlooked, ignored, or misunderstood. Being less rigorous about what it would scrap allowed waste in one area to go down but led to productivity problems in other areas, and, some time later, to reduced sales. The downward spiral was underway. These negative aspects of the interdependencies are often made worse by an organization's pyramid structure and emphasis on competition. A reliance on win-lose instead of win-win erects barriers between people and departments, and information that might reveal the unintended consequences of actions in one area rarely gets shared. We learn by taking action and getting feedback. If we can't get the feedback, it's hard to learn. **Optimization requires a win-win orientation and systems to make cooperation happen.**

The Bigger the Loop, the Better

The companies just described got good results from breaking down barriers within the organization: Their executives threw loops around the entire organization and asked, "What can I do to make this system as a whole operate better?" Eventually, the loops we draw extend beyond our organizations:

A company looked and looked but couldn't find a cause for severe problems that suddenly appeared in its products. Finally, it discovered that a supplier five tiers *back (the supplier of the supplier of the supplier . . .) had made a minor change in materials that had a very major effect down the line.*

The company was lucky they were able to uncover the problem. It had recently reduced its number of suppliers, working on a long-term basis with fewer suppliers rather than continuing its old "revolving door" practice where work was awarded primarily on price tag. Working in close cooperation with fewer suppliers allowed this company to expand its improvement efforts beyond its corporate boundaries, to throw a larger loop around most of its supply chain, and thus to learn more rapidly how to make the entire system work well for its customers. **The bigger the loop, the bigger the gains.**

A SYSTEM WITHOUT AN AIM IS NOT A SYSTEM

The need to unite an organization as a system is widely felt. I've asked innumerable middle managers what they would most like to improve about their organizations, and almost all have responded, "Break down barriers between departments." For these barriers to be broken, an organization must have a shared *aim*.

Although many organizations today would say they have an aim, few have one that employees know about, understand, and actually work toward. Without a shared aim the elements of the organization have no guidepost by which to navigate. They operate as separate fiefdoms, each pulling in its own direction

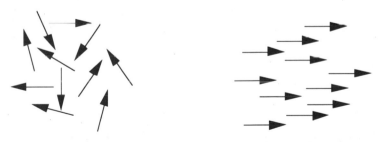

ORGANIZATIONAL ALIGNMENT

One manager told me, "We found many of our fiefdoms even have castles with moats!" Until all the pieces of an organization are headed

31

in the same direction, they will never function as a system. The barriers will remain as long as people and departments are pulling in different directions.

Ask most recent MBAs what the aim of a company (*any* company) should be, and the ready answer is "to maximize shareholder wealth." Such an aim works poorly in aligning the arrows for a sustained period. The best aims—those most likely to produce organizational cohesion—are connected to customer needs:

- "To provide vehicles that help people and goods move freely"
- "To provide products and services that help companies manage more effectively"
- "To provide healthcare services that improve the quality of life for patients and their families"
- "To move freight across North America"

Companies that have aims attached to a particular product or service—"to provide outstanding carburetors" or "to provide outstanding rail service"—often run into problems because those specific products or services can become outdated. For example, virtually all engines now use fuel injectors instead of carburetors, and some carburetor producers have been caught short, not thinking about their business from the perspective of customer needs. Railroad companies that thought of themselves as being in the "railroad business" instead of the business of "helping people move goods across the country" were blinded to the opportunity to integrate services such as trucking with their rail operations.

Finding a customer need, filling it well, and providing high value with low waste is starting at the head of the Deming Chain Reaction. Organizations that do this well receive all of its benefits: increased customer satisfaction, expanded revenues, better job security, and increased shareholder wealth. That is why management must develop an effective aim and ensure it is incorporated into the organization's short- and long-term strategies and actions.

THE BIGGEST OPPORTUNITIES LIE IN THE SYSTEM

Another way that a systems view influences managerial thinking is by making us more cognizant of the way in which all the elements of a system contribute to its success.

Standard practice is to believe or at least act like problems would go away if only employees would do their jobs either faster or the right way every time. This approach to improvement leads us to hold people culpable for problems. When a problem occurs, we keep asking "why" until we find a "who." How well does this work in practice? Not very well.

Using data to guide our search for causes and to evaluate changes has led 4th Generation managers to see that performance is largely determined by the system within which employees work: its policies, processes, procedures, training, equipment, instructions, materials. These factors powerfully affect how well an employee can do his or her work. Individual skill, ability, and motivation are important but play a much smaller role than previously assumed. When problems arise, therefore, it is more effective to focus our attention first on the other elements of the system: hence the increasingly popular phrase, **blame the process not the person.** We need to ask, "How did the process *allow* this to happen?"

> *David Couper, the former chief of police in my hometown of Madison, Wisconsin, was aware that the public often thirsted for blame when serious problems arose. But, after learning about 4th Generation Management, he changed his own response to problems such as when officers were involved in high speed chases. "First, I get the details of what happened," he said. "Then I ask what policy, process, or system might have contributed to the problem."*
>
> *He no longer wasted time trying to figure out who was to blame for a problem; rather, he and his officers spent their time more fruitfully by looking for processes and methods they could change to prevent recurrence. Doing this changed his life, he said, as well as the atmosphere of the entire department. "I used to dread coming to work having to deal with the 'whos,' now I look forward to coming to work to deal with the 'hows.'"*

Chief Couper's approach reflects a belief that most problems are the fault of flaws in a system and therefore can only be effectively addressed by management.

Worker-controllable Problems

The idea that most problems are due to a the system or process and not to the individual worker is not new. By the early 1950s, Dr. Joseph M. Juran had found in studies in a wide variety of companies that an average of only 20% of the production-level problems turned out to be worker-controllable. By "worker-controllable," he meant that people

- had the means for knowing what they were supposed to do.
- had the means for knowing what they were actually doing.
- had the means to close the loop between what they were doing and what they should be doing.

Dr. Juran found that the lion's share of problems—a full 80%—were, in this sense, beyond the control of the individual worker. Thus, if our employees all did their jobs as well as possible every time, no more than a fifth of our problems would go away. In other words, the vast bulk of problems lie in the processes, the methods, the systems, the policies, the equipment, the materials—things that only management can change.

Dr. Deming says in his experience the ratio may be even worse: perhaps 96% of problems can only be removed by management, leaving less than 4% the responsibility of individual employees. Does that mean managers, as individuals, should be blamed for that 80% or 96% of the problems? That's the same trap. We must work to overcome our natural instinct to blame the person closest at hand. Executives and mid-managers alike must look at what it is that constrains them to act the way they do: what past practices, policies, guidelines, unspoken taboos, and personal experiences shape their decisions, their approaches ... then work together to change anything that needs changing—so together they can eliminate the 80% to 96%.

As long as we personalize problems—think about them only in terms of *who* is at fault—we're going to continue to have them, because the causes more likely reside in the system than in a person. Blaming people is a low-yield strategy for improvement; the biggest opportunities, the biggest leverage, lie in improving our work processes.

Pushing for Deep Fixes

We can expand on this idea of fixing problems within systems even further:

Steve, head of development for a small software firm, had just gotten into work one day when he got a call from David, the firm's president.

"Get on a plane! We're only three days away from sending our new product to the first test sites—and I just found out we don't have a signed contract with the distributor! We've got to get

a contract signed before the product is sent out. You've got to fly to the coast to finish the contract negotiations by Wednesday, so it can be signed on Thursday. I don't know how it happened that we got this far without a contract!"

There weren't any options for Steve to consider. He hopped on a plane and spent the next two days rushing from meeting to meeting, FAXing contract drafts back and forth between offices, and finally sending the contract overnight express to the last person who had to sign it. The ink was barely dry when the new product hit the market.

If you work for a perfect company, you may be thinking to yourself, "How stupid of that firm to jeopardize a major effort like that with such sloppy planning." But if you work for a typical company, you're probably saying, "Things like that happen all the time around here."

Fortunately, Steve's company knew something about process thinking. The managers decided to learn more about this situation. They asked: "Was this a one-time event or is it symptomatic of other problems we're having?" The answer was that they often ran into problems like this. A little more investigation showed that a common thread was "contracts." Any time the company needed to deal with contracts, many critical steps fell through the cracks.

This example illustrates what my colleagues and I have come to call **Levels of Fix.** The notion is simple: many problems in an organization arise from the same deep causes. Thus the deeper we can push a fix, the more problems we'll be able to solve or prevent—and the more rapidly we'll improve. In practice, it's helpful to think about three levels:

- **Level 1: Fix the Output**—Promptly correct problems that appear in existing output or that occur during the delivery of a service.
- **Level 2: Fix the Process**—Change the process that allowed the problem to occur; develop ways to prevent its recurrence.
- **Level 3: Fix the System**—Change the system that allowed the faulty process (that led to the faulty product or service) to operate with these flaws.

For Steve's company, the Level 1 **output fix** was flying him to the coast to get the contract signed: that fire-fighting was critical to save this product launch but did nothing to prevent the same problem from reappearing. The Level 2 **process fix** for this company was to look at the process of negotiating and signing contracts. They ended up creating a checklist of contract issues that each manager would review before entering negotiations with a potential supplier, customer, or partner. Contract issues are now dealt with up front, long before they lead to last-minute panic. These changes helped clean up that faulty process but neglected a still deeper issue: how that faulty process had been allowed to exist in the first place.

In searching for a Level 3 **system fix**, the executives of this company found that almost every area of the company had problems with legal issues: employee benefits, trademarks, copyrights, contracts, international trade, purchasing agreements, and on and on. They also discovered that many times managers didn't need a detailed legal opinion that would take days or weeks to research; instead, often a ballpark response given that day allowed them to respond quickly to issues without getting the company into legal quagmires. Part of the system-level fix they put in place was to make it easier for managers throughout the company to contact a lawyer and to get quicker responses when they encountered a potential legal issue.

High-level managers, in particular, should look for these common problems and push for deeper and deeper levels of fix. Tim Ball, a consultant and friend from New Zealand, told me years ago:

> *"You know, Brian, I've found that I can take any five problems from anywhere in a company, and if I push deeper and deeper, I find that they all stem from the same core issues."*

The challenge in Level 3 system fixes is to find these same deep core issues, then take action to remove them. That's how we slow down the flow of moles that we need to whack. What do these deep issues tend to look like? Dr. Deming captured most of them in his famous 14 Points, including:

- Lack of a clear aim (constancy of purpose) for the organization.
- Barriers between departments or businesses; failure to optimize the company as whole.
- Management by rewards and punishment on achievement of goals (3rd Generation Management).
- Reliance on inspection and rework to fix problems rather than on effective prevention.
- Failure to understand that suppliers are part of our system; reliance on pitting supplier against supplier using price-tag purchasing.

Some of these built-in system flaws can be solved only by dedicated efforts to uproot and change the destructive practices; but others are nothing more than policies we can change relatively easily. Tim Fuller's assembly operation, for example, achieved major gains by changing a *policy* about when to start the work: there was no extra machinery, no retraining, no change in paperwork, no redefinition of what the basic work was. The old policy of starting work on incomplete kits was simply a built-in flaw in the system. Our work as managers is to become detectives, using data to search for clues that lead us to such flaws. Solutions are often simple and obvious once a flaw is isolated.

USING LEVERAGE POINTS

By pushing for deeper levels of fix, we are leveraging our efforts, attempting to remedy many problems by attacking one deeply rooted cause. This same notion is true in other ways as well. Every system, no matter how large or how small, has steps, pieces, or components that, when improved, substantially improve the performance of the system as a whole. These **leverage points** are small in number but big in effect.

Thinking in terms of leverage points is important, from both a practical and a theoretical view. Time and time again I've encountered organizations, divisions, departments, and even individuals who deceive themselves into thinking they can manage 20 priorities. These issues attained priority status presumably because of their potential impact on the organization's success. But by having 20 "priorities," we end up having none. Organizations that can focus on the one, two, or perhaps three most important leverage points have much more success. For example:

- Most customer complaints typically concern only a handful of your products and services.
- The biggest budget overruns arise from only a few sources.
- The majority of defects or errors in a process will occur at only a few of the process steps.
- Most revenues come from only a few customers or types of customers.

An important way to identify leverage points is thus to separate the **vital few** from the rest. To be clear about who our top few customers are, for instance, and what few problems account for the most customer dissatisfaction. These few will provide opportunities for great leverage. In the 1950s, Dr. Joseph M. Juran demonstrated the importance of such thinking in quality improvement and called it the **Pareto Principle**. Vilfredo Pareto was an Italian economist who in the early 1900s observed that a relatively few people held the majority of the wealth. Dr. Juran pointed out that this principle applies in a wide variety of situations. He also called it the **80/20 rule,** since, in his observations and tests, roughly 80% of the problems were typically caused by only 20% of the contributing factors.

The **Pareto chart** powerfully brings home this idea. It is a type of bar chart that captures the impact or frequency of different problems. The chart below, for instance, shows the frequency of different types of injuries. As you can see, in that company, three types of injuries—contusions, strains, and sprains—accounted for the vast majority of incidents.

Seldom can we solve a complex problem all at once. Usually, we need to focus in on specific components of the problem, which is what

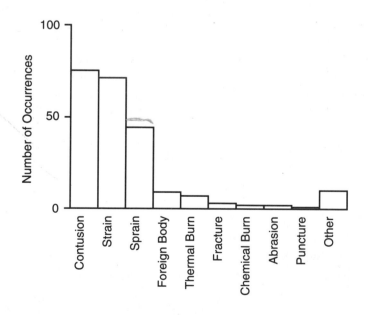

PARETO CHART OF INJURIES

Pareto thinking and Pareto charts help us accomplish. Generally, we get much greater leverage by focusing on reducing the largest source of trouble than we do from working to totally eliminate any of the smaller sources.

This idea of focusing in leverage points surfaces in two other ways when we seek to improve processes: critical paths and bottlenecks.

Critical paths

> *In our new product development process, we shortened the time for a number of operations, only to find it had no effect at all on our overall development time.*

Where did this company go wrong? They shortened the time for operations that were not on the **critical path.**

In the sketch below, each arrow represents the calendar time required for an operation. The bold arrows indicate operations on the critical path; they determine the minimum time required for the process. Each of the critical path operations cannot start until other functions are completed. Shortening the time for other operations will not shorten the overall project time.

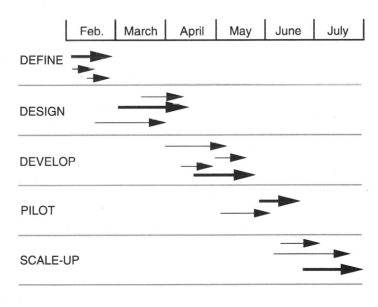

A CRITICAL PATH

39

Bottlenecks

The flashing lights warned drivers that three lanes would narrow to two for several miles before expanding to three again.

It seemed that everything had to go to Mary for approval ... and Mary was often tied up in other key activities. Delays were inevitable, and many projects took longer than planned.

The new measurement equipment was wonderful—microscopic details scarcely visible before were now clear. But it was in great demand ... and expensive, *so much so that an additional machine was out of the question.*

These examples illustrate **bottlenecks**, points in a process that limit the output of the process as a whole. Knowing how to manage a process in light of its bottleneck(s) is critical to improving overall capacity.

Leverage-point thinking

Knowing where the leverage points are in our organizations is critical in determining priorities for both our long-term and short-term strategies. This knowledge helps us focus on improving the right things. Here are some questions that help stimulate new thinking about leverage points:

- If we were to improve this, would it have the most impact on expanding the number of customers who will be pleased to buy our products and services?
- If we were to improve this, would it have the biggest impact on solidifying the loyalty of the customers we now have?
- If we were to join forces with another organization to tackle this opportunity, would it have a substantial impact on our capabilities?
- If the market were to change in some probable ways, is this our area of greatest vulnerability?
- If we were to improve this, would it have the greatest impact on reducing our overall cost structure?
- Why are we doing this at all?
- Why are we doing it this way?

It is unlikely that you'll be able to develop exact answers to these questions, but even rough answers will indicate where a leverage point may be. If an opportunity doesn't seem to have much leverage, look for something else to work on. And, of course, the more we have appropriate data to support our answers, the more effective we're likely to be.

SHAPING THE FUTURE

Applying the system principles discussed in this chapter can have a profound effect on both our organization's immediate future and its long-term prospects. Identifying leverage points and thinking about what's best for the system as a whole can help us overcome long-standing barriers to improvement. Defining the aim of our "system" and communicating that aim to all employees will help people determine their priorities and enhance their customer focus.

But the impact of systems thinking can extend even further. By thinking in terms of systems, by drawing larger and larger loops, we can help shape the future. As you and your organization begin to expand the boundaries of your systems to include your customers, suppliers, communities, and competitors, think about expanding the time boundary as well. Consider, for instance, what kind of environment will allow all your stakeholders to win not only today but also for decades to come.

For example, many chemical companies are working cooperatively with competitors to provide a cleaner environment and thus are helping to shape the regulatory requirements of the future. They could, of course, wait for the others to develop regulations, but often this leads to a mix of useful and useless (or even counterproductive) requirements. Some might argue that these companies are only being self-serving. And in a sense they are. But such efforts will only be successful in the long run if these companies truly dedicate themselves to creating win-win not only for themselves but also for their customers, suppliers, shareholders, and communities.

Similarly, companies in many industries are working together to develop common standards to eliminate differences that really have no practical value. These efforts have led to the development of common connectors for electronic devices, shared methods for measuring the properties of materials, and common software standards, to name a few. Among other benefits, this allows suppliers (and other companies that supply related products) and their customers to become more efficient.

41

As we come to see our organization as a system, we appreciate more and more the importance of the basic principles discussed above:

- Optimizing the pieces destroys the effectiveness of the whole.
- Interdependencies are often complex and widely separated in time and space.
- Optimization requires cooperation, win-win.
- The bigger the loop, the bigger the gains.
- A system without an aim is not a system.
- Blame the process, not the person.
- Push for deep fixes.
- Look for leverage points.
- Shape the future.

Applying these lessons will help focus our attention on improvements that will bear the biggest fruit. We can capitalize even further on these improvements through the third theme introduced early and discussed in the next chapter: rapid improvement requires rapid learning.

4
RAPID LEARNING, RAPID IMPROVEMENT

A senior manager's curiosity grew as he and several other managers reviewed two improvement teams that had nearly eliminated problems that had plagued the company for years. The teams made their presentations, discussed the results of changes they had already made, and recommended further action.

At the end of the meeting, the senior manager said, "There is not a single solution you have discussed today that hasn't been around for a long time. I've heard them all before. How is it that you're now able to make substantial improvements when you weren't able to in the past?"

A team member was quick to answer: "It's the data, the process focus, and the teamwork." The others nodded in agreement.

"Can you say a little more?" said the manager.

For one thing, said the teams, the solutions they ended up using were only a few out of the dozens of possibilities that had been considered over time. The data, process focus, and teamwork allowed them to identify which of the ideas, in what configuration, would work in practice.

This company had overcome a common problem. Every day, in every organization, people have *opinions* about how to make things work better, and, every day, we take a lot of actions based on these opinions. Still, the same problems keep rearing their ugly heads, over and over again. We keep "solving" these problems and reinventing the same wheels because we lack effective mechanisms for *learning*. And without effective learning, we lack sufficient knowledge to *improve rapidly* . . . in other words, without an effective way to find out where the moles are coming from, to block off the key tunnels, we just keep on playing the same old whack-a-mole games day after day.

Rapid learning is thus the third critical mindset that fuels 4th Generation Management. Together with an understanding of the links between quality and productivity and of systems thinking, it helps to create a foundation for translating theory into effective action. **Rapid learning is the best survival skill we can grow in our organizations.** I recently heard a radio commentator remark that if the effort to develop electric cars succeeds, the playing field will be level again for all car makers because the old manufacturing technologies will be useless. I disagree. Some automakers have invested a great deal of time, money, and effort in learning how to learn faster: how to gather data and use it effectively to shape decisions, how to root out the deep causes of problems, how to run experiments to determine the optimal operating conditions of complex machinery, how to rapidly improve design processes. There is no doubt. These companies will be better able to adapt their operations, to learn new technologies quickly, and to *improve* on the new technologies than those organizations who have not learned how to learn rapidly. The bigger the change, the farther the old guard will be left behind.

LEARNING FROM DATA: PLAN-DO-CHECK-ACT

The cornerstone of rapid learning is **Plan-Do-Check-Act (PDCA).** The basic notion of PDCA is so simple that when I first heard it I felt I understood it in five minutes. Now, more than a decade later, I think I might understand it some day.

    P: plan what you're going to do and for how you will know if it works

    D: do; carry out the plan

    C: check; evaluate the outcome, learn from the results

    A: take action

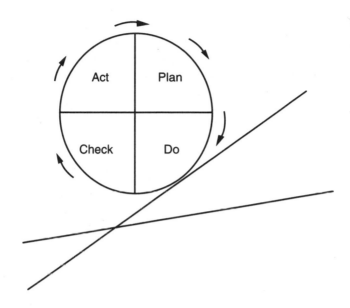

THE PDCA CYCLE

The PDCA wheel is a simple, flexible model that has been adapted to a broad range of situations. Let's look at some examples.

- A custodian found people continually putting trash into the aluminum recycling bins. He came up with an idea, made a simple cardboard baffle with a hole in the shape of a can, and wrote on it "aluminum cans only." He tried out this new baffle on three recycling containers. Each day, he looked at the results. The conclusions were obvious: almost no undesired trash in the bins with the new baffle. He then took action to put baffles on all recycling containers. He solved the problem within a week. With one turn of the PDCA wheel he made a plan, carried out a small-scale test, and checked the results. With another turn he spread the solution to all recycling bins.

- To close the corporate books each month, a company makes a schedule, plans the tasks, then holds a postmortem to determine the effectiveness of their work and to examine departures from schedule and any errors, rework, or delays. Lessons learned from the postmortem are used to improve the plan for the next month's closing process. This PDCA wheel turns once a month.

45

- A management team got serious about improving its annual planning and review system under the theory that this system had a profound impact on the organization as a whole. To begin their work, they reviewed what had happened the previous year and compared the *plan* with what they *did* and the *results* they achieved. They studied the deviations, failures, and successes, and concluded (among other things) that the company started more projects than could be successfully completed in the desired time frame. After more investigation, they made changes that reduced future project delays and provided more accurate information on *actual* time needed to complete different types of efforts. The PDCA wheel for this key system turns on a large scale once a year, each year providing the company with better and better means for planning, doing, checking, and taking action.

PDCA is the scientific approach applied to the workplace. But despite its seeming simplicity—or maybe because of it—I've yet to find anyone who has come to appreciate its power and elegance before they've spent years wallowing in it. Even those of us who are familiar with its applications are delighted (or dismayed by our ignorance) when a new manifestation of PDCA takes us by surprise. Over the years, I've come to realize that **PDCA is the essence of managerial work: making sure the job gets done today *and* developing better ways to do it tomorrow.** A manager's job is to ensure that we and our employees plan the work that needs to get done, carry out the plan, study the results to see if we got what we expected, then take action to recover from shortfalls and to capture and preserve any lessons. How often, how fast, and how effectively we rotate the PDCA cycle determines how well we get the job done *and* how fast we improve.

The Importance of Check

In an early experience with PDCA, staff to the top executives of one of the largest and most respected companies in the United States were lamenting the fact that they could not get the company to do a good job of planning. Time after time managers and employees alike went off half-cocked and got less than optimal results. "What do you know about how to help a company improve its planning?" they asked me. They described planning courses galore, company-wide drives on planning, pocket cards with the basic ingredients of a successful plan. But still they fell far short of where they needed to be.

"You're not so good at P," I said. "How are you at C?" It turned out that they'd never given the C, the Check step of PDCA, any attention at all, so they had never learned what they were doing wrong or where they could improve.

All of the PDCA cycle is important for rapid improvement. But among the steps, "C" (Check) is the driver of rapid *learning*. Without it, improvement is nearly impossible. Performing a Check is something that few organizations do regularly or well. Instead, they only execute the Plan and Do portions of PDCA—with the emphasis heavily weighted toward Do! This incomplete execution of PDCA is what many people think of as "decision making." By getting conscientious about Check, by treating decisions as experiments from which we must learn, we get *all* the components of PDCA to fall into place.

Like many states, the state I live in keeps a record of the number of points accumulated by any licensed driver: so many points for a speeding ticket, so many for an accident not involving property damage, and so on. Get 12 points and you lose your license; with 6 to 9 points you used to receive a letter requesting your appearance for a discussion with a counselor in a "driving interview." Several million dollars were spent each year by the state to pay for these counselors and the driving interview process to improve safety.

Instituting this interview procedure was a decision; it had not been viewed as an experiment, except by one man who had the authority to treat it like an experiment. He had every tenth motorist with 6 to 9 points set aside and not invited in for the driving interview. After several years, he had accumulated a substantial amount of data. Analysis of these data held many surprises. The driving records of people who had been through the driving interviews were no better than those of the people who had not gone through them.

When presented with this conclusion, the employees and other champions of the driving interview process naturally objected and challenged the analysis. Another, more thorough analysis was conducted, examining such things as subsequent minor accidents, serious accidents, serious traffic violations. The analysis controlled for factors such as previous driving record, age, sex, and so on—meaning those factors were not allowed to skew the interpretation of the results.

The answers in all cases turned out to confirm the initial analysis: no beneficial effect from the driving interview, and, if anything, possibly even a slight negative effect. The program was subsequently abolished with a savings of several million dollars per year to taxpayers and reduced hassles to drivers who accumulated points on their licenses.

The person responsible for this large scale PDCA, the late Lorris Dusso, was truly the exception. As he discovered, a **Check** uncovers things we would just as soon not know: it forces us to look at the huge waste in each of our activities; it exposes all the nonproductive (or just plain stupid) things we have unknowingly been doing for years; it creates the gut level energy to do a better job of taking **Action,** of **Planning,** and of helping manage the **Doing.**

When an executive group creates new policies, or chooses a particular course of action, the managers work hard to identify how they will know if the decision meets its objective. They try out the decision on a small scale (with a small PDCA) and then, after sufficient time has passed to truly judge the impact, do a postmortem. Over a series of decisions, they have identified patterns of problems in their decision-making and implementation processes and have systematically improved their ability to make and carry out decisions. This PDCA wheel is turning constantly, with each new decision being taken as an experiment that presents another opportunity to learn and improve.

Using PDCA Effectively

There are several keys to getting the most out of PDCA:

1. Adapt to the situation.

The preceding examples reflect situations that vary in their potential impact, the resources required to make the change, and the people's knowledge about the situation. There is no need to spend months studying whether to add baffles to recycling bins: the change is simple, requires few resources, and has few potential negative side effects. That level of change therefore emphasizes the Do and Check steps more than the others. The executive team trying to improve its corporate planning efforts obviously faces a much more complex situation, one that requires a great deal of effort in all stages of PDCA. In fact, in most situations (including some of those just described), it is more appropriate to start the cycle with Check rather than Plan, because we usually have to figure out what the current situation is before we charge off making changes ("decisions"). This sequencing of the PDCA cycle is commonly referred to as CAP-Do (**C**heck-**A**ct-**P**lan-**D**o).

2. Try ideas first on a small scale.

Had the state executives who were in power when the driver counseling program was suggested known about PDCA, they might have been able to try it in one county before implementing it statewide. Trying out ideas on a small scale can potentially save our organizations immeasurable amounts of effort and money:

> *A manager had been authorized to build a new facility that would cost millions of dollars. After choosing a design, he had the architect build a scale model the size of a large dinner table. The price tag: $40,000.*
>
> *Everybody who was going to work in that new facility spent time looking at it, walking around it, thinking about what their jobs would be like.*
>
> *The maintenance person said, "You know, there's a valve right in here behind that wall. . . . That valve is going to go bad some day and there's no way I can get at it to change it. If you don't want this plant down for two weeks when that thing goes, you'd better find a different place to put it."*
>
> *An operator said, "Look, you've got instrumentation up on the third floor but the controls are down by the machines. I'd be up and down these stairs forty times a day trying to get my job done. Get 'em all on the same floor."*

Did this manager waste $40,000? He probably gained $200,000 . . . or $500,000 in benefit from trying the facility design on a small scale and finding out what wasn't going to work before building the full-scale facility. How much the company really saved we will never know.

In general, the simpler the small-scale test, the better. You might start with a paper-and-pencil analysis and compare alternative decisions on characteristics such as expected benefits, cost, ease of implementation, potential negative effects, and so on. Narrow the field to one or two alternatives, discuss them with those who would be affected by the change, or do a detailed walk-through with the people who will implement the change. After refinements, do a trial implementation with only a few people or one department or one machine—whatever makes sense in your situation. With each PDCA cycle, the stakes increase. Challenge yourself to find ways to do small-scale tests quickly.

3. Decide ahead of time how you will assess progress.

Nothing is more wasteful than to plan a change, make the change, and be unable to tell whether it had any significant effect. Yet deciding "how we will know if things are better" is a step often overlooked in the planning stage. Before making a change, write down the expected benefits and how you will know if they've been achieved. As you carry out the plan, capture notes on key events, anything related to what does or does not go according to plan. Then force yourself to study the results. It will be a humbling exercise! Document the lessons learned and take action. Keep it up. The next experience will also be disappointing, but less so. Momentum will build as you continue to turn the PDCA wheel.

4. Integrate PDCA functions.

In many organizations, the elements of PDCA are present but divided among separate departments.

As shown on the left side of the diagram, one group plans, another is responsible for execution, a third measures or audits progress (part of Check), and yet a fourth interprets the results (also part of Check) and decides what actions are needed (Act). This fragmentation makes turning the PDCA wheel nearly impossible and leads to little or no progress. To be effective, the entire PDCA cycle must become the basic mindset of every employee, every department, every function. When

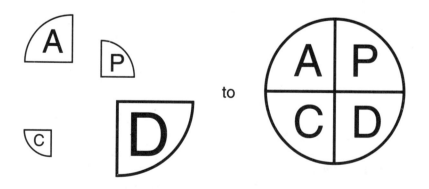

INTEGRATING PDCA

all employees become immersed in all four elements of PDCA, they begin to feel truly empowered to improve their jobs and the products and services they deliver to customers.

NO SUBSTITUTE FOR KNOWLEDGE

PDCA and the scientific approach in general thrive on new ideas—ideas about how to make things work better. Without new ideas, there is no improvement. A 4th Generation organization wants ideas from everyone. But there are many ways to *turn off* these ideas. Here are some I hear every day:

- We've never done it that way before!
- If it ain't broke, don't fix it!
- Be realistic!
- That's really weird.
- What if everyone did that?
- We'll never get that approved.

Such statements stop creativity in its tracks, harming our ability to learn rapidly and thus improve rapidly. It's far preferable to have employees pay attention to their work, formulate theories, try out new ideas—dare to be creative. The epitome perhaps is summed up by one of the more inventive companies in the world: its 11th Commandment is "Thou shalt not kill an idea."

Creative managers—or, perhaps, "managers of creativity"—want a creative environment. They share information constantly, not on a need-to-know basis, and do whatever they can to boost others' self-esteem and inspire confidence. They understand that it is by intuition that we discover; by logic and data that we prove. They also understand that intuition is most valuable in an employee who has a lot of knowledge and experience.

Creative managers love to hear expressions like these:

- I don't know much about that. Tell me more.
- What are the options?
- I'd like your help on this.
- Let's give it a try.
- I've got a wild idea.

51

- Are there other ways we can do this?
- Let me hear other people's ideas.

These statements, and the intent behind them, bear even more fruit when we prepare the soil—increase people's "stores of knowledge." We need to make sure that all employees learn as much as possible about the systems within which they work. They need to know about the needs of the organization's customers and suppliers as well as about the needs of their immediate customers and suppliers. They need to understand the basic "theory" behind the work they do, whether it be chemistry, psychology, finance, or some other discipline. This knowledge, plus an environment receptive to rapid improvement where managers are eager to learn and to try new ideas on a small scale, helps engender a "fire in the belly" for creativity, learning, and improvement.

There is "no substitute for knowledge," as Dr. Deming says. Only through knowledge will we create a steady stream of ideas from all our employees on how to improve quality and better serve our customers; ideas we can test using data and PDCA; ideas that can kick-start the Deming Chain Reaction to give us higher quality, higher productivity, more satisfied customers, greater job security, and greater return on investment.

Summary

As economic and market conditions have changed in recent decades, new management principles and methods have emerged to create a new business consciousness that I call 4th Generation Management. The key elements are a dedication to quality as defined by the customer, a scientific approach to rapid learning, and an All One Team environment. These elements are interdependent: none can be practiced effectively without the others. Three fundamental building blocks also influence our ability to achieve the needed results: seeing that quality and productivity are two sides of the same coin, viewing organizations as systems designed to serve customers, and focusing on rapid learning, rapid improvement.

EPILOGUE

About six months after the executives described earlier learned about the loss of a major customer, they got some surprising news.

"You won't believe this, but we've got another shot at the Franklin account," Ed told me.

"What?" I said. "I thought they were going elsewhere. What changed their minds?"

"For one thing," said Ed, "the other guys weren't perfect either. Then they began to haggle on price. But what tipped the scales in our direction was that some of our friends over there started hearing about the improvements we've made. Now they want to come visit and see for themselves what's going on. 'Then,' they said, 'maybe we'll sit down and talk business again.'"

"Amazing," I said. "What made them interested in seeing firsthand what you're up to?"

"We let the word out that we had made significant changes in our new product development process and had already seen some major gains in two other development efforts we had underway," said Ed. "They were particularly impressed that we managers had gotten involved personally in making the improvements. And now I think we've really got a shot at recapturing their business!"

Ed was justifiably excited. Losing the Franklin account had been a major blow. But it had an important side effect: causing the senior executives to rededicate themselves to making fundamental improvements in how they managed the company. They now knew at a deeper level that it was the right thing to do and would help prevent anything like this from happening again. The surprising thing was that unexpected success fell into their laps only six months later.

Changes like the ones this company made—and continues to make—don't come easily. They require new thinking, new skills. The magnitude of these changes is well captured in an analogy:

For many years, the best-known way of doing the high jump was called the Western Roll. The jumper ran toward the bar and launched over the bar face forward in a rolling motion.

53

Then, in the 1968 Olympics in Mexico City, Dick Fosbury startled the world by setting an Olympic record and winning the gold medal with a new technique he had been working on for several years: the Fosbury Flop. Within a few years, more records were being set, all by people using his new method of going over the bar backward.

Dick Fosbury caused a "paradigm shift" in the sport of high jumping. He replaced one model with another entirely new model. Now virtually everyone uses the Fosbury Flop. Even high school athletes.

Does that mean it was in any way wrong to use the Western Roll before Fosbury came along? No. Why not? It was the best-known method at the time. Would it be wrong to use the Western Roll today if you wanted to be effective in international competition? Of course. What's the difference? It's no longer the best-known method. We now know a way to get better results.

Now think about that in terms of generations of management. It doesn't mean that it was wrong to use older forms of management. It just means that now there is a better-known way.

As I mentioned earlier, in all my contact with hundreds of companies and thousands of managers, I've never found one, myself included, to whom all of these new ideas come naturally. Some elements of 4th Generation Management will come easily to some people but be harder for others. But we will all be doing some things that go against our instincts. Will it be easy? I haven't found a manager yet, myself included, who found it easy to make these changes.

Back to the high jumpers for a moment. How do you think other high jumpers who were expert at the Western Roll felt when Dick Fosbury developed a better technique? Do you think they were just delighted? No—they were apprehensive, threatened. The first thing they tried to do was get it outlawed. Do we ever do things like that?

Some tried to change, tried to learn the Fosbury Flop. How do you think it felt the first time they ran up to the bar and tried to go over backward? Natural and graceful? Or awkward and clumsy? They were a flop . . . but not a Fosbury Flop!

But nobody, once they mastered the new approach, has ever wanted to go back to the old ways. Fosbury Floppers won't go back to the Western Roll—at least not if they want to compete successfully. (Though some former Western Rollers may have snuck out in the middle of the night a do a few Western Rolls for old time's sake!)

Personal Transformation

Fourth Generation Management is a new approach to management. For an organization to be fully effective, every manager, indeed, every employee, needs to master this new approach. It will require concerted organizational focus.

However, for each of us, it is ultimately a personal transformation that will take place. We must learn to live and breathe a system-oriented, data-based customer focus and to trust each other.

Here's an excerpt from a recent letter addressed to Dr. Deming and me:

> *"I really want to thank both of you for what you have taught us. My company is experiencing many benefits from your lessons. But for me, even better than the gains at work have been those in my personal life. I now take a totally different approach with my children. Instead of getting upset with a poor grade and demanding improvement in the future, I now try to help my children understand the causes of the problems they are having, then seek to find ways to help them learn the things they are having trouble with. It's made a big difference in the way they relate to me. Instead of being afraid of me, they now enjoy our time sitting together working on what they're learning."*

We all have a long way to go. There are no quick fixes. Major benefits that far outweigh the investment are readily available from year one, but reaching the full potential will take time. In the rest of this book, we'll look more closely at the elements of 4th Generation Management, and how they can help us become better managers so we can create stronger, more effective organizations both in the short run and the long run.

Part Two

Building a True Customer Focus

PROLOGUE

Our executives had gotten together to meet with our new consultant, said Janine. One of the first things he asked us was what we were doing about quality and a customer focus.

We ranted on for almost half an hour talking about the wonderful things we were doing to get closer to our customers, Janine continued. We told him that each of us had started meeting with at least one key customer every quarter. We hosted an annual golf outing for executives from these key customers. We put up posters in every building reminding employees that The Customer Is Number One. We held meetings throughout the company talking about how important customers were to us and how all of our incomes depended on customers being happy with us. We had periodic customer surveys. In short, we thought we were doing a pretty good job of being customer focused.

Our consultant sat there quietly listening to us. After we were all done, he said some nice things about what he had heard, and then said he had a few questions for us.

"Which of your products or services is most important to your business? And who is the most important customer for that product or service?" he asked. There was a pause before someone mumbled an answer.

Then he asked, "What are the most important characteristics of that to that customer, and how do you rate on those characteristics?"

There was dead silence in the room. Finally, Mark answered ... though we all knew it was just a guess. "Good, good ... that is what you think," said the consultant. "Can you please show me the data you have on that customer's perceptions?"

Again, there was silence in the room. Everybody avoided looking directly at him. "Ah, well," he said, "perhaps you can show me your plans for improving customer satisfaction for this customer."

Just looking at the faces around the room, I could tell that everyone felt the same way I did: like the fairy tale emperor

59

standing in a public square when a little boy yells out, "The emperor's got no clothes on!"

It was a jarring experience, one that I'll never forget. At first we were angry, but after we cooled down, we saw the deep wisdom in these questions. We suddenly realized we didn't even understand what one of our customers needed and wanted, much less all of them.

This company was rather rudely awakened to a new vision of what being "customer focused" means. Though they were truly committed to customers and to quality improvement, they realized they hadn't gotten very good at listening to the Voice of the Customer—what customers say about their needs and their perception of how well we and our competitors meet those needs. Thus none of this company's strategic or operating plans or daily management decisions were based on thoughtful analysis of:

- the most important customers of their key services and products
- the most important customer needs they were, or could be, addressing
- the most important features and characteristics of their current offerings
- how they compared to competitors in relation to those characteristics

Thus, though they had high hopes about what their company was doing, they couldn't be certain any strategies or tactics would have an impact in the marketplace. In that one meeting, the senior managers realized what a long road they had ahead of them if they really wanted to walk the talk.

Imagine walking through your organization and asking people you run into, "Who are our organization's most important customers? How does what you do help the company provide value and quality to those customers?"

What results do you think you would get to this informal survey? Would other employees' answers be consistent with yours? Would everyone be able to answer? When each employee is able to answer those questions, and there are data to back up the answers, you are beginning to develop a true customer focus.

Why have a customer focus? The answer should be obvious: if we please customers they will send us money. If we don't, they won't . . . as this next company discovered:

A computer software company spent several years carving out a niche with products that allowed people using different mainframe computers to communicate with each other. Having successfully established itself in the marketplace, the company eagerly sought other needs to fill. After considerable research, they were excited to find a void that no other company had stepped into. Months of development were devoted to creating a new product to fill this void, a product unmatched in the marketplace. Finally, they released the new product ... only to find that no one wanted to buy it. They soon realized the gap was there for a good reason: no customers needed products to fill it.

This software company learned its lesson the hard way. The developers never bothered to check their "breakthrough" ideas with their customers. Unfortunately, mistakes like these are far too common. Thus a major benefit of a true customer focus is being able to **identify and eliminate work in our organizations that has little meaning or value to customers.**

When we routinely deliver high value, customers become loyal "partners." They stick with us and bring other customers. They are wonderful allies against those who would switch suppliers in a moment based on price tag alone.

But achieving a true customer focus is more challenging than it may sound. The difficulty is not that we don't know what to do—the basics of defining quality and understanding customers have been known for years. And it doesn't lie in being unaware that a customer focus is important. In a recent survey my company conducted, we asked a large sample of executives to name the top three issues facing their company. Nearly 60% listed the need to become more customer focused.

What *are* the barriers then? A key underlying problem is demonstrated by the following experience:

George joined a large consumer durables company as its market research director. As he poured over the company's customer information, he was impressed with the quantity and quality of the information on the end user, but surprised to see no real data on retailers—a critical part of the customer chain.

George thought his top priority was to close this gap by initiating a survey of key retailers. When he mentioned this to another executive, he learned that "nobody talks to retailers" without the permission of Henry, the vice president of sales. So George told Henry about his desire to contact retailers ... and was stunned when Henry made it clear that he didn't want George bothering his customers! "If you need any information on retailers, ask me," said Henry.

George's next move was to take his predecessor to lunch. He found out that earlier attempts at retailer contact had revealed a host of problems and complaints: medium and small retailers complained that salespeople didn't call frequently enough; backorders on shipped goods were much more frequent than with competitors; the sales force didn't seem to know much about the company's newer products and didn't want to discuss them when customers asked; point of sales materials were not being offered; and purchasers were complaining to retailers about inadequate information on the use of a new product.

George, of course, realized immediately why Henry didn't want anyone "bothering his retailers." As George's predecessor pointed out, sales had become alarmed that "their dirty laundry was being aired." They saw surveys as a threat rather than as a source of valuable information that could be used to improve not only the sales process, but the company's products and services as well.

George's predicament resulted from two converging forces: Henry's certainty that (1) any problems would be blamed on people instead of processes, and (2) knowledge is power. So, like most of us, Henry fought for survival by jealously guarding information about retailers.

A more powerful approach is to blame processes instead of people, and to adopt the view that customers belong to the *organization,* not to any one functional area. We need to help everyone understand that our future success is directly tied to our ability to serve and delight customers. And we need to create systems to translate that knowledge about customers into strategic direction and daily action. Creating systems that cause this to happen is management's job.

Though your organization undoubtedly has some people who already have in-depth knowledge about customers, the need discussed here is somewhat different: **to develop customer information that will be helpful to *all* employees and to create systems that make sure this information is shared and used.** The following chapters address these issues by providing ideas for the kinds of customer information we should gather, analyze, and share. They also identify ways to remove barriers that stand in our way and describe new approaches that are helping some companies develop and maintain a true customer focus.

5
VOICE OF THE CUSTOMER

A company that primarily produced film also had a small division that developed and marketed cameras. The revenues for that division were abysmal, and at one point it was on the verge of being shut down. In desperation, the manager pleaded for one last chance to make the division profitable. He got it.

This division knew that the only way it could compete in a market that had several well-established, well-respected brand names would be to develop something that no other company offered. They had already found that customers could not articulate answers that would give them the insight needed to develop innovative products. In search of inspiration, people from this division started working with people from the film division. They saw many rolls of film being processed that had poor photographs. They then went out to the retail stores and talked to customers picking up their photos. The most common problem they encountered was one of underexposed film.

"Do you know why these pictures are so dark?" the company representatives asked.

"Oh," the customer might say, "it was Johnny's birthday, and we turned down the light when we lit the birthday candles. I knew that it might not turn out but I wanted to take a picture anyway."

"Didn't you have a flash?"

"I'm sure I did somewhere," came the reply. "But I didn't have time to go find it."

Or, from another customer, "Well, the sun was going down, but I wanted to get one last picture of everyone down on the beach."

We probably all know how this company solved those customers' problems. They developed a camera with a built-in flash unit. And got a big surge in the market.

Inspired by this success, they tackled the second most common problem: photographs that were out of focus.

> *"These photographs seem blurry," a representative would say to another customer. "Can you tell me about that?"*
>
> *"Well, my eyesight isn't too good any more," came a reply. "And I have a hard time looking through the little window. My eyes just don't focus well that way."*

To solve this problem, the engineers licensed what was then a new infrared technology developed for slide projectors. The result: autofocus cameras. Again, they got a big surge in their market.

> *Many customers had still another type of problem.*
>
> *"Did you suspect this roll of film was going to be blank?" the company representative asked.*
>
> *"Oh, no," was the answer. "I thought the film had caught on those sprockets, but I guess not."*

Again, back to the lab. The result this time: auto-loading cameras. And again, another surge in the market.

Unfortunately for this company, there is a sad postscript to this story. The company put all these wonderful features into separate cameras but subsequently lost much of its gained market to competitors who combined them. Its experience still holds lessons for us:

- It did not rely solely on market surveys, questionnaires, or customer complaints to get customer information. Instead, the company combined *general knowledge about customers* with *specific data on customer needs* it obtained by looking at the results of the actual use of its product.

- Customer information was obtained directly by the people who needed it to do their work—the engineers, product managers, and technicians responsible for designing new products.

These lessons have much broader implications than just shaping new product development decisions. An organization as a whole will benefit most when every employee relies on the Voice of the Customer to make decisions. The rest of this chapter reexamines some long-standing notions about customers through 4th Generation lenses, explores several more recent innovations in understanding how customers perceive quality, and discusses common barriers that stand in the way of developing a true customer focus.

WHO IS A CUSTOMER?

Ask marketing or sales people about customers, and they usually speak at length about the distinctions between end users, decision makers, and influencers, and about all the subtleties of closing sales. "I need to understand all these players if I really want to understand my customers," these people say to me. And they're right. But although this depth of knowledge is critical to them, it is not so important for the majority of our employees.

A good starting point for employees is developing a shared understanding of:

- Your **major customers** or **categories of customers.**
- How your products or services reach customers: the **value chain** (or "customer chain") involved in creating and delivering products and services.
- What characteristics are most important to various customers and how **each step in the customer chain adds value** for the end user.
- How your organization works as a system; how employees' work fits in, how they and their **internal customers**—people inside the organization to whom they hand off their work—**add value** in the eyes of the customer.

We need to keep the message simple so employees can put their own work into perspective. This is seldom as easy as it sounds.

Identifying Major Customers

A hospital executive team wanted to improve quality and reduce costs. They set out to identify their major customers, and immediately ran into difficulty. Should they think of patients as customers? The families of patients? Physicians? Health-maintenance organizations? The companies that purchase insurance that use the hospital? The hospital's Board of Directors? The communities where satellite clinics are located?

It took months of investigation, discussion, and refinement before that executive team agreed on three categories they would define as their customers:

- Patients and their families
- The physicians who chose to use that hospital's facilities
- The employers who bought medical insurance that used their hospital

They concluded that the other candidates were *stakeholders*: people or groups who could affect or be affected by the hospital's work, but who were not primarily *customers* of its services. Communicating these distinctions and what was most important to each of these customer groups to all of their 2,000 employees took more time. But this was a key step in getting all to focus on doing what was important to the customers and to eliminating non-value-adding activities.

Knowing what is important to different customer **segments** is also important. One useful way to segment customers is by customer status:

- Current customers
- Former customers
- Competitors' customers
- Users of substitute products or services

Our tendency is to focus most on current customers. This is appropriate since keeping an existing customer is always much cheaper than recruiting a new one. But to expand our market we need to understand the needs of the other three groups of potential customers as well. Their needs are often different in subtle ways that we may be able to address by relatively minor changes in our offerings. Keeping an eye on users of substitute products or services is especially important in reducing the chances we'll be blindsided by changes in technologies or market perceptions.

Customers are commonly segmented based on demographic factors such as age, income level, geographic region, and so on. Though this is a useful and necessary approach, there is one caveat. We should make sure that individual customer needs are known first, then create **need segments** to group customers with like needs. Demographics come back into the picture as convenient but approximate ways to identify which customers fall into which need segments. If we go directly to demographics and stop there, we run the risk that neither individual customers nor their needs will ever get known.

Value Chain

In many companies, products and services go on to other companies who add additional value before the offerings get to the final customers, as in the following examples:

- A consumer products company sells to wholesalers who sell to retailers who sell to customers.
- A hotel chain sells support services to franchises who provide hotel services to guests.
- A chemical company sells paint to an automobile company, who paints cars that are sold to dealers, who in turn sell the cars to drivers.

A food company kept running into trouble when people from different parts of the organization tried to work together. People who thought they were discussing the same customer needs were, in reality, often talking about entirely different issues. To solve this problem, the company created standard definitions that all employees began to use: its retailers are now "customers" and the people who use the food are "consumers."

Helping all employees understand the larger system in which your company operates helps them to make better decisions. In particular, knowing what value each element of the chain adds and knowing what characteristics are important to each link in the chain are basic building blocks for an informed workforce.

HOW CUSTOMERS DEFINE QUALITY

A chemical company was mystified about why its revenue figures continued to increase only modestly. It had, after all, invested a lot of time and research into making sure its products had the most sought-after attributes identified by customers. Finally, the senior executives started talking directly to customers, asking broad, open-ended questions: "What do you like about doing business with us? What don't you like?" The customers responded with many things that were on their minds.

The executives were shocked to find that customers loved their products but hated everything else about doing business with them. The complaints were numerous: inaccurate bills, trucks showing up with dirty or incorrect fittings, failure to return phone calls quickly, and on and on. In the customers' eyes, the product simply wasn't worth the hassle!

The moral of the story? To customers, "quality" means more than just the characteristics of the product or service they receive. Customers pay attention to *all* their interactions with your company. The products and services you sell are not just the physical item or one-time experience that the customer gets but rather all the services that go with it: the 800 number for technical help, warranties, need-based selling, reservation services, and so on. You are selling a "bundle" of products and services to your customers to satisfy some need. Poor quality of the services associated with a product can drive customers away almost as quickly as poor quality in the product itself. On the other hand, if the service and product together are perceived as a good value, you will develop loyal partners who will be pleased to do business with you.

A Model of Customer Perceptions

As a frequent hotel guest, I find there are some things that **must be** present or I am disappointed. A characteristic that falls into this category is having a room available when I check in with a guaranteed reservation. There are other characteristics where **more is better**, such as the size of the room, the size and thickness of the towels, the quickness of the check-in. Of course, there are limits! I wouldn't want a towel the size of a bedspread, or need a room the size of a football field. Finally, there are some characteristics that have **delighted** me by their presence because they met a need I didn't expect the hotel to address. For example, I spend a lot of time in the evenings on the phone catching up with voicemail and contacting other consultants. When I'm in my office, I always use a speaker phone because it allows me to move around and take notes more freely. When a hotel in Dallas provided a speaker telephone in my room, I was delighted—and began to wonder why other hotels didn't do the same.

These three categories of customer perceptions—Must Be, More Is Better, and Delighter—have been summarized by Dr. Noriaki Kano, as shown in the diagram on the opposite page.

- **Must Be**—characteristics or features we take for granted, like clean linens and hot water in a hotel room. Since we expect

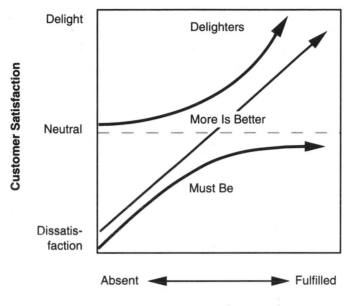

Presence of the Characteristic

KANO'S MODEL OF CUSTOMER PERCEPTIONS

them to be there, we notice more when they are missing than when present. Thus "absence" annoys us but "presence" only brings us up to neutral. In fact, *all* of the Must Be's must be present; if *any* are missing, we will be disappointed. But even when all are present, we still only get up to neutral.

- **More Is Better**—in this category, we are disappointed if a need is poorly met but have increasing satisfaction (and perhaps even delight) the better that need is met. For example, slow response to a customer query will disappoint that customer; instantaneous response may delight the customer; something in between would probably evoke no response at all.

- **Delighter**—these are the features or characteristics that surprise customers—in a good way! They solve a need the customer didn't know we could solve, or didn't think anyone would solve. Since they are unexpected, there is no negative effect if they are absent; but when present they have a positive effect.

Remember, too, that customers are a moving target. We need to stay close to them if we are to serve them well. A Delighter one year quickly becomes a Must Be the next: TV remote controls were Delighters a few years back, but now they are Must Be's for most people. In addition, many times, customers cannot articulate their needs, either because they don't know how or because they don't think it's in the realm of possibility to have those needs met. It is *our* task to describe and deliver the means for meeting those needs if we want to delight our customers.

Value of the Kano Model

The notion that there are different categories of customer perceptions may seem old hat to specialists. But it is refreshingly new to others. When taught to employees, it can aid their understanding of customer needs.

1. It helps employees set priorities in their own work. Working on a Delighter generally has little effect if the service or product is missing crucial Must Be's—such as going to a hotel with speaker phones only to find that no room is available despite a guaranteed reservation. We should first get rid of the things that are disappointing customers or driving them away: these are usually Must Be's. Then we can turn our attention to the More Is Better features and Delighters.

2. It helps people avoid the trap of thinking that "no complaints" equals customer satisfaction. Many companies keep score on customer satisfaction only by the number of customer complaints they receive. The implicit assumption is that if there are no complaints, customers are satisfied. The absence of a negative has never created a positive. Eliminating dissatisfiers stops driving customers away but does not and never will create a loyal, delighted customer. Also, a lack of customer complaints may mean that customers are simply unaware of any alternative, better product or service, *not* that they are satisfied or delighted with ours.

Finding the Must Be and the More Is Better characteristics is relatively easy: customers will tell us what annoys them if we just ask. Finding the Delighters is much harder. Customers are seldom aware of these. Our challenge is to create them—get ahead of the customer—as the camera company did in our opening example.

Targets or Goal Posts?

We have all needed to have a household appliance repaired or wanted to have a meal served in a hotel room. In such cases, we're usually told the service will arrive during some time interval: "We'll be there between noon and 5:00"; "Your breakfast will arrive between 6:30 and 7:00." Such specification limits do not represent my needs as a customer. I'd much rather be able to count on having the repair person arrive at 3:00 P.M., or having my breakfast arrive at 7:00 A.M. That way I don't have to waste *my* time because my supplier doesn't have a more predictable process.

Here's another example:

> *An automobile company worked very hard to provide high value to its customers. Besides improving its own processes, it subcontracted only with suppliers who had proven track records of consistently producing high quality. Several years ago, this company was surprised to find that transmissions from a subcontractor had lower warranty costs, ran quieter, and shifted smoother than the ones it produced at its own facilities. The surprise arose because this company was sure its employees were being very conscientious in performing the work.*
>
> *A detailed investigation found that the company's own transmissions were meeting specifications in all components (as were the subcontractor's). The key difference turned out to be that the subcontractor's transmissions had much less variation around the target values for a number of important characteristics. That is, the subcontractor didn't stop working once all characteristics were within the specifications, it worked hard to get all key components closer and closer to the target.*

The lesson this company learned shattered its long-held belief that meeting specifications was achieving quality. It realized it was paying a high price by being satisfied with anything between the specification "goal posts": frustrated customers, higher warranty costs, and higher assembly costs. It realized it needed to continue striving to get closer and closer to the target, well inside the specification limits.

This notion of having a target value with greater and greater loss the further you get away from it was developed by Dr. Genichi Taguchi, who was awarded a Deming Prize in 1960 for this contribution. It is now known as the Taguchi Loss Function, as shown on the next page.

The curve on this graph captures Dr. Taguchi's finding: we can reduce loss by getting closer and closer to the target. And, vice versa, loss increases the farther we get from the target. If I tell the hotel staff that I'd like breakfast at 7:00 A.M., I can still easily adapt my schedule if it's delivered a few minutes early or late. If it comes 5 or 10 minutes

TAGUCHI LOSS FUNCTION

early or late, I'm likely to be in the middle of some other task. Fifteen to 30 minutes early or late, and my schedule is completely upset; it's likely I'd be in the shower or perhaps will have had to leave to make my morning meetings. Thus the **loss** to me is greater and greater the farther the service gets from my target. Goal posts do not reflect this increasing loss at all. If the hotel said they treated "7:00 A.M." as "anywhere between 6:45 and 7:15," that suggests that anything between those goal posts is equally acceptable, but that 6:44 or 7:16 would somehow be totally unacceptable. In other words, there is "no loss" between the goal posts and "total loss" outside the goal posts. That obviously is not how I as a customer perceive the value of their service.

To deliver world-class quality to our customers, we must understand *their* perceptions of value. We must help employees understand the customer's target; we must develop methods for reliably getting closer and closer to that target, reducing the variation about the target. We'll do a far better job for customers this way than if we communicate it's okay to settle for just getting barely inside the goal posts.

Understanding customer targets, their Must Be's, and their Delighters requires good timely information about customer needs. The next logical question is how do we get such information.

Getting Customer Information

The market research staff had just completed their presentation to senior management. A customer survey had found the company deficient in "reliability." The managers couldn't believe it. They had test results to show the superior reliability of their products. But their customers obviously didn't agree. The managers decided they'd better take action. It would be expensive to improve reliability, but they didn't seem to have any choice.

Then Mary had the good sense to say, "I wonder what they mean by 'reliability?'" Everyone scoffed, "Anybody in this business knows what reliability is." But they took a moment to speculate what customers might mean by reliability . . . and were surprised when they came up with a long list of possibilities!

The survey had done exactly what it could be expected to do: answer some important existing questions and raise new questions—questions that cry out to be answered. Had the company gone ahead with the proposal to enhance reliability, it would have been a waste of time and money. More specific information was needed to know if and how to change their offerings. So instead of jumping to a solution, they followed up the survey with focused interviews of selected customers. "What do you mean by 'reliability'? . . . Can you tell me more? . . . What would be an example of that?" They also asked customers to compare different candidate offerings, such as "Which of these three would you prefer? Why? . . . How much improvement would that represent over what we offer today?"

What they learned surprised them: Few customers used the "standard" industry definition; some even meant such things as whether the phone calls were returned promptly, others whether the product worked in a wide variety of environments.

Like the camera company introduced earlier, this company came to understand the need for a variety of sources of customer information. Some of the most important sources are shown at the top of the next page.

Each of these sources has its strengths and limitations. Across the board, all suffer from the same malady: few organizations have created methods and processes for systematically capturing, analyzing, integrating, and using the information. For instance:

- The primary purpose of the basic or reactive functions such as customer service, sales, claims/credits, and technical support is

73

SOURCES OF CUSTOMER INFORMATION

Basic or Reactive Sources	Advanced or Proactive Sources
• Customer service	• Focused questioning of selected customers
• Technical support	• Observing customers using the product or service
• Claims/refunds	• Monitoring customer satisfaction
• Sales force reporting	• Monitoring of broad market trends

meeting an immediate customer need. Yet with a bit of extra planning and work these functions can yield useful information as a simple by-product of their primary functions: data on common problems, frustrations, delights, why customers are buying from us, who else they are buying from, why. The real challenge is to capture the information in the format that is useful to other functions such as planning and product development.

• The proactive techniques take even more energy and planning up front than do the basic techniques and incur additional expense. For them to be fully effective, we have to know a lot about what we want to learn and what we're going to do with the information once we get it. Thus, as a general rule, it's best to look first at any data we already have, even if we suspect the information is less than ideal. Existing data will answer some questions and will help us articulate additional questions so we can better focus future data collection. **Money spent gathering new data when we haven't learned how to use what we already have is often money wasted.** That said, many companies don't begin to get more customer focused until an objective third-party study raises the awareness that they don't know what customers really think.

Of all these sources, perhaps the one we need to beef up most is direct contact with customers:

A company's top managers were very concerned that customers kept saying their company was seen as "older" when its major competitor was viewed as "youthful." The managers became intent on providing a more youthful image for the company: creating new ads for both TV and print media, updating the packaging designs, and so on.

They decided, though, to do a little more investigation before beginning this major effort. Deeper probing with selected cus-

tomers revealed that by "older" they meant the company rated high on "stability, good, old-fashioned values, and reliability"—all of which were important positive attributes in the customers' eyes. With this information in hand, the managers quickly dropped their "youthful image" campaign!

Even more information can be obtained by observing customers using our products and services:

Dennis was a middle manager for a company that manufactured and sold plastic components. He wanted to drive a strong customer focus at his organization, so he decided to spend time at key customer sites, getting to know the people who used his company's products.

Most customer employees were reluctant to talk to him at first. After all, when was the last time anyone had really helped them with anything? The first person who was willing to talk to him was Cheryl. He asked Cheryl if there wasn't something his company could do to make things better for her. She thought for a moment, then took him to the receiving dock where his products were unloaded. She opened one of the boxes and told him to look along the edges of the plastic parts that were stacked inside. He could see that the parts had rubbed together during shipping and that the finish was blemished. Cheryl and her coworkers had to polish the finish slightly before they could use the parts. She suggested his company put little pieces of cardboard in between the parts as they were packed.

Dennis went back to his company that same day and discussed Cheryl's suggestion with the shipping staff. It turned out her idea was simple to implement and wouldn't cause any problems at their end. The next day, a box arrived at Cheryl's company with cardboard shims in place, and her name in bold letters on the box. The parts no longer needed reworking. Cheryl was a hero among her cohorts, and Dennis had a key ally.

With Cheryl's cooperation, Dennis understood more and more what characteristics were important to this customer. One day he noticed a stack of a competitor's products waiting to be used. He could see by a close examination that these products had a flaw that could cause serious problems for Cheryl's company, a flaw that his own company had experienced but learned to contain. Dennis showed Cheryl a simple test that would reveal this problem. The test saved Cheryl's company and its customers *hundreds of thousands of dollars—earning more goodwill and loyalty for Dennis and his company.*

Finding the Time

Though the benefits of capturing and using customer information are innumerable, several roadblocks stand in our way . . . the most common of which is simply finding the time to gather the information. Which, in practice, means making it a priority. Two tactics can help us achieve that goal:

- Making sure that everyone understands the importance of having and using customer information. When we know what customers value and are willing to pay for, we will be better able to judge how well we're doing our jobs.
- Picking one or two issues or problems that are of great importance to customers, then *making* the time to eliminate some complexity or waste, some whack-a-mole associated with those issues. That will free up small amounts of time and increase energy to make further improvements.

We will make time once we develop a mindset that the effort needed to build and sustain a customer focus is not *extra* work; it's work that lies at the heart of the organization, that keeps it alive, that brings meaning and focus to everything we do. This work is one of the most important investments a company can make to ensure its continued survival.

THE CUSTOMER WITHIN

The concepts described in this chapter apply equally to customers within and outside our organizations. Most of our employees, in fact, deal with **internal customers:** the people or groups to whom they hand off their work. Few deal directly with **external customers:** the people *outside* our company who purchase or use our products and services. Although treating other employees who depend on our work as customers can be very helpful, it can also cause problems.

We started developing stronger customer awareness in our employees several years ago, says Fred. Very patiently, we taught people about processes, and about treating the next step of the process as your customer. The result was a Pandora's Box of trouble.

People would turn to their internal supplier and say, "I'm the customer, and the customer is king. You'll do what I want, when I want it. You're the supplier. It's your job to do it for me in the way I want it done."

We finally had to scrap the whole notion of internal customers because no one could get their work done. People were being pulled in too many directions trying to please all their internal customers, and forgetting about the real customers.

This company ran into trouble when internal customers assumed too much power over their internal suppliers. Though we want to please our internal customers, **we must not lose sight of the fact that external customers are the most important judges of quality, not us.** We have to pay attention to the entire customer chain and make sure that what we do for an internal customer is clearly connected to our external customers' needs. In the next chapter, we'll see some of the methods that companies are using to make sure that everyone in the organization keeps the needs of external customers foremost in their minds.

6
CUSTOMER-FOCUSED
STRATEGIES

Earlier, I told the story of a management team whose innocence as to a customer focus was abruptly exposed one day. The managers had all been committed to serving customers ... but they had failed to develop the *means* to create a coordinated customer focus that would drive strategic, annual, and daily decisions. Despite all the work those managers put into creating an awareness of the importance of a customer focus, employees still lacked the knowledge and skills they needed to act in the best interests of customers.

A fundamental tenet of 4th Generation Management is that **nothing happens in a predictable, sustained way unless you build mechanisms that** *cause* **it to happen in a predictable, sustained way.** Our practices and policies (stated or unstated) have a profound effect on how employees make everyday decisions. This chapter explores some ways organizations are turning the theory of customer focus into action.

NEW POLICIES

In one sense changing a policy is very easy; just change some writing on a page! But, in another sense, it's one of the hardest things we'll ever do because we have to find ways to get the policy known to and followed by employees. What follows is a discussion of techniques that several companies are using to make this kind of broad change happen.

100% Satisfaction

Some companies have adopted the policy of 100% satisfaction: "If you are ever dissatisfied with this product or service, for any reason, please let us know and we'll give you a full refund. No objections, no exceptions." This approach sounds costly, but it doesn't have to be:

> One of the biggest things we did that really convinced employees that we were serious about change was instituting a 100% satisfaction guarantee. If a customer asked for a refund, we did it. No questions asked, except to try to understand and to learn so we could do a better job in the future. Among other things, the sum of the refunds we issued made the cost of failure very visible.
>
> It was amazing what this did to our relationship with our customers. They were really surprised at first. When they called in to ask for a full or partial refund, they were ready with a long list of reasons and arguments. Our simple "OK" took the wind out of their sails. Many of them even came to our defense, gave a more in-depth response about what happened, and ended up declaring that a full refund wasn't appropriate. We became partners with our customers, not adversaries.
>
> But even three years in, some employees still questioned whether we really meant it. A pivotal event changed even those skeptics' view. One lot of product we sold was contaminated, and it contaminated a customer's new $40,000 instrument. We not only replaced the product, we bought the instrument from them for the full $40,000. This story got around our company quickly and made believers of the last holdouts. It turned out not to cost us that much because we were able to refurbish the instrument and resell it ... but even if it had cost us $40,000, the lesson would have been well worth the money.

Why did this manager believe the cost was worth it? Because the company had retained a customer, quite possibly for many years to come, who would likely repeat this story to many other potential customers. And because all employees now knew the company cared, really cared, about quality.

Companies using this approach have found that few customers abuse the policy. They've learned to trust their customers, just as they are learning to trust their employees and suppliers. The result is that these companies lose a fraction of a percent in sales, but reap huge dividends in customer loyalty and future sales growth. It allows them to delight customers and replaces adversarial customer relations with cooperative discussions aimed at finding permanent solutions to problems. It helps companies learn faster about what changes would have a big impact.

There are several traps we need to avoid in order for a 100% satisfaction policy to work. One company instituted such a policy but made no other changes: they gave customers their money back but didn't seek further information, make improvements, or practice prevention. This annoyed the customers even more. Another trap is making this change *before* managers and employees have learned to work together and to trust each other. Imagine being told you have to guarantee 100% satisfaction for customers while working for managers whose first instincts are still to blame people. How nervous would you be about making a mistake? How much more likely are you to make mistakes when you feel nervous? How likely are you to distort figures or distort systems to prevent your manager from ever learning about an unhappy customer?

Thus, changing to a policy of 100% satisfaction *will* be costly unless our companies are willing to analyze the source of dissatisfaction and correct the causes, not just the symptoms. Completing the learning and improvement cycle saves us in the long run, leading to better products and services, and more delighted customers.

Everyone Owns Customers

An earlier example in this section described a marketing director's problems when a vice president acted as if sales alone "owned" a certain type of customer. This attitude is common, but many companies are making great strides to change it. Here are some examples of approaches that typify true customer-focused thinking:

- A company that produces power supplies and other computer components recently received the Malcolm Baldrige National Quality Award for its management practices. One of its strong points was treating *each* employee as a "customer contact" employee. All employees are taught about the business, about the products, about customers, and about how to interact with customers. Employees take pride in what they're doing. Customers or potential customers who breeze through a facility are typically greeted by enthusiastic employees who proudly explain what they do and how it adds value to the products and services that they sell. These employees often ask if the customer has suggestions for improvement—and, of course, there are systems in place that help them take action when customers respond.

- Another company, anxious to close a significant sale it had been trying to close for years, sent its president, a sales manager, and a production worker with its sales representative to visit the customer, a trip of over 1,000 miles. All the men wore suits. They were introduced by name, not title. The deal was made, everybody was delighted. Only then did the customer find out that Joe was a production worker, not a senior manager. "He had such detailed knowledge about the product and how it's made ...," they said. "Such enthusiasm for the product and company. What really sold us was Joe's earnest insistence that 'we want your business.'"

- A telecommunications firm has come to view all of its 50,000 employees as its sales force. But just viewing them that way doesn't make it happen. They found that they had to train all 50,000 employees on the nature and benefits of the products and services they offered. They had to provide ways for this sales force to get more information when interested customers had questions they couldn't answer. They had to develop ways for all employees to take orders. This was a mammoth undertaking and was not achieved in a few months; but it was achieved. Chief among the many gains is better service to customers: faster and more complete responses to their questions.

- The customer service personnel at a major corporation spend a full day each month out in the field having face-to-face contact with the people that they usually only talk with by phone. This greatly reduces the burnout, isolation, and "us-them" mentality that the customer service staff say they inevitably develop when isolated from direct customer contact.

- A company that produces very expensive industrial equipment in a competitive global industry charters a large jet once a quarter and flies a diagonal slice of 200+ employees to a customer site. Employees get up early, often flying out by 5 or 6 A.M. and not returning until midnight. All wear identical sweaters with the company's logo, leaving behind them all the usual ways to sort people into bins. It is impossible to tell who is a secretary, who is a maintenance person, who is an executive, an engineer, or a production worker. They all mingle together, strangers, getting to know each other as peers, getting to know the customers they visit, seeing their product in the customer's facilities right beside competitors' products, and hearing from the people that use the product what they like and don't like about the products and services they receive. These employees come back with an obligation and a desire to tell their coworkers what they have seen, what they have learned, and how a little dent here or a slight delay there isn't such a minor thing after all. In fact, they not only tell their coworkers, but their friends and neighbors as well. They have new pride, new enthusiasm, new energy, new commitment. They have become All One Team.

- A manager of one of the best-managed automobile plants I've ever seen said, "We go to enormous lengths to keep reminding people that they're not just putting screws in a door, they're building $20,000 automobiles, the second largest purchase of most people's lives." They hold a lottery each day so three randomly chosen employees get to drive brand new cars home for a night. They get to experience all the fresh smells, the glossy paint, the wonderful feel of a new car. They get to show it off to their neighbors, and to see what it's like to find "minor" imperfections. And they bring back powerful messages into the organization. Every week, other employees visit dealers and find out what the dealers like and don't like about the cars they are getting. The employees go down in the pits and talk to the mechanics to find out what they like and don't like. Also once a week, a customer who has purchased a new car takes delivery right at the factory, in a large all-purpose room much like a high school gymnasium, with 500 employees in the bleachers observing this emotional event.

The moral? **We have to go to great lengths to keep reminding people that they're not just an unimportant cog in a big wheel.** They are part of a powerful system that produces high value for customers. Here's another example that makes this point:

In a manufacturing firm, each employee gets the opportunity to experience nearly every job in the manufacturing process by following a product through the entire production sequence. This helps them understand what happens through the whole chain, to see how their jobs fit into the system as a whole and how their jobs affect the final quality of the product.

83

These examples show a variety of ways that companies are getting employees to feel ownership of customers. These methods share the following traits:

- Involving the entire workforce in customer contact
- Treating all employees as peers working together; eliminating much of the artificial status conferred by dress code, title, or job category
- Helping everyone to begin to see beyond their own individual jobs—how they aren't just making travel reservations, or lubricating equipment, or polishing floors ... but are part of a system that provides a product or service that makes an important difference in their customers' lives

Are such extremes necessary? The answer, in short, is yes. Our society is much more complex today, as are the products and services we sell. Knowledgeable employees who know and care about the customer provide a critical edge in the marketplace.

Increasing Customer Complaints!

In most organizations, employees have been taught that decreasing the number of customer complaints is a good thing to do. Their companies mistakenly equated "no complaints" with "customer satisfaction" and thus sought to reduce the number of complaints. A goal to reduce customer complaints leads to a number of dysfunctional behaviors:

- Employees argue over whether a particular inquiry was a complaint or not.

  "This customer said she couldn't read the tiny type in the legal notice. That's not a complaint, is it?"

  "Carlos wanted to know if we could make the frames a bit thicker. Does that count as a complaint that they're too thin?"

- Employees waste time arguing over which department should be charged with the complaint.

- Customers are sent the message, "We don't like complainers; if you don't have anything good to say, we'd rather not hear from you."

The customer who complains wants to continue doing business

with you and assumes that you want to know about the problem and will do something about it. Complaints are Blessings from the Sky . . . appreciate them . . . welcome them.

The trick, however, is to increase complaints while improving the quality of your products and services. One sure way to increase complaints is by delivering poorer service to customers, or giving them worse products. That is not what I have in mind here. Rather, the goal is to make it as easy as possible for customers to give you their comments.

Many companies now have toll-free 800 numbers that provide instant responses to customers 24 hours a day. One luxury automotive company even provides its customers of new models with a free cellular phone that has the customer service number programmed right in. All the customer has to do is hit one button to get instant toll-free access to the company. Not only does this provide near-instantaneous support for the customer, it also gives the company feedback it might not otherwise get. Another car company provides a free one-year membership in a national automobile association to new-car purchasers: their customers get free road service, and the company gets data back from the association on exactly what kinds of problems their cars develop in the first year.

Even if an organization lacks official customer service or technical support departments, it undoubtedly has some way of fielding customer inquiries, questions, and complaints and trying to turn around a dissatisfied customer. Like many other customer-contact positions, customer service representatives and technical support staff are rightly focused on helping individual customers with their particular problems. Unfortunately, this single-minded focus on fighting the immediate fire prevents them from getting data that could be used to identify ways to prevent recurrence of the problems, or to identify product or service enhancements. Capturing information from these customer contacts can help us drive for deeper levels of fix by learning how to avoid the problem in the future or next generation of the product or service. Here are just two examples of data being collected:

- Information on whether a product or service works the way the purchaser thought it would work.
- Attempted uses of a product or service that are beyond its intended use or its capability: this helps to identify potential changes in how current products or services are marketed, as well as providing ideas for possible new products.

85

Turning complaints into sales

A U.S. government survey included the following findings, lessons that are familiar to most of us by now:

- In a survey of consumers with service problems, more than 70% of the respondents said they did not complain.
- Where complaints about minor losses ($1 to $5) were resolved to the customer's satisfaction, 70% of the complainants said they would maintain brand loyalty. When minor complaints were not satisfactorily resolved, 46% still indicated they would repurchase the problem product or service.
- When customers had major complaints (potential losses exceeding $200), 54% of those whose problem was resolved satisfactorily said they would maintain brand loyalty, whereas only 19% of those whose complaint was not resolved satisfactorily said they intended to repurchase the product or service.
- Perhaps more importantly, among those customers who did not complain despite potential major losses, only 9% said they would continue to purchase the offending product or service.

The main point: Effective, proactive handling of customer complaints presents a major business opportunity. No matter how much potential loss there is to our customers, whether large or small, we can increase the likelihood that they'll purchase our products and services again if we are good at resolving their complaints.

In addition to retaining the complaining customer, some companies have even found that when somebody calls you to complain or ask for a credit, it provides an opportunity to sell some additional product. One telecommunications firm has turned this to good advantage. First, they handle complaints and refunds efficiently and effectively, which earns them goodwill from their customers. Second, by deeply understanding their customer's needs, they are able to use this contact time with customers to make suggestions on additional service features or products that might be of particular benefit to that customer.

UPGRADING EXISTING FUNCTIONS

To develop a strong customer focus, we will undoubtedly have to develop some new structures in our organizations to enhance our ability to gather information, analyze it, and act on the Voice of the Customer. Equally important will be taking a fresh look at existing functions to see how we can make them more supportive of a customer focus.

Customer Service and Technical Support Functions

The company that is clear about its aims for customer service and technical support functions and develops ways to measure its effectiveness can use PDCA to continuously upgrade performance. Some examples of measures or indicators of effectiveness are:

- Percentage of customers whose need is satisfied after one contact
- Percentage of customers who report being very satisfied with the support they received (for example, when called back to see how satisfied they were)
- Average time to satisfy customers
- Average time to accomplish a successful preventive fix
- Percentage of inquiries that are repeats of problems customers reported three months ago (this assesses whether the information being gathered is being used effectively to prevent problems from recurring)

These measures are useful if they drive rapid improvement; destructive if they are used to blame people. There must be follow-up action to use data to pinpoint specific problems and their sources. The continued emphasis is on "what can we change in our processes and systems to serve customers better, and thus make these measures even better."

Many companies have found that one of the most important factors in increasing customer satisfaction is giving customer service and technical support staff the power and authority to resolve issues themselves. To be comfortable with that decision, these companies work hard to develop staff who are familiar with the policies and practices of the organization, and who have in-depth knowledge about all their products and services. Management must also provide a mechanism for responding to customer questions or issues the employees do not feel comfortable resolving on their own.

Business Planning

Traditional annual or strategic plans often start from some targeted growth rate in sales and profits.

> *"As you all know, our strategy calls for a 10% growth in both revenues and profits each year. Thus our targets for next year will be $1.3 billion in revenues and $200 million in profits. These are very ambitious targets given the nature of the changes going on in our industry, but I know that if you really put your minds to it, you can all do it. Our investors are counting on you. So we'll need to have your rough-order-of-magnitude budget information within the next few weeks. We'll review those rough projections soon afterwards and get back to you on how they all add up. You'll then get your individual targets by early next month, which will provide you with ample time to come up with your final plans before the end of the year."*

In this "planning" process—which is loosely named, since the only plan that typically results is a budget—managers make forecasts, create budgets, and only then ask themselves, "What do we have to get customers to do to make this forecast?" The answers, usually, are along the lines of: "We'll have to get a price increase from them," or "We have to get them to buy more of this and that."

This approach to planning and budget starts at the end of the Deming Chain Reaction rather than at the beginning. And, as many companies are now discovering, it tends to produce weak results. Things look good on the books: continued growth in revenues, continued rises in profitability, continued decreases in costs. The numbers look good; the ship seems to be in good shape. But the sales have been gotten at a price. Costs have been reduced, but the causes of those costs are still buried in the organization. The organization, like the Titanic, is headed for an iceberg, the real issues lying hidden in an illusory appearance of steady progress. Many organizations are able to continue the illusion of prosperity for some years, until everything seems to come unglued all at once. The investment community then wonders how such a respected safe haven for investors could have suddenly fallen so far, from the top of the list of most admired companies to the bottom in a few months.

The principal causes of this approach to planning are well known, including the short-term thinking of so many of us who invest (or speculate) and the issues that are reported in the media. It's hard for an organization to turn that financial focus into a customer focus. The culprit from the investment side is over-reliance on a few financial indicators by investors who do not yet know how to diagnose the problems in 3rd Generation companies or the characteristics to look for in 4th Generation organizations.

A customer-focused approach to strategic and annual planning begins with customers, not financials. It begins with the attitude "how do we provide even higher value to our customers with lower cost." We look at data on how the needs of our major customers or customer segments are changing, on the markets for our current and potential products and services, on the industry as a whole. We look at environmental factors such as changes in international forces, in regulations, in technologies, in demographics. We look at our internal capabilities, such as trends in process improvements and quality, cycle time, and costs. We review our track record in identifying needs and developing effective new products that reach the market quickly and find receptive purchasers. We take an honest look at our capability to attract, secure, and retain customers.

All of this information is then integrated into an understanding of our current and potential markets and our ability to respond to and shape the evolution of those markets. This understanding defines our strategy. We develop tentative action plans that identify new products to develop, new markets to serve, key processes to improve, and waste to eliminate. We then make predictions as to the impact of those changes on revenues, costs, cash flow, and profit. That leads us to the first draft of a budget. Examination of that budget then tells us whether we can afford to do all that we'd like to do, and if not, how much we have to cut. A second hard look at the customer-focused actions we have outlined is generally necessary along with some painful paring and focusing of efforts.

To some, the final plan may look much the same as those most organizations currently use, but in practice, the results differ radically. The driving force of a 4th Generation plan is serving customers, with the understanding that we need revenues and profits to do that; in a 3rd generation approach, the driving force is revenue and profit, with a grudging admission that we need to deal with customers to get the revenues and profit. The latter attitude creates an environment where employees feel that customers are merely vessels into which they have to stuff product. All too soon, customers come to recognize this tone ... and then become increasingly elusive. Companies wind up bribing customers through rebates, discounts, and end-of-the-quarter, end-of-the-year special packages. Customers become addicted to such special treatment and are very difficult to retain once those special concessions can no longer be afforded.

The issue is one of cause-and-effect: Will focusing on customers bring profit, or will focusing on profit bring customers? The answer is the same, time and time again. We get better results by building plans and budgets around serving customer needs. There is a big difference between forcing the company to grow and allowing it to grow as it provides more and more valuable services to customers.

Adding a Customer Element to Regular Meetings

Maintaining a customer focus requires frequent attention: one beginning step many companies have taken is to have the first portion of their regular management meetings devoted to quality. This tactic allows for regular reviews of progress. Here's a sample agenda:

Agenda

- Overview of agenda
- Review of indicators
    - customer satisfaction
    - other quality indicators
    - other indicators
- Summary of recent customer information
- Customer issues needing immediate attention
- Status reports on customer issues targeted for prevention or breakthrough
- Summary of decisions and action items
- Meeting evaluation

CUSTOMER-FOCUSED AGENDA

A System of Customer-focused Meetings

Many companies are taking this idea of adding "customers" to their agendas one step further. They have developed a system that I've come to call "rolling customer-focused meetings." The sequence goes like this:

- Stage 1: The first-level managers meet with the front-line staff to examine the work for the coming period (day/week/month). They discuss any problems they've had or might have. They discuss customer feedback. They identify issues needing resolution, which are entered into their problem-tracking logs. They resolve and deal with as many issues as they can. Issues they cannot deal with or that seem to have larger implications are logged and continued onto the Stage 2 meetings.

- Stage 2: The second level of management meets with their first-level managers. The pattern of discussion is repeated. Issues that bubble up from the first-level meetings are dealt with as much as possible. Those that cannot be dealt with at that level, or seem to have larger implications are continued on to the next level.

- Stage 3 and beyond: The process continues level by level to the top of the organization. The higher levels of the organization use various channels for getting decisions and messages rapidly back through the entire organization.

- Periodically, the issues logged at each level are examined for patterns. The logs provide data on the types of problems encountered, how often each type appeared, which are resolved, which continue to resurface, and so on. This data can tell us what deeper levels of fix are needed to prevent recurrence.

A number of characteristics affect how well this system works. One of these is the organizational structure. Organizations that link together employees along process lines can resolve most issues at lower levels because people can easily get and share the information they need to make decisions. The system works quickly and effectively. In organizations that have taller chimneys—long chains of command that prevent most employees involved in a process from dealing directly with one another—most issues hit a barrier at the first level and never get resolved. Large organizations with a strong functional orientation find that many day-to-day issues need to go near the top of the organizations before the official organization chart is prepared to address them, because people at lower levels are prevented from seeing enough of the picture to take informed action. Informal shortcuts or patches can be organized but tend not to have lasting benefits.

The speed with which the entire cycle of meetings is completed is also an important characteristic. Some organizations repeat the entire cycle *each week*, others, once a month. Others in a crisis repeat the cycle daily in targeted areas. Organizations with many levels will have more trouble using this approach than those with fewer levels.

The tenor or tone of the communications is also of fundamental importance. They need to be customer-focused, candid, nonblameful, open. They must also be action oriented so that it's clear what people should do during and after the meetings.

Organizations that are clear about the aims or purposes of this system (or any other system) of meetings will be in a good position to improve their effectiveness quarter by quarter, year by year, through the PDCA cycle. For example:

- If enhancing customer satisfaction is one of the aims, as it should be, we should track customer satisfaction data that reflect the consequences of changes made.

- If an aim is "to resolve problems at the lowest possible level," the logs should include data that can be analyzed in terms of how many issues were resolved at a given level, and how many had to be passed up the ladder.

- If another purpose is "to resolve issues in a timely way," the logs would need to include data on when a problem was first identified and how much time elapsed before it was resolved.

- If still another aim is to prevent recurrence of customer problems, the data can be summarized over time and patterns identified. If a particular problem keeps resurfacing at the same rate over time, the meetings are obviously not helping to identify the root sources of that problem. There are many reasons why the meetings may not be helping: for instance, it may be that the type of data being gathered is inadequate for the purpose, or that the data are not analyzed appropriately. Further study will be needed to find out what additional information or analyses could help employees prevent recurrence.

Here are three examples of applications of such a system of meetings:

Example 1:

A large telecommunications firm has a system that involves the first five levels of management (with the top several corporate levels yet to be involved). Once a month for over two years, roughly ten operating level employees who have responsibility for a small geographic area have been meeting with their manager for a full day. A large portion of this meeting is devoted to customer issues such as new problems that have arisen in the field, design improvements, held services (when they can't get a job done within the targeted time), key commitments in the short term and for the year, sales opportunities, and so on. Other portions of the meeting are devoted to issues such as training. The meeting is held out of the office, and the company buys lunch (something the employees perceive as a major benefit). Later in the month, the first-level managers meet for a half-day under the leadership of a second-level manager to discuss similar issues. And so on up to higher levels of management.

"At first we fought it," said one executive. "It's been two years and we're just starting to feel comfortable with the system. Now we're even bringing in individual contributors from other functions as needed. It's required patience and persistence. But this system has helped us be much more customer focused and helped us to deal with some tough issues such as down-sizing. Now, we'd never want to go back to the old way!"

A key step was reorganizing key functions needed to get the job done. Operations that used to exist in their individual silos are now working together. They've eliminated a lot of "us versus them" thinking. Local areas have taken control of customer issues.

Another ingredient in their success is a parallel employee development system that provides people with a variety of work experiences. Service installers, for instance, spend time in the office regularly so they'll understand what's it like to be on the telephone, trying to take orders and keep all the details straight. Office workers periodically don their steeled-toed shoes and go out into the field so they'll know what it's like to be up in a bucket in below-zero weather, with the wind blowing, and not have all the information needed to do the job.

"Before, we used to manage toward objectives," said one of this company's managers. "Now we manage toward zero problems and zero response time. Before we had different objectives,

now we have common objectives. By working together on common problems, we've made real progress on issues that have been around for years. For example, we've reduced the number of 'held services' [those they are unable to deliver within the targeted time] to essentially zero; we had none last year. Before, we used to have 10 to 15 percent."

Example 2:

An automobile plant has a weekly cycle of customer-focused meetings. The entire assembly line is divided into teams of approximately 20 workers each. On Monday mornings, from 8:30 to 9:00 A.M., each team meets with its "team coordinator" to discuss problems that keep them from producing high-quality output: parts that won't quite fit, shortages, equipment not quite working like it's supposed to, and so on. Issues that can be addressed at that level are taken care of; urgent issues that need an immediate resolution are communicated to a place where action can be taken. On Tuesdays, from 9:00 to 10:00 A.M., the team coordinators meet in groups of about ten with their "area coordinators." Again, they focus on surfacing issues, resolving those that can be resolved, taking those that require immediate action to an appropriate place, and then carrying those issues that cannot be resolved to the next level. On Wednesdays, from 9 to 10 A.M., the area coordinators meet in groups of about ten with their "sector coordinator," following the same kind of agenda. On Thursday mornings, the plant manager and the five sector coordinators meet from 9:00 A.M. to 12:00 noon to conclude the process.

At each of these meetings, other people are brought in and involved as appropriate, so the actual number of participants is often 50% greater than if only the regulars were there. On Friday mornings, or at any other time when an urgent need arises, the plant manager gives a brief summary of the highlights of the issues identified and actions taken to all 10,000 employees via closed-circuit TV.

Example 3:

A major retailer has a system of rolling meetings that also cycles every week. In Phase I, the sales force does its usual work with customers on Monday through Thursday, but they also capture market issues such as quality problems, opportunities for increased sales, competitor activities, and support problems. This information is passed on to the regional sales managers, who will attend the meetings in the next phase.

In Phase II, 50 to 75 people meet for a half-day on Friday mornings. Attendees include:

- The president, the three vice presidents, plus several selected other members of their staffs
- Selected regional sales managers, 3 to 5 at a time out of a pool of 50 (rotated so that each of them attends periodically)
- Selected sales staff (also rotated)
- Central warehouse managers (two to three at a time out of six)
- Guests

A standard agenda and seating arrangement has been honed over many months. Each issue that is raised is assigned to either an appropriate functional manager or a standing cross-functional team of high-level managers whose job is to deal with cross-functional issues that do not have an obvious functional home. The goal is to identify issues and take action immediately so the company can be in a position to respond by the beginning of the next week to what's happening in the marketplace.

Phase III: Results of the Friday morning meeting are discussed directly with sales, warehouses, and other locations on Friday afternoon through closed-circuit broadcasts.

Phase IV: Regional teleconferences from late Friday afternoon through Monday morning are held to discuss implications of the Friday morning session and any new issues surfaced by viewers of the Friday afternoon telecast.

Each issue raised is logged, with notes that identify the originator, the issue, who is responsible for resolution, and how to get in touch with that person. Notes are kept on whether the issue was strategic, tactical, or administrative and on the type of issue (whether quality, communication, pricing, customer service, etc.). The status is regularly updated, and, when resolution is reached, special notation indicates what channels of communication should be used (memo, electronic mail, voice mail, teleconference) to get the message back out to the organization. This allows them not only to keep track of where each issue is but also provides a rich source of data for deeper levels of fix.

LEADING THE CHARGE

As we all know, few employees will be enthusiastic about going the extra mile, making the extra commitment to customers, unless they see us, their leaders, doing the same. The way that top management spends its time and the questions they ask of each other and of the rest of the organization are critical in determining the focus of the organization.

To create a customer focus, top executives must enjoy interacting with customers and helping them solve problems. Though it sounds trite, we must love the products and services that we sell and the customers we sell to. We must constantly talk positively about customers, what's going well with them and what's not. We must be keen to take immediate action when customer problems appear.

Key Questions for Managers

Here are some key questions we can use to check whether our actions are helping to build or destroy our organization's customer focus:

1. If I were to act in the best interests of our customers, what would my decision be?
2. What can I do personally to better understand our customers' needs?
3. What can I do to help my employees put a customer focus into action?
4. What are the systems by which we achieve a customer focus? Which of those are most in need of attention? What is my schedule for regular PDCA to continuously improve each of them?

These questions, asked on an ongoing basis, provide a framework for assessing and upgrading our customer focus.

Other Executive Responsibilities

Besides asking the preceding questions, executives must also be prepared to take action. We need to start doing this work ourselves, looking at data and information our organizations already have. We must have regular meetings with key customers or customer groups, asking questions that probe both specific issues and broad themes:

"What do you like about doing business with us?" "What don't you like about doing business with us?"

In these interviews, we must not spend our time defending current services or products. We must listen to what our customers have to say. Often we "know" why something hasn't been fixed, but it's time to open our minds to our customers' views, to challenge our own thinking.

Several key ingredients to making executive meetings with customers effective are:

1. Let people know in advance that you're coming, what questions you're going to ask, and that you're going to do something with what you learn.
2. Though you usually ask broad, open-ended questions, they should be well thought out in advance. Try to work them into the conversation naturally.
3. Take notes, capturing thoughts in the customer's own language.
4. After the visit, write a summary of what you heard and what actions will be taken. Send copies to appropriate coworkers.
5. Get back to customers quickly with what you're going to do and by when.
6. Take action.
7. Follow through.
8. Do it all over again on a regular basis.

KEYS TO A CUSTOMER FOCUS

Creating a true customer focus takes energy, creativity, and perseverance. The role of executives is particularly crucial, because your attitude and efforts will shape the entire organization. In particular, you must have regular contact with customers, ideally through site visits (as described above). You will also need to take responsibility for creating systems and methods that encourage and maintain employee knowledge and enthusiasm for delighting customers. For this to happen:

- A customer focus must be in line with the organization's strategy; that is, employees must feel that by helping customers, by taking the time to gather and analyze customer information, they are helping the organization achieve its strategic goals.

- Employees must have some appreciation for and understanding of the organization's most important customers or categories of customers.

- There must be systems for effectively dealing with immediate customer issues such as complaints, claims, refunds, technical support.

- Information on customer problems, needs, and expectations must be gathered from a wide variety of sources, analyzed, integrated, communicated and widely acted upon.

- Management meetings and other systems must continually drive for deeper and deeper levels of fix in ways that drive higher customer value and lower costs.

- And, perhaps most importantly, we must not only hear but also act on the Voice of the Customer, translating what we learn into specific action plans at all levels of the organization (strategic plans, annual operating plans, development or improvement plans, marketing plans, etc.). At every level, our plans and actions must be tested against, "Is this getting us closer to what our customers need and want from us?"

If you try to address the problem piecemeal, you will probably fail. In shifting from the Western Roll to the Fosbury Flop, high jumpers didn't just have to add a backward turn into their process. They had to reassess their timing, pace, and position from the moment they started approaching the jump until they landed on the other side.

Summary

Knowledge about how to get customer information and what the information tells us has in most companies been restricted to a few specialists. This knowledge must become more widespread so all employees can readily hear the Voice of the Customer. The Kano Model illustrates different reactions customers have to changes in different characteristics and the Taguchi Loss Function makes visible the need to focus on getting ever closer to our customers' targets. Organizations are changing policies and practices so that all managers and other employees feel responsible for customer satisfaction and know how what they do affects customers. Better results are coming from systems of customer-focused meetings and from other methods for responding rapidly to changing customer needs and concerns.

EPILOGUE

An astute customer knows that you can tell a lot about the quality of an organization's products and services from interactions with its employees: Do they look up and smile as you go by? Do they seem to be enjoying their work?

I often seize an opportunity to talk with someone when they are out of earshot of other employees. My first question is, "**What's it like to work here?**" I once asked this question of a housekeeper who came in to clean my room in a fairly expensive hotel in Cincinnati.

> The housekeeper looked up at me out of the corner of her eye and said suspiciously, "Why do you want to know?"
>
> I replied, "I'm just curious. I travel a lot. And I like to know how people feel about their jobs, their work."
>
> "You're not going to tell anybody, are you?" she asked.
>
> "No," I replied (meaning nobody in the management of her company).
>
> "You won't get me in trouble?" she said, trying to disguise the skepticism in her voice.
>
> "No," I assured her. (And I didn't.)
>
> "It's terrible."
>
> I said, "What do you mean?"
>
> "It's so disorganized," she answered.
>
> "Can you give me an example?" I asked.
>
> "Well, like today. I don't have enough sheets. And I'm going to have to go from floor to floor to find somebody else who can spare some sheets. Yesterday it was towels. The day before that, pillowcases."

I probably don't need to say much more to tell you how that place felt to me as a customer. That very trip I had to go to three rooms to find one that I could live in. In the first room, the bathtub had six inches of dirty water in it. I went back to the desk, stood in line again, and got another room. That one was fine, except somebody else was already living in it. I went back to the desk again. Finally, the third time I got a room that was habitable. Each time the desk clerk was as nice as could be to me.

Two weeks later, at a similarly priced hotel in Chicago, I asked another housekeeper the same question. "What's it like to work here?"

She said, "It's wonderful."

"What do you mean?"

"I'm an immigrant," she said. "I've been in the country for five years and I've had several different jobs. A couple in department stores, and one in another hotel. This place is different."

"In what way?"

"Here, they love us. They don't hate us."

I was stunned to hear such powerful words.

"Can you tell me what that means to you?" I asked.

"Here, when you have problem, they try to figure out how to help you instead of yelling at you and blaming you for the problem. If we need more training, they give us more training. If the problem was caused by trouble in another area, they go help there. It's just wonderful. I love working here."

You've probably guessed that this hotel greatly impressed me with the quality of its services and the environment. A basic message we can all learn from its housekeeper is that **our employees won't be able to treat our customers any better than we treat our employees.** If we respect our employees and help them, they'll respect the customer and help them. But if we blame our employees—look down on them— they'll do the same to our customers.

A hotel chain that received the Baldrige award for its effective management practices has a motto that employees carry on a small card in their pockets: "Ladies and gentlemen serving ladies and gentlemen." It's a powerful message backed up by effective management.

The point is that we will not be successful in building a strong customer focus unless we pay attention to all the core elements of 4th Generation Management: Quality, a Scientific Approach, and All One Team. Employees will not be able to give customers the attention they deserve if they fear making a mistake, if they get blamed for problems that are outside their control, if chaos prevents them from doing their work efficiently, if decisions depend on a manager's whim instead of data and logic, or if managers focus more on figures than on customers. They need to believe they are an important part of a team that operates to serve customers.

Part Three

Managing in a Variable World

PROLOGUE

A longtime employee for a specialty materials company, Jerry eventually became the manager of one of its flagship facilities. Yet no matter how high he moved in the organization, there was always someone higher up asking him to explain deviations between what was planned for the month and what was actually achieved. Every month was the same. Some figures were higher than planned, some lower. And every month Jerry came up with explanations: production was down because there had been some material shortages; costs were up because a key supplier had raised its prices; safety incidents were down because supervisors were keeping a better watch over their work areas. And, every month, Jerry would tell his boss he was taking action to correct any problems with that month's figures ... but he knew from experience that "action" didn't necessarily equal "improvement." Jerry suspected, deep down, that few of the "reasons" he dredged up month after month really had much bearing on the deviations he explained. Occasionally, of course, a major problem or a new breakthrough clearly had a significant impact on results ... but for the most part it seemed that some months just happened to be better and some months just happened to be worse.

A diligent worker, Sylvia had never had any trouble finding part-time jobs during the years when her children were in school. When the last of them went off to college, she wanted a full-time position, one with growth opportunity, and finally landed a job as a teller in a local bank.

Several months into the customary probationary period, Sylvia was unhappy with her progress and confused by the company's reactions to her performance. "Some days my manager tells me what a great job I'm doing," said Sylvia. "Other days, she tells me I'm doing a horrible job. For the life of me I can't figure out what's going on. I work as hard as I can every day. I'm always careful to be extremely polite to customers. I try my hardest to do the work exactly as I was trained. I know I have more problems on some days than on others, but it usually doesn't seem to be linked to anything specific. I don't know what I can do to get consistently better results."

Everyone has had experiences like these. Some of us regularly see figures: costs, revenues, production, sales, errors, defects, customer satisfaction ratings. Those figures are rarely the same twice in a row and there often doesn't seem to be any good reason why. Others of us just work as hard as we can every day, and sometimes the results are good and sometimes they aren't. So what do we do? We look around for explanations. And generally we find something (or someone!) that we can blame for poor results or credit for good results. Sometimes we make changes, hoping to preserve the good and prevent the bad. Yet, despite our good intentions, we continue to have good days and bad ones, good months and bad ones.

Intuitively, of course, we all know that nothing ever happens exactly the same way twice. The cause of this phenomenon is **variation**. Conditions are always changing; the world is filled with variation. What few people realize, however, is the important role that *understanding* variation plays in effective management. Variation is like a fog hindering our sight, a fog that obscures the sources of problems, disguises true improvements, and confounds our perceptions of performance.

> *Joy, a product manager for a pharmaceutical company, was about to give up. Engineers had been working on the "child-proof cap problem" for months, to no avail. Whenever they made the bottle caps tight enough to pass the "child-proof test," they found that most adults had trouble opening the bottles, too. When they made the caps so that adults could open them, they wouldn't pass the child-proof test. The engineers had made numerous changes, trying to find that right balance between child-proof and adult-proof, but they couldn't find it. Joy was certain it was a no-win situation.*

Typical reactions might be to call in the engineers or the equipment operators and make sure they knew that their jobs and the company's future depended on solving the problem. Perhaps there would also be a temptation to get more-competent employees in there to run the process, to buy new equipment, or to have technicians "baby-sit" the process—continually adjusting it to get caps that are tight enough to protect children but not so tight that adults can't open them.

One of a 4th Generation manager's first steps would be to find some way to make the problem more *visible*, to develop a better understanding of the current situation. Following are a few sketches that help. The first picture below simply represents what Joy's company needed: a cap that was tighter than Point A so that children would have a tough time opening it, but not tighter than Point B, where most adults would also have trouble opening the cap.

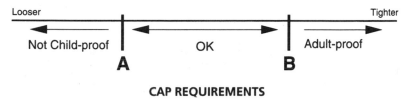

CAP REQUIREMENTS

A second sketch below shows some sample output from the capping process. Each dot represents the measure of tightness of one cap. You can see that not all caps achieved the same tightness. This plot has the classic "bell-shaped" curve—with middle values being more common.

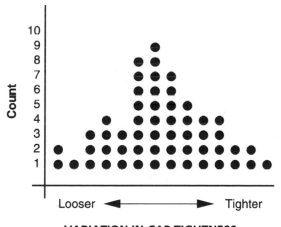

VARIATION IN CAP TIGHTNESS

Joy's problem can be seen more clearly when we combine these two pictures, as shown in the diagram on the next page. As Joy came to realize, none of the changes made in the process had changed the **amount of variation**. When the equipment was set so that all the caps were tight enough to protect children (the top sketch), many caps were too tight for adults to open. And when it was set so that all the caps could be opened by adults (the lower sketch), many could also be opened by children.

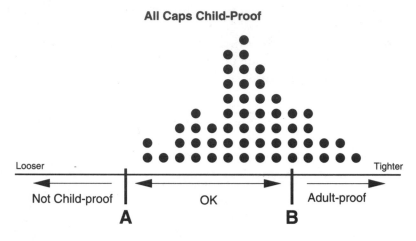

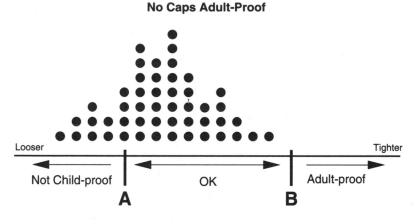

ACTUAL CAPABILITY VS. DESIRED LIMITS

Data points like these represent the **Voice of the Process:** the output is telling us what the process is actually capable of producing. The solution to Joy's problem rested in her ability to bring the Voice of the Process (what the process could do) in line with the Voice of the Customer (what the customer wanted the process to do). In her case, this translated into understanding and reducing the variation in the process.

Joy's situation is far from unique. Variation surrounds us. It influences results, the information we receive, and thus our business decisions. Here's another example:

> *A small company launched a new product that turned out to have amazing success. Though there were a few bad months, sales kept increasing month after month after month. The revenues this product brought in provided a much-needed relief to the company's line of credit and supported new expansion efforts. Then, suddenly, there was a downturn. Three bad months in a row.*

How would you react to the dip in sales of this key product? Try to motivate your sales staff? Reduce prices? Place additional ads? Mail promotional materials to potential new buyers? Call previous buyers or prospects and see why sales had dropped? Do nothing?

What if I assured you that an unusual event caused those latest figures—that something specific had happened to cause that dip, such as the appearance of a new competing product. Would that change your reactions? And what if the opposite were true? What if I could assure you that the dip in sales was just part of the normal variation in sales—that nothing special had happened—and that next month you were likely to have sales at or above the previous figures *even if you did nothing*? How would that affect your reactions?

Luckily, there is a body of knowledge about variation that helps us answer such questions. Variation is not an unfathomable black box. Quite the reverse. Variation has many signals that provide clues about what's going on, **signals that are critical for effective management**. With an understanding of variation, the people we met in the preceding examples would be in better positions to determine appropriate actions. They would better understand the conflicting messages they continually receive: "Caps are too tight ... uh, no, now they're too loose"; "Sales are great ... oops, now they're not so great"; "Your performance was great yesterday, but what happened today?"

Knowledge about variation is a key element of the Scientific Approach. Our ability to produce rapid, sustained improvement is tied directly to our ability to understand and interpret variation. Until we know how to react to variation, any actions we take are almost as likely to make things worse, or to have no effect at all, as they are to make things better.

One of my favorite quotes from Dr. Lloyd S. Nelson sums up this need:

"Failure to understand variation is a central problem of management."

Of all the issues I've worked on with managers over the years, the basic principles of variation have probably had the most profound impact, made the most dramatic changes in their view of the world. This part looks at what it means to have a worldview that incorporates knowledge of variation. We'll see how an appreciation for variation can help us pick out the signals in the fog, become much more effective managers, make better decisions, and drive more rapid improvement.

7
PRINCIPLES OF VARIATION

One year Jeff's department had a travel expenditures budget of $100,000, but the actual expenditures were $110,000. He wasn't sure whether to tell his staff they'd have only $90,000 to work with the next year (so that if they came in $10,000 over again, they'd hit his real target of $100,000), or just to be realistic and set the budget for $110,000 since that's how much money it seemed to take.

A team had six months to complete a project, but they finished in five. Based on this experience, their manager scheduled the next similar project for five months.

Mary reviewed the figures for a third time. It looked like her expenses for the year were going to be under budget by $80,000. Management always used last year's expenses to budget for the next year. So she knew she had to get busy and spend that $80,000. Otherwise her budget would be cut next year.

When she came on board, Dolores was worried about having to pick up all the new skills for her job. Fortunately, she befriended the person who had been hired several months earlier. He taught her what he had picked up.

Last month, Jules had to hire two temporary workers at the last moment to get the monthly invoices out on time. This month, he had the workers lined up at the beginning of the month so there wouldn't be a scramble.

Ethel monitored the warp on the plastic moldings quite carefully. If there was the slightest hint of curly edges, she knew the pressure was too high and she'd lower it accordingly. If the edges were too thick, she knew she'd gotten the pressure too low and would raise it.

Each week, Pete ordered enough inventory to bring levels for all products back up to four times the previous week's sales.

Like these people, each of us makes decisions every day based on information we receive. The question is whether our decisions are making things better, not having any effect at all, or even making things worse. To answer that question, we need to understand a few basic concepts about variation. And for that, I'm going to call on an enterprising fourth grader named Patrick Nolan for some help.

SOURCES OF VARIATION

Patrick Nolan needed a science project. After consulting with his father, a statistician and consultant, Patrick decided to collect data on something he cared about, his school bus. For several weeks he recorded the time the bus picked him up in the morning. He would look at his watch when the bus reached his stop, jot down the time in a ledger, and make a dot on a chart to represent that time. At the end of the project, he had a chart where pickup times for successive school days were plotted in time order.

An example based on Patrick's work is shown on the next page. Not unexpectedly, the pickup times differed from day to day. Just how much they varied is shown in the chart: you can see that most times fall within a band that is indicated with lines, but there were two days on which specific events delayed the pickup time considerably. As the notes show, one day there was a new driver; on another, a faulty door opener. These two unusual events obviously added to the variation in pickup times. But even without them there was still variation in the process.

Think for a moment about some of the things that might affect the pickup time: the amount of traffic, the weather, how long the bus driver waited for the children at previous stops, what time the driver

110

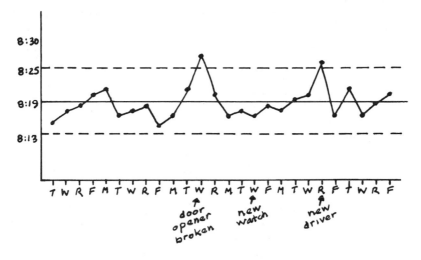

PATRICK'S CHART

got started, and so on. These are called **common causes of variation**. Common causes

- Are present all the time in a process, though their impact varies
- *Individually,* have a small effect on the variation
- *Collectively,* can add up to quite a bit of variation

All processes have common causes of variation. Some also have other sources. For instance, the factors that led to two abnormally late pickup times for Patrick—the new driver and the faulty door opener—are called **special causes of variation**. Special causes

- Arc not always present in a process; they appear sporadically
- Come from *outside* the usual process (the faulty door opener and the poorly trained new driver, for example, were outside the ordinary process of picking children up and taking them to school)
- Can contribute either a small or large amount to the total variation, but typically have a much bigger impact on variation than any single common cause

All measures are subject to these causes of variation. Sales figures, for example:

- **Common cause** factors could include weather conditions that influence shoppers' moods, delays in processing orders if a clerk is out sick, fluctuations in consumer confidence, etc.

- **Special cause** factors could be anything from a preannounced price increase to a price war, to a major cleanup after a flood.

The time it takes to close the books at the end of the month is another example:

- **Common causes** could include having an accounting clerk get interrupted by a five-minute phone call, having slow computer response occasionally, having trouble deciphering some hand-writing.
- **Special causes** might be anything from having the computer crash to having a facility in the path of floodwaters that prevents employees from getting to needed records, to having a change in tax regulations.

You can do this same exercise for your process: Factors that are always present in the work but whose impact varies from day to day or month to month are common causes. Factors that disrupt the usual flow are special causes.

A Model of Variation

In decades of teaching about variation, I've discovered the importance of having a simple, visual model of common and special cause variation. One of the best devices for this purpose is called a **quincunx** (pronounced "kwin-cunks"), shown in the diagram on the following page. It was invented in the 19th century by a man named Sir Francis Galton to study probability and genetics. A quincunx has a hopper of beads at the top, and a mechanism for dropping one bead at time down through a funnel. The beads bounce through a grid of pins, then come to rest in a series of slots below the pins.

The rows of pins represent common causes: the many factors *within a process*. Special causes are represented by a bump that causes the funnel to move. The rows of pins, like common causes, are always present, always acting on the process, and each individually has a small effect on the final result. A bump to the funnel, like a special cause, comes and goes, and typically has a bigger impact on the results than any common cause.

Imagine a quincunx operating with only common causes—only the pins—influencing the outcomes. Bead after bead drops through a

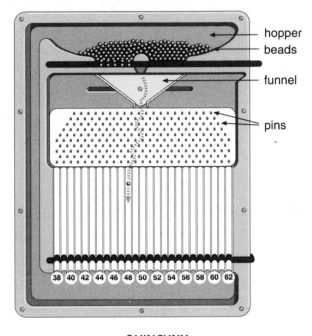

QUINCUNX

stationary funnel. The beads bounce through the pins, and land in slots below, labeled from 38 to 62. The following plot shows one possible outcome of 25 bead drops. As you can see, the effect of the pins is random: some beads end up high, some low, and some in the middle.

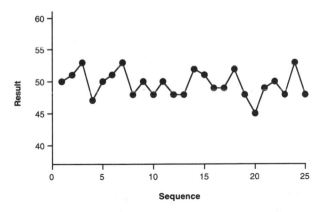

PLOT OF COMMON CAUSE VARIATION

If we kept dropping beads and plotting the results, the chart would eventually stretch straight out before us as far as the eye could see, like a highway across the desert. Though we don't know where the next bead will fall, we are reasonably confident it will fall somewhere on that highway. For that reason, a process that has only common cause variation is said to be **stable** or **predictable.**

COMMON CAUSE HIGHWAY

As Patrick found out, however, sometimes a process also has special causes. In our quincunx model, a special cause is represented by a bump that moves the funnel. What would this do to our highway? We can't predict exactly how far or in which direction the funnel will go. A process with special causes might be better represented by a highway through an earthquake zone: likely to shift suddenly to the side by several feet or more.

SPECIAL CAUSE HIGHWAY

For that reason, processes that have special causes of variation—bumps to the funnel—are said to be **unstable** or **unpredictable.**

114

Applying the quincunx model

Let's look at Patrick's experience in terms of the quincunx. We said traffic was one source of common causes in his process: traffic is always present, always acting on the process. It can't be represented by one pin that the beads either hit or don't hit. It is better modeled by rows of pins, representing dozens or perhaps hundreds of cars, vans, trucks, motorcycles . . . each of which individually has a small effect on pickup time. Other common causes include weather . . . how many children take the bus on a given day . . . what time the driver starts the route . . . which traffic lights are red, yellow, or green. We would need to add one or more rows of pins for each of these common causes. Think about a bead dropping through a quincunx with many common causes—many rows of pins. The cumulative effect of these rows of pins can be quite large even though the contribution of any single row is small.

The special causes in Patrick's process—the faulty door opener and new driver—we model with a bump that moves the funnel. They represent special, specific factors outside the usual process that are not present all the time. Before a special cause appears, we have no way to predict how much the funnel will move. Special causes add additional variation to a system beyond that contributed by common causes.

To summarize, processes with only common causes are **stable** or **predictable**; you might hear them referred to as **in statistical control**. Processes with special causes are **unstable, unpredictable,** and **not in statistical control**.

Process with only common causes	Process with both common causes and special causes
Stable Predictable In statistical control	Unstable Unpredictable Not in statistical control

Structural Variation

Many processes have yet another source of variation, what I call **structural variation.** Earlier, I described a company that saw a drop in sales of a key new product. This company would have been disappointed had their "highway" of results lain flat before them. They wanted sales to climb steadily, to have the highway head northeast

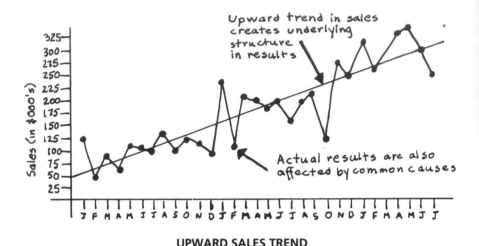

UPWARD SALES TREND

instead of due east. If sales had truly risen *steadily,* a plot of the outcomes would have looked like the smooth straight line in the sketch shown above. But, like many processes, sales has common cause variation as well as structural variation. So a plot of the actual sales had variation about the line.

Here, the structural component of the variation was an underlying upward trend in sales. We can simulate a trend with the quincunx by starting with the funnel at one end and moving it up (or down) the same amount (perhaps one unit) after each bead drop. The pins, or common causes, always add to the variation in results, but overall the trend would still be in the direction in which we were moving the funnel. Other types of structural variation include seasonality and, in manufacturing companies, factors such as tool wear or degradation of chemicals in baths. To model seasonal variation, on the other hand, we could move the funnel slowly back and forth, right to left then back to the right, and so on, dropping beads as we go.

Basics of variation

Patrick Nolan's experience, the quincunx model, and the other examples illustrate the basic principles of variation that every manager and employee needs to understand to make effective decisions. This understanding prepares us for the topic covered in the next chapter: what effect different actions have on variation.

116

8

THE PRICE OF IGNORANCE

Meet Walter, a fictitious operator of a drill press. Walter's job is to do what we all want to do: produce output that meets customer needs. Today, Walter is drilling holes in components for a customer who needs those holes at a spot 50 cm from the edge. We will mimic this process by dropping beads through the quincunx and moving the funnel to simulate actions he takes on the process. We'll start with the funnel targeted over the slot labeled 50.

> As Walter came to work he ran into his manager, who reminded him that they had some big orders today, so he'd better get busy.
>
> "Our customers come to us because we deliver high quality," the manager reminded Walter. "They want us to make sure that all the holes are drilled at 50 so that the final assemblies work properly. They'll accept 49 and 51, but they really want the holes at 50. They're waiting for these components, so you'd better get busy."
>
> "You bet," said Walter. "50 it is. I always do my best to provide the customers with what they want."
>
> Walter soon got the drill press up and running. While waiting for the components to come off the line, he remembered the newspaper he'd brought with him that day so he could check yesterday's sports scores. A pair of tickets for the next game was riding on the results. Walter picked up the paper, intending only to glance at the scores and the standings ... but it was some time later when he realized the press had been running without him. He rushed to the machine and saw that 25 components had come off the drill. Walter could see that not all of the holes ended up at 50 and became concerned.

Walter has shown us **Rule 1 of the Funnel: Negligence**. He let the process operate without interference; or, as translated into our quincunx model, he left the funnel alone. The outcome of his negligence is shown in the following chart: the 25 data points represent the location of the 25 drilled holes. The results are plotted in the order the components came off the press. As you can see, many of the holes did not fall where Walter's customers wanted them to be.

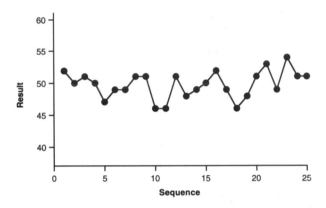

RESULTS FROM RULE 1: NEGLIGENCE

"Look at all the variation in these results," Walter thought to himself. "Our customers aren't going to be too happy. I'd better pay more attention. I can't just stand here; I've got to do something! Maybe if I make adjustments whenever the hole isn't in the right place, I'll get better results."

Walter formed a plan of attack that we'll call **Rule 2: Adjust for the Deviation.** In Walter's second strategy, if the hole is above or below where it's supposed to be, he will adjust the equipment in the opposite direction. Again, we'll mimic his actions on the quincunx by moving the funnel as shown on the top of the facing page. So, if the bead lands high, say at 52, we'll move the funnel *down* by 2 units to adjust for that deviation.

Walter sure felt better now that he was paying attention to the process. When the first hole came out at 51 (one unit above the target), he adjusted the machine settings down to 49 before drilling another hole. The second hole came out at 51 again—still one unit too high—so he adjusted the settings down another unit before drilling the third hole. On the bottom of the facing page is the chart showing his results this time.

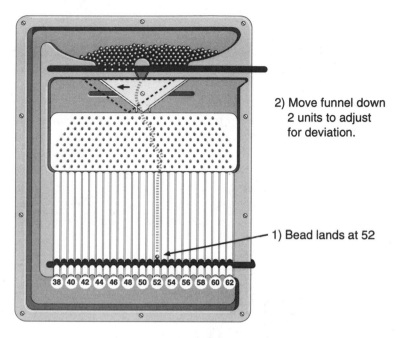

2) Move funnel down 2 units to adjust for deviation.

1) Bead lands at 52

38 40 42 44 46 48 50 52 54 56 58 60 62

WALTER'S SECOND STRATEGY

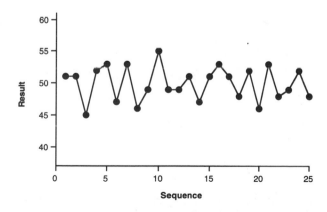

RESULTS FROM RULE 2: ADJUST FOR THE DEVIATION

119

Walter swallowed hard when he saw the results of his adjustment scheme: they seemed to be even worse than when he did nothing at all. When he left things alone, he had 15 out of 25 results the customer would accept. Now he only had 9 acceptable results.

"Well," he thought to himself, "if I don't get fired for reading the newspaper on the job, I'm sure to get it for these results. Our customers aren't going to be happy at all!"

He thought for a few minutes. A light bulb went off in his head. "I know what the problem is! I was adjusting the funnel based on where it was last positioned, forgetting all about my original target. Maybe if I use 50 as a constant reference point, and make my adjustments from there, the results will improve."

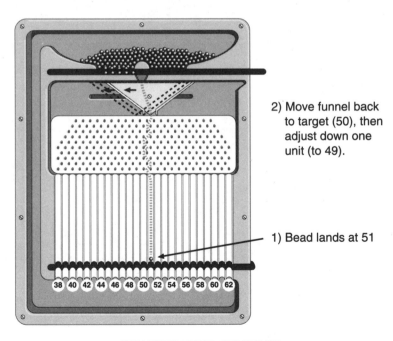

2) Move funnel back to target (50), then adjust down one unit (to 49).

1) Bead lands at 51

WALTER'S THIRD STRATEGY

So Walter tried this new strategy, which we'll call **Rule 3: Adjust Relative to Target**. In this strategy, Walter always returned the machine settings to their original position before making his compensating adjustment; in the quincunx, we move the funnel back to the target of 50 before making the adjustments. The second bead, for instance, landed at 49, so we moved the funnel back to 50, then up by one unit. When the next bead landed at 51, we moved the funnel back to 50, then down by one unit.

Walter began cranking components off the line, measuring the hole location on each one and making adjustments accordingly. He soon starting seeing results even farther from the customer's target. The placement of the holes oscillated wildly, one way too high, the next, way too low. Obviously this strategy wasn't what he needed.

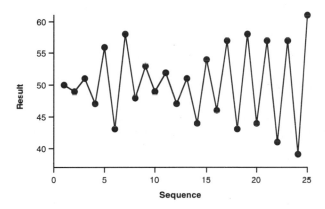

RESULTS OF RULE 3: ADJUST RELATIVE TO TARGET

Walter was having a bad day. No matter what he did, the variation kept getting worse and worse.

Soon, his manager came to seek him out. "This latest batch was awful," said the manager. "George called me to say this is not what he hoped we'd do for them. He said that if we can't make them all at 50, at least try to make them all the same. It's the variation that's killing them."

As the manager walked away, Walter breathed a sigh of relief. At least he wasn't fired yet. And he was even getting another chance. He thought for a few minutes about what he could do to make all the holes the same. Finally he decided that he would move the funnel so it was always targeted at the most recent result. That way, at least, maybe he could get a string of them that were the same value.

Walter's new strategy illustrates **Rule 4: Each One Like the Last One**. Under this new scheme, he would target his equipment to match

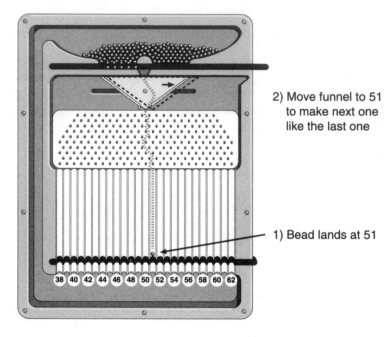

2) Move funnel to 51
to make next one
like the last one

1) Bead lands at 51

WALTER'S FOURTH STRATEGY

the last results. So if the hole ended up at 47, he would adjust the setting to 47; if it wound up at 51, he'd change the settings to 51. Below are the results from this strategy.

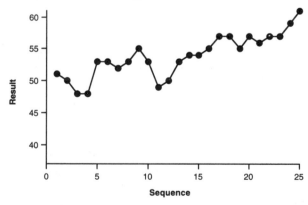

RESULTS OF RULE 4: EACH ONE LIKE THE LAST ONE

Poor Walter just can't seem to win. The results of his latest strategy seem to be wandering aimlessly away from the target. And now he was fresh out of ideas.

122

Comparing the Results

Let's compare Walter's results. The diagram below shows all four charts side-by-side. The first plot is what happened when Walter let the drill press operate without any interference. That was Rule 1: negligence. He then tried to adjust for the deviation, Rule 2—but that just caused the spread of points to increase (mathematically this will increase the width of his "highway" by 41% in the long run). With Rule 3, adjust relative to the target, the results showed every indication of bouncing wildly in opposite directions. When these strategies failed, Walter gave up on trying to get everything at 50 and tried to make each one like the last one, Rule 4. Under this latest strategy, he felt like he was taking a random walk through a forest: with each step he was likely to be farther away from home, "off to the Milky Way."

We can learn several important lessons from Walter's experience:

- Each of the strategies sounded logical.
- The disastrous outcomes were obvious to us only because we plotted the results over time.
- Until Walter has a better understanding of variation, his company will be better off paying him to read a newspaper!

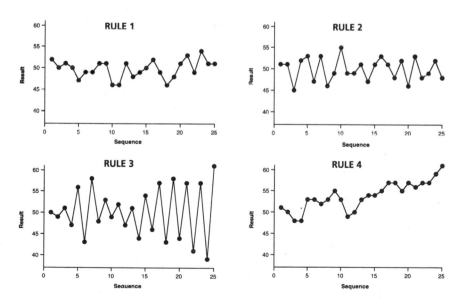

SIDE-BY-SIDE COMPARISON OF WALTER'S RESULTS

The Rules and Real Life

"That's all well and good, Brian," you may be saying. "A nice little parable. But nothing like that happens in real life." Unfortunately, actions like Walter's happen all the time, every day, in every organization at high levels and low. Let's take another look at the examples at the beginning of the previous chapter and the kinds of decisions these employees made based on their most recent results:

- Jeff's department had a travel expenditures budget of $100,000 one year, but the actual expenditures were $110,000. He wasn't sure whether to tell his staff they'll have only $90,000 to work with the next year (so that if they come in $10,000 over again, they'll hit his real target of $100,000)—**(RULE 2: Adjust for the Deviation)**—or to just be realistic and set the budget for $110,000 since that's how much money it seems to take **(RULE 4: Each One Like the Last One)**.

- A team had six months to complete a project, but they finished in five. Their manager scheduled the next project for five months **(RULE 4: Each One Like the Last One)**.

- Mary reviewed the figures for a third time. It looked like her expenses for the year were going to be under budget by $80,000. Management always used last year's expenses to budget for the next year. So she knew she had to get busy and spend that $80,000. Otherwise her budget would be cut next year **(RULE 4: Each One Like the Last One)**.

- When she came on board, Dolores was worried about having to pick up all the new skills for her job. Fortunately, she befriended the person who had been hired several months earlier who taught her what he had picked up **("worker training worker"; RULE 4: Each One Like the Last One)**.

- Last month, Jules had to hire two temporary workers at the last moment to get the monthly invoices out on time. This month, he had the workers lined up at the beginning of the month so there wouldn't be a scramble **(RULE 4: Each One Like the Last One)**.

- Ethel monitored the warp on the plastic moldings quite carefully. If there was the slightest hint of curly edges, she knew the pressure was too high and she'd lower it accordingly. If the edges were too thick, she knew she'd gotten the pressure too low and would raise it **(RULE 2: Adjust for the Deviation)**.

- Each week, Pete ordered enough inventory to bring levels for all products back up to *four times* the previous week's sales **(Amplified Rule 2)**.

You might notice that none of these examples followed Rule 3, which, indeed, rarely if ever happens in practice; it just doesn't seem to come up as a natural way to compensate for variation (though it sounds logical to most people when they hear it explained). But Rules 2 and 4 do capture actions that people instinctively take. Rule 2 is based on the suspicion that the *last deviation* will repeat: for example, if the last result was over by $10,000, we tacitly assume that the same deviation will occur next time so we adjust down by $10,000. Rule 4 is based on the suspicion that the *last figure* will repeat: we assume that if this project took five months, the next one will too.

Actions like these just compound the problems from the common causes, special causes, and structural variation already present. Rule 4 situations always remind me of the "telephone" game where a message is whispered around a circle of children, each child repeating the message they thought the previous child said. The final version usually bears little resemblance to the original message—an outcome that is just as true for most communication in business situations today.

Tampering

The quincunx holds many valuable lessons for us, not the least of which is seeing how our failure to understand variation can affect results. All of the preceding examples reflect **overreaction to variation**, or **tampering**: making continual adjustments to a stable system, result by result, hoping to make things better. Tampering can be done by anyone: a manager, an operator, or even a machine:

> *A chemical company started noticing increased variation in a key raw material purchased from another chemical company. They asked the supplier what had happened about April when the increased variation starting appearing. The supplier found that was when the new sophisticated $1 million equipment had gone on-line. The customer asked them to please go back to the old way of producing the material.*

> ———

> *One Fortune 50 company found that about half of its automatic compensation devices in its machining operations were increasing variation, not reducing it.*

125

But of all the sources of tampering, the most deadly is management asking for explanations when in fact the variation is due to common causes. Look for instance at the report below.

COST BY COMPONENT
PERIOD 12, 19XX

	Actual	Plan	Variance Fav.(Unf.)	Volume	Usage	Spending	Price
Pulpwood	$131.63	$139.29	$ 7.66	$	$(1.98)	$	$ 9.64
Waste	27.18	33.61	6.43		2.36		4.07
Other Raw Materials	28.93	30.74	1.81		1.46		0.35
Labor	30.10	26.14	(3.96)	(1.30)		(2.66)	
Repairs	22.52	24.34	1.82	(1.22)		3.04	
Steam	32.01	35.37	3.36	(0.25)	0.82		2.79
Power	73.79	70.90	(2.89)	(1.76)	(2.20)		1.07
Wrapper	2.99	2.90	(0.09)				(0.09)
Clothing	11.11	10.18	(0.93)	(0.50)	(0.41)		(0.02)
Supplies	7.95	8.37	0.42	(0.42)		0.84	
Other Expenses	3.91	4.33	0.42	(0.22)		0.64	
Mill Burden	66.57	67.67	1.10	(3.38)		4.48	
Mill Depreciation	50.42	48.55	(1.87)	(2.42)		0.55	
Total	$489.11	$502.39	$13.28	$(11.47)	$ 0.05	$ 6.89	$17.81

MANAGER'S REPORT

Almost every manager I've met gets reports like these. Typically, they circle or highlight big negative variances, then ask someone, "What happened? What are you doing about it?" By asking for explanations, demanding action based on one or two points, we are tampering, overreacting to variation, which often just increases variation and costs. Are you reacting to figures like this? Causing people to take action on common cause variation? Are you seeing trends where there are no trends, and missing trends when there are trends? Remember Walter's lessons. Rule 2 *increased* variation 41%. This can have a big impact!

Think of yourself as a big gear. You turn a fraction of a degree: "WHAT HAPPENED?" The next level of gears have to move a bit more to keep up: "I don't know. I'll go see." Those gears turn the next level of gears, on down through the organization, until you get to the smallest gears who are turning frantically trying to keep up: "I'm looking! I'm looking! I'm looking! I'm looking!"

"Why are costs up? What are you doing about it? Why are revenues down? What are you doing about it?" The big gear turns a notch and the little gears whirl in frenzy trying to keep up. If you don't know whether it's a common or special cause, a better motto would be "Don't just do something—stand there!" It won't create rapid improvement, but at least you won't actively be making things worse.

What happened?

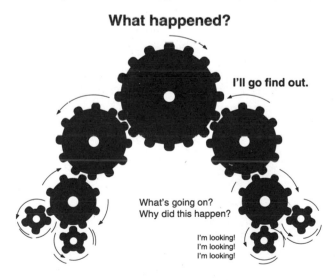

I'll go find out.

What's going on?
Why did this happen?

I'm looking!
I'm looking!
I'm looking!

THE BIG GEAR TURNS

Tampering is a major source of increased costs. It is one of the biggest sources of waste. It accomplishes nothing except to give the false sense that we're taking action. It leads to higher costs, increased variation, and more wasted effort:

- People's time is chewed up developing and submitting explanations:

  One company currently spends approximately $4.5 million annually just on employees whose full-time jobs are to make budgets come in on target each month. Most of their actions are tampering, are increasing *variation in other key aspects of the business.*

- After a while, people learn what explanations will be accepted. Sometimes, they just rotate through a fixed set. The net effect: no organizational learning.

- Other people spend time adjusting month after month, churning up the organization: marketing campaigns start and stop, sales puts on a push, then the rest of the organization scrambles to deal with an influx of orders—and when the rush is over, sales drop below their previous levels, leading to idle time.

- People learn false lessons and put in false solutions: Sales are down so they send out a direct mail piece and sales go up; we believe the two are related—even though sales may have gone up anyway—so when sales are down again, we do another direct mail piece.

And these consequences don't apply just to our businesses. They can have very real personal effects as well.

"I have a heart condition that is associated with a greater risk of strokes due to blood clots," said the man. "So I take a blood-thinning drug. This drug regulates a particular characteristic of the blood related to clotting. My physician would test my blood periodically, and adjust the dose of the drug based on the results. Recently, we started plotting the results of this test ... and came to realize that we were essentially using Rule 2 of the funnel to manage a stable system! Our attempts to control this characteristic led to even greater variation than if we had just left things alone. We keep the plot up to date now and know better than to tamper with this system as long as it's stable!"

THE VP'S DILEMMA

> *Ed was a regional VP for a service company that had facilities around the world. He was determined that the facilities in his region would get the highest customer satisfaction ratings in the company. If he noticed that a facility had a major drop in satisfaction ratings in one month or had "below average" ratings for three months in a row, he would call the manager and ask what had happened—and make it clear that the next month's rating had better improve. And most of the time, it did!*

Ed was doing the best he could to encourage consistently high customer satisfaction ratings in his region. But let's look a little more deeply and revisit the questions at the beginning of the previous chapter: are his actions making things better? having little effect on the status quo? making things worse?

An excerpt from one of his periodic reports is shown on the next page.

I'm sure you've seen reports like this. What would you pick out? The locale that scored the highest went from a 49 in February to a 94 in March—up more than 90%! Surely a reason to celebrate (after making sure the number 94 wasn't just an accidental transposition of another 49). You might write a letter of congratulations to that manager, one that would go into his or her permanent record. The locale ranked sixth unfortunately went from 90 to 69—down 21 points. They are still in the top ten but obviously slipping badly. The locales ranked 13th and 14th both plummeted 34 points! Surely heads should roll there!

The manager of locale #11 provided me with even more data. The customer satisfaction ratings for his site, going back two years are shown below Ed's report. I've added some lines to this chart to indicate the centerline and width of the highway of variation. As we can see, all the data points fall on the highway—which means this process is stable, in statistical control. As far as we can tell, all of the ratings are produced by the same set of common causes. A lot of little things (the pins) add up in one direction one month and in another direction the next. There's nothing special about the high months or the low months. Nothing special about the latest data point or the seemingly abrupt changes. If this company continues to do what it has been doing, it can expect the customer satisfaction ratings to continue to fall anywhere between 22 and 100. How does that make you feel as a manager? Are you happy with those limits? This manager was not at all happy!

129

INTEROFFICE MEMO

To: All managers
From: Ed J.
Date: April 17, 19XX
Subject: March Customer Service Scores

5

Bad news! We dropped five points! We should all focus on improving these scores right away. I realize that our usage rates have increased faster than anticipated, so you've really got to hustle to give our customers great service. I know you can do it! Particular areas we need to pay attention to are:
- Prompt service
- Cleanliness of facilities

	Site	March	February
1.	Cleveland East	94	49
2.	Bloomington	85	87
3.	Chicago	82	90
4.	Erie	79	72
5.	Toledo	73	58
6.	Hoosier Dome	69	90
7.	Milwaukee	68	79
8.	Detroit	65	35
9.	Dubuque	62	85
10.	Springfield	57	57
11.	Oak Park	57	58
12.	Cincinnati	50	25
13.	Dayton	48	82
14.	Schaumburg	46	80
15.	St. Paul	45	39
16.	Cleveland West	43	65
17.	Mpls-Central	35	62
18.	Dearborn	27	48
	North Central Region Average	60	65

REPORT ON CUSTOMER SATISFACTION RATINGS

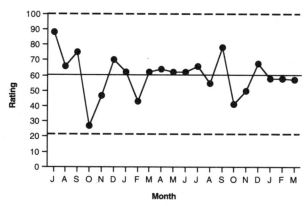

CUSTOMER SATISFACTION RATINGS

We'd like to drive these figures higher through increased customer satisfaction. But very often the variation inherent in the figures—here 22 to 100—is so great we wind up having little idea how the locale is really doing, and whether any of the changes being made are helping. These charts have many lessons for us. Among the most important: *Our indicators of performance are far more variable than we'd like to believe.* In other words, our view through the fog is much less clear than we thought.

Many people resist this learning. Throughout my career, I've had many conversations with managers about plots like the one on the previous page. Inevitably, they go something like this:

> *"Brian, I live in the real world. I don't have the luxury of looking at data from 20 or 30 months ago. I have to manage with the most recent information. I've got to live in the now!"*

> *"OK," I say, a bit tongue-in-cheek, "here's a chart that shows the most recent figure."*

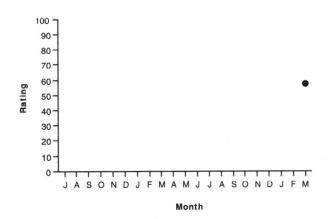

> *"How would you react to this customer satisfaction rating?" I ask the manager. "How can you plan? How can you tell whether this locale is getting better or worse, or staying the same?"*

> *"Well, that's not all I look at. I also like to have the previous month."*

> *"OK, here's a chart with the two most recent figures."*

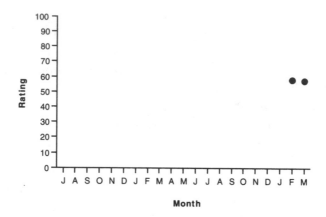

"Why do you like to have last month's figure?" I ask.
"So I can see how I'm doing, what my short-term trend is."
"And how are you doing?"
"Oh, down a little. Not too much change," says the manager.
I probe a bit further. "Anything else?"
"I also like to look at the same month last year."
"OK, here's a plot that shows it, too."

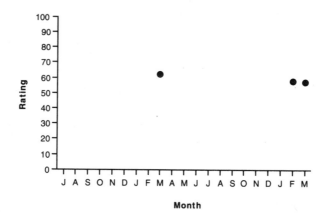

"Why do you like to have the same month last year?" I ask.
"So I can compute my long-term trend."
"How's your long-term trend?"
"Not so good."
And when I ask, there's always an explanation of the reasons
for both the long-term trend as well as for the latest result.

Do you look at data this way? This month versus last month? This month versus the same month last year? Do you sometimes just look at the latest data point? The last two data points?

It took me a long time to realize that I was at an advantage since I had studied statistics before I became interested in management. I couldn't understand why people would only want to look at two data points. Finally it became clear to me. With any two data points, it's easy to compute a trend: "Things are down 2% this month from last month. This month is 30% above the same month last year." Unfortunately, **we learn nothing of importance by comparing two results when they both come from a stable process ... and most data of importance to management are from stable processes.**

Look again at the three-dot chart (p. 132) and the chart with "all the dots" (p. 130) that represents performance over a two-year period. Which one would help you do a better job of planning and predicting? Of being able to tell whether any changes truly made things better? Most managers, once they've seen all the data, are reluctant to go back to looking at figures any other way.

INOCULATION

The world we live in is a messy place. Our systems all have common cause variation and some have structural variation; most also suffer from special causes and the effects of tampering, overreacting to variation. Though some variation is inevitable, we can greatly improve quality and reduce costs by eliminating as much variation as we can. The first step is to **plot the data.** The second step is to **stop tampering.** To do that, all we have to do is to stop doing things we now do that are making things worse. If I convince you of nothing else in this book, it'll be worth the time and money you've invested if you learn just two lessons: *plot the data and stop tampering.*

But of course, there is much more. I'm not advocating that we sit around reading newspapers all day. An inoculation against overreacting is progress, but won't lead to rapid, sustained improvement. How, then, *should* we react to variation? The answer, as we'll see in the next chapter, takes us back to young Patrick's lessons.

9
STRATEGIES FOR REDUCING VARIATION

A company makes large complex engines that are bought by other companies and assembled into final sophisticated products. A major customer complained that the fuel consumption varied too much from engine to engine. The supplier company looked back at its records and found the ten engines with the worst fuel consumption and the ten engines with the best fuel consumption. It then tried to identify differences between these engines.

Was this a good strategy or not? Will it lead to rapid improvement? The answer: **It depends on whether the system that produced the high fuel-consumption engines was the same as the system that produced the low fuel-consumption engines.** That is, are they from the same highway or from different highways?

What do I mean by that? Think back to the school bus example. Patrick experienced two days when special causes led to later pickup times than usual; the variation in the rest of the days was due to common causes. Suppose we picked out one of the early pickup times and one of the later times that were both still within the highway of common cause variation. The question, again: "Is the system that produced the early time the same as the system that produced the later time?" And the answer, in this case, is yes. The same factors influenced both points.

Think about the quincunx. When the funnel is steady and only common causes (the pins) are at work, a low point occurs when a bead

135

happens to hit the left side of a series of pins. A high point occurs when a bead happens to hit the right side of a series of pins. If we look to see what caused the difference, we'll find nothing of value. The pins are the same in both cases, and no row is making an overwhelming, unique contribution to the result. **In a common cause situation, there's no such thing as THE cause.** It's just a bunch of little things that add up one way one day and another way the next. So we don't learn much by trying to find differences between high points and low points when only common causes are at work.

The engine producer faced the same issue: Is the system that produced the high fuel-consumption engines the same as the system that produced the low fuel-consumption engines? Subsequent data analysis showed that, indeed, all of those engines were produced by the same set of common cause factors that just happened to add up on the high side one day and on the low side another.

In a way, these engineers were lucky. It could have been much worse. They could have found a factor that they thought explained the difference between the ten best engines and the ten worst when really it was just coincidence. They would have learned a false lesson. They could have taken action to put in a solution to prevent that sort of problem in the future. This almost surely would have added to cost and increased bureaucracy, and would not have been effective. As Will Rogers reminds us:

> *"It's not what we don't know that hurts, it's what we know that ain't so."*

The false lessons cost us. Better to know how to use data wisely.

Think back to the school bus for a moment. What if we compared one of the late times that was produced by a special cause with the times within the common cause variation. "Is the system the same?" No. There was something fundamentally *different*. On one day there was a new driver. On the other day, the door opener wasn't working correctly. Something special, specific, had bumped the funnel.

Suppose you were the school bus supervisor for Patrick's school district, and you received complaints from teachers that the children on this route often arrived late. How would you react? The biggest delays, of course, occur when special causes arise. To counteract those sources of variation, you'd need to discover **what was different** on those particular days and take corrective action to prevent those special causes from reappearing. For example, provide better training for new drivers and perhaps improve the preventive maintenance schedule to prevent problems such as the door opener.

Once we've succeeded in eliminating delays due to special causes, what next? To change the common cause variation, we'll need to **reconfigure the system** somehow. We could, for instance, tell all bus drivers not to wait as long at each stop for children who might be late (though parents and children might complain about that course of action!). Or we could start the route earlier, select a new route that has fewer traffic lights, or reassign some children to other routes. Each of these changes affects the number of common causes or reduces their impact.

The differences between common cause and special cause variation thus *require* us to use different managerial approaches to deal with each if we are to be effective. With unstable processes, ones with special causes, we are interested in finding out what was different when the special cause appeared. With a stable process, one with only common causes, the answers are often more subtle.

One of the biggest revelations in dealing with variation is that *most problems arise from common causes*. Yet, paradoxically, it still pays to work on special causes first. Special causes present us with a chance to learn the easy way; let's take advantage of that opportunity. In addition, if we do not eliminate special causes first, they will cloud our vision and make it difficult for us to tell what the common cause variation is saying and make it difficult for us to judge the effect of changes. If we tried to work on common causes first—before removing the special causes—we'd waste a lot of time and effort following false leads. In this chapter, we'll look at the important differences between these approaches and their implications for managerial action.

IMPROVING AN UNSTABLE PROCESS

Luke couldn't have been happier with how his facility was working. Day after day, things clicked along like clockwork. Then one day he arrived at work to discover the place in an uproar. The final product had a severe flaking problem. Customers would never accept it. Luke knew something had changed, but what?

Luke's experience beautifully illustrates the cardinal rule of special causes: they provide us with an "easy" chance to learn, and we'd better take advantage of it! Not all special causes announce themselves as loudly as the one Luke encountered, but all are telling us the same message: something has changed, something has bumped the funnel . . . and if we look for what was *different now*, we may be able to find that special cause. In Luke's case, after several weeks of frustration, they discovered that the very day the process went sour was the day they began using raw materials delivered by truck instead of by rail. No one had a clue why that should make a difference, but that was about the only change they could find. Further investigation revealed that the settling of the materials during the truck transport was much different than the settling that had occurred during rail transport: there was more separation of material, with small beads making their way to the bottom and larger beads to the top. This seemingly minor change caused the material to behave entirely differently in the formulation process. This knowledge helped them back another, better analysis of the trade-offs between truck and rail transportation.

A common mistake in reacting to special causes is to change the process so that it will accommodate special causes in the future. For example, they could have added a mixing step in this process to counteract the separation. But adding steps like that tends to add cost and bureaucracy. In most cases, it's far better to work on the source of the special cause to prevent recurrence. In this case, the immediate remedy was simple because there was no difference in costs between truck and rail; they simply went back to shipping by rail. But they didn't stop there. They went on to understand the effects of different amounts of separation. This led them to understand how much separation was possible and to develop a simple test that was used to assess separation.

The **special cause strategy** for improving unstable systems is

- **Get timely data so special causes are signaled quickly:** Timely data is essential to effective action against special causes. This is true whether the effect is negative or positive. To get data quickly we might use an approximate figure we can get right away—on projected customer ratings, for instance— rather than waiting days or weeks for a more accurate figure. It's often also useful to look for ways to monitor process factors that are highly correlated with process outputs, such as "on-time" departures as an early process indicator of customer satisfaction with arrival times.

- **Put in place an immediate remedy to contain any damage:**

This step is the Level 1 Fix (p. 35), playing whack-a-mole, putting out the fire. How will we get *this* project back on schedule? What will we do about *this* angry customer? What will we do about the product we've already sent out?

- **Search for the cause—see what was *different*:** What occurred, when, where, and with whom. Also note what did *not* occur: Are there related problems you might have expected to see but didn't? When didn't it occur? Where didn't it occur? Which employees or groups did not have the problem? Look for deep causes. Keep asking "why, why, why" until you get the deepest cause you can affect.

- **Develop a longer-term remedy:** We've learned something very useful. Now when the source of the special cause has been identified, we're in a much better position to develop a long-term fix that can prevent its recurrence, or, if results are good, preserve and maintain the benefit. Generally, this means changing some higher-level system.

What does it mean to change a higher-level system? It's likely that the faulty door opener in Patrick's case was due to either inadequate maintenance policies or poor purchasing policies (perhaps buying on initial price tag alone instead of total lifetime cost). Actions to prevent problems with a new driver might include more effective training for new or substitute drivers, or, if the problem was traced to frequent turnover, working even farther upstream to eliminate the factors that made experienced drivers quit. The fixes for these problems are high-level, wide-impact policies and practices well beyond the reach of Patrick or his bus driver.

Poor purchasing practices, for instance, could lead to

- erratic FAX machines in the office,
- breakdowns in production,
- computer crashes in payroll processing,
- delayed arrival of stationery, and
- equipment failures in the research labs.

To payroll processing, a computer crash looks like a special cause, but a higher-level manager may be able to see the connectivity among all these problems and put in a deeper fix.

That's why management must be involved in tracking down and

eliminating the deep sources of special causes, or in helping to capture a favorable special cause and making sure it continues to happen. It is also management's responsibility to verify the effectiveness of any changes (was the problem truly solved or did it reappear?) and to ensure that any improvements are maintained.

To summarize, a special cause is something different, something outside the normal process that is severe enough to give results a jolt. The jolt may be positive, but it is more commonly negative. In either event, the special cause has presented us with a chance to learn the easy way. But we must act quickly or the trail will grow cold...and bad special causes have a way of coming back and hitting us again, often worse the next time. If we wish to learn rapidly, we need indicators that give us a clear signal when something affects our results, and we need to act rapidly, capture the lessons, and build ways to ensure future success.

IMPROVING A STABLE PROCESS

Some people have been led to believe that when a system is stable—when only common causes are present—they should leave it alone. At least they can predict the results; they have confidence the results will fall somewhere on the common cause highway.

Unfortunately, just because a process is stable doesn't mean that it meets customer needs or our needs. The fact that it is stable tells us nothing about how *wide* the variation is or whether its average is at an appropriate level. As the child-proof cap example at the opening of this part showed, sometimes the **spread of variation** is too wide. In that example, the company couldn't produce "child-proof" caps without also producing "adult-proof" caps. In another situation we may care much more about the **level**. For example, in the case of safety, we obviously want to reduce the total number of incidents, not just their variation; the same is true for reducing the time it takes to process orders. Or suppose that sales or customer satisfaction ratings are too low, then we'd want them to increase. Discovering that a process is stable does *not* mean we need be satisfied with its variation or its level. It does not mean we should settle for whatever the process is currently delivering. **Leaving the process alone is not improvement.**

Improving a stable process requires a different approach than does eliminating special causes. For one thing, the same set of factors (the same rows of pins) is operating all the time. Trying to find out what was different, as we would with a special cause, is a low-yield strategy. In a common cause situation, every data point has information, so **all the data are relevant and useful**—there is nothing particularly important about the latest point, or highest point, or lowest point, or the points we don't like. Think about the quincunx: one bead comes down and happens to bounce left at almost every row of pins. Another follows, but it happens to bounce right most times. There is no point asking, "Why was that bead high? Why was that bead low?" A number of small things just happened to add up in one direction one time and in another direction the next.

The sources of common cause variation typically lie hidden deep within a system. And unlike special causes, there are no obvious signals calling out to us, nothing that says, "here's a common cause, come look!" With common cause variation, quick fixes that really work are the exception: taking that route usually leads to statements like "We've solved that one 20 times!" The straightforward special cause strategy—"track down the signal and look for what was different"—no longer works. Instead, we need strategies that help us deeply understand the workings and interactions of factors that are present all the time in the system. These strategies fall into three categories:

- **Stratify**—sort data into groups or categories based on different factors; look for patterns in the way the data points cluster or do not cluster
- **Experiment**—make planned changes and learn from the effects
- **Disaggregate**—divide the process into component pieces and manage the pieces.

Each of these strategies helps us to generate lots of ideas or theories about causes and solutions, and to separate those that yield pay dirt from those that are empty tunnels. We end up **localizing** common cause variation, pinpointing it at its source. Once we know that, we can develop measures to counteract the common cause variation by **making fundamental changes in the system**, reducing the number of rows of pins in the "quincunx" or at least minimizing their impact.

Although the people who work in a process are often in a position to identify special causes, uncovering common cause variation may require management involvement because these strategies may require additional data collection efforts or may even disrupt a process temporarily. Managers must also be involved in identifying and implementing countermeasures for both special causes and common causes.

Stratify

The city vehicle supervisor was surprised to see how much the maintenance division was spending on fuel pumps. Was there some sort of epidemic going on at the city garage? He asked the mechanics to look into the problem.

The mechanics dug back through their records and collected information on all the vehicles in the past year that had fuel pumps replaced. The initial surprise was that almost all the problems were with heavy equipment—garbage trucks, for instance; few of the lighter vehicles—police cars, pickup trucks—had needed to have fuel pumps replaced. It was a pattern that no one had really paid much attention to.

None of the mechanics could think of reasons why the problem should appear only in the heavy equipment, so they came up with other factors that might provide them with more clues. They looked at the age of the vehicles, other repairs performed, and the type of fuel used. They discovered that vehicles of all ages had the problem, that it didn't matter what other repairs had been performed, but that the problem only appeared in diesel-powered vehicles.

What was it about diesel fuel in heavy equipment that could lead to problems with fuel pumps? Nothing jumped out at them at first. Then they looked at where the fuel was coming from—different vendors, different fueling locations—and, Aha!, discovered that the problem only appeared in vehicles that used the fueling station on the east side of town. With a little more investigative work, they discovered that the fuel tanks at that location had sprung a leak, and water got into the fuel mixture—leading to rusted fuel pumps.

As these mechanics discovered, the challenge with common causes is continually one of focus. With vague, unfocused problems such as "we're spending too much replacing fuel pumps," we tend to get big, vague solutions that don't work very well. If we focus in on the problem—"we tend to have rusted fuel pumps on diesel-powered heavy equipment that gets fuel from the east side location"—we are much more likely to develop effective solutions. The answer is often very simple, as it was in this case, once we do enough focusing.

Stratification helps us identify and eliminate common cause variation by revealing patterns in the data that point to the source of trouble. In focusing, we look for contradictions that we can study and explain ... something that makes us say, "Aha! So that's where the problem really is!" Focusing allows us to identify the leverage points where a little effort brings major improvement.

To perform stratification analysis, we must have information on conditions related to the data, such as the type of job, day of the week, time, weather, region, equipment, employee, product, and so on. You may have some of the information you need readily at hand, but early on most organizations find that the information they need most is not available, either because it hasn't been collected, or because it is "in the computer" and somehow inaccessible to humans. In such cases, you may need to collect new data.

Experiment

Common cause variation, as stated previously, stems from the interaction of large numbers of factors in a process. Identifying which factors are contributing the most variation can often be tricky and time-consuming. In most cases, employees have a lot of ideas about what *might* work better, but nothing that is clearly supported by data. Rather than simply ignore these ideas—these *theories*—we can learn a lot by planning and trying out these ideas and monitoring the effects: experimentation.

Experiments come in all shapes and sizes. They can be as simple as changing the sequence in which information is given to customers, or as complex as testing multiple combinations of many factors. As discussed in Chapter 4, there are two keys to effective experimentation: having good ideas to test and having good ways to assess and learn from the results. A "good idea" is one that's based on a deep understanding of customer needs, coupled with in-depth knowledge of how a process does or should work. Being able to "assess and learn" from the experiment depends on how well we plan in advance ways to assess the results of the test. An experiment is often just a slight formalization of what we do intuitively: try a change and see what happens—though we should use the PDCA framework:

Plan: Have an idea, a theory, or hunch about something we want to change. The theory can be about causes of problems ("I think people don't understand their jobs") or about potential solutions ("Our budget projections might be more realistic if we required detailed timelines before approving final funding requests"). Develop ways to assess the results.

Do: Test those ideas.

Check: Study the results—what did we learn?

Act: Capture the improvement, modify it, abandon it, or try it under different circumstances.

Disaggregate

"Say, Brad, I wanted to tell you that the number of customer complaints about late shipments has really dropped in recent weeks. Can you fill me in on what your crew has been doing?" asked Phil.

"Sure," answered Brad. "Originally, I was charting data on the total cycle time for the whole order-entry-to-shipping process, but those figures had been steady for weeks. So I started having each of the managers look carefully at their separate pieces. Ed charted the data on just the order entry phase, Betsy on assembly, and Vince on the packing and labeling area."

"Then what happened?"

"I asked each of them to watch their data carefully and see what they could do to make their area better. We also met weekly to make sure we weren't causing each other problems. Vince's data showed that his area—packing and labeling—was the most time consuming ... which we thought was strange, since the procedures are pretty simple. Then one of his labelers discovered that assembly usually didn't deliver the assembled product to the labeling area until they had several pallets' worth of material. So there was a big time lag none of us had seen when we were look-ing at the time for the process as a whole."

These managers applied a concept called **disaggregation** to improve their process. To "disaggregate" means to divide a "collective"

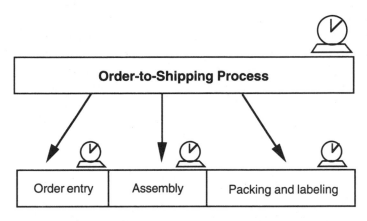

DISAGGREGATING THE SHIPPING PROCESS

or "aggregate" thing into its component pieces. Every process has multiple steps or phases that can be monitored and improved individually. Brad's group disaggregated the process into three components: order entry, assembly, and packing and labeling.

This approach exposed a time lag that they addressed by rearranging the workspace to eliminate the transportation step between the last two functions. The packing and labeling area was moved next to the assembly area, so completed assemblies are put on a table and picked up immediately by the packing operators.

In disaggregation we're making the elements of a process visible through *measurements and data*, indicators that reflect how well different parts of the process are working. Through disaggregation, we make process characteristics—such as the quality of outputs, time used, errors made, costs—more visible.

At first, the concept of disaggregation sounds like it runs counter to everything else I've said in this book: throughout I've urged you to "look at the system as a whole" and *not* to optimize individual pieces. But when we manage it properly, disaggregation *does* help optimize the system as a whole:

- Working on a smaller piece of the puzzle gives us a simpler "cause structure." For instance, there are far fewer potential causes of variation in one component of the process than in the whole order-entry-to-shipping process. By disaggregating the process we make it easier to find where and why the big delays occurred.

- There may well be special causes buried in components of a process that don't show up when the process is tracked as a whole. Senior executives, for example, are unlikely to see special causes, because the figures they look at represent the sum of variation across many sources—and any special cause in one small area is likely to get masked when added to common cause variation from other places. Disaggregation helps maximize the chances of a special cause being detected.

Disaggregation only works when each piece of the process has an aim tied to serving the next step and is consistent with the overall aim of the process; we must know the definition of a "good job" for each chunk. That's why we have to be careful not to look at data on the components out of the context of the system as a whole. Though the "manager" or "owner" of each of the smaller pieces needs to be responsible for improvement within that component, the work needs to be integrated by those responsible for managing the process as a whole. A system of regular meetings in which the work on and in the components is discussed in terms of the whole is essential (a system of such "rolling customer-focused meetings" was described on pages 91–95).

Which Tactic to Use

It is often best to use these common cause tactics in the order presented:

- **Stratify:** This requires the least investment of time or resources when we have *existing* data on factors related to our processes. By stratifying the data we may be able to uncover patterns that provide clues that will help us focus our search for solutions.

- **Experiment:** This tactic usually requires more investment than stratification, but less than disaggregation. If we have data, we may be able to learn a lot easily with stratification. If not, and we have some compelling ideas, let's try them on a small scale.

- **Disaggregate:** This is more complex than stratification or experimentation, but is also more powerful. When we have many eyes, many sensors watching the disaggregated process, we can learn more rapidly—as long as we have an effective management system to keep the components integrated.

MAKING VARIATION VISIBLE

Some years ago, a manager learned about the high price of tampering and began charting his data. He would show charts like the one below to his boss, a tactic that saved him from having to come up with explanations for common cause variation each month.

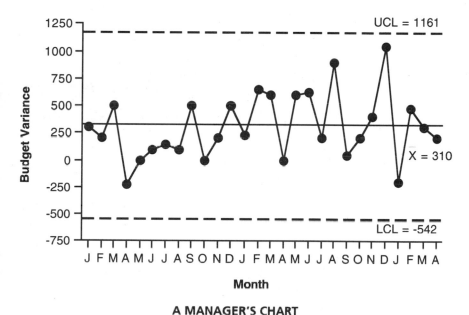

A MANAGER'S CHART

Such charts are **statistical control charts**, an example of which we saw earlier with the Regional VP's data (p. 130). Like the highway sketches shown earlier, a control chart has

- data plotted in **time order**;
- a **centerline,** typically the mathematical **average**; and
- lines called **statistical control limits** that indicate the width of the common cause variation, the edges of the "highway."

Creating a control chart is not rocket science, a fact few people appreciate until they have created several themselves. The next pages show one way to create a control chart. I urge you to take five minutes and carry out the calculations; I've never met anyone who understood

147

Creating a Control Chart

1 Assemble the data.

3 Calculate the differences (ranges) between adjacent points.

	Measurements X	Range R
1	28	2
2	26	3
3	29	1
4	28	4
5	32	2
6	34	0
7	34	1
8	35	8
9	27	4
10	31	7
11	24	4
12	28	3
13	31	0
14	31	4
15	27	0
16	27	1
17	26	5
18	31	1
19	32	0
20	32	3
21	29	1
22	30	2
23	32	1
24	31	2
25	33	

Total = 748

Average $= \dfrac{748}{25} = 29.92 = \overline{X}$

4 **Determine the median range, $\tilde{R}$** (pronounced r-tilda). One way to do this, shown here, is to list the ranges from largest to smallest and find the middle of the list. Here there are two center values, both 2, so $\tilde{R} = 2$.

These ranges help us determine the width of the common cause highway.

8 7 5 4 4 4 4 3 3 3 2 2 2 2 1 1 1 1 1 1 0 0 0 0

2 Calculate $\overline{X}$, the average. This becomes the centerline of the common cause highway.

5 **Multiply R̃ by 3.14.** This gives the distance from the centerline to the edges of the common cause highway.

> ## Calculations: 2 x 3.14 = 6.28
>
> (Formula: R̃ x 3.14)

6 **Calculate control limits.** Add the result from Step 5 to X̄, the average, to get the Upper Control Limit (**UCL**). Subtract to get the Lower Control LImiit (**LCL**).

UCL	LCL
29.92	29.92
+6.28	−6.28
36.20	23.64

(Formula: Control Limits = X̄ ±3.14 R̃)

7 **Plot the data in time order** and **draw a solid centerline** at X̄, the average.

8 **Draw dashed lines** to indicate the edges of the highway (the control limits).

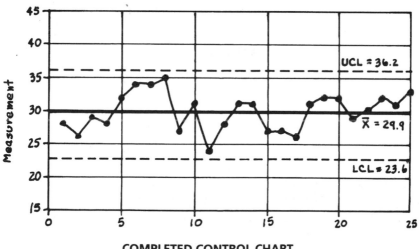

COMPLETED CONTROL CHART

and valued control charts until they understood how the charts were created. After working through the example provided, I also urge you to create a control chart on figures that are important to you, such as sales, customer information, defects, budget variances, and so on.

Interpretation of the Control Chart

What can we tell from this control chart? There are no points outside the limits, and thus no obvious signals of special causes. Using the terminology introduced earlier (p. 115), this process is stable, predictable, in statistical control. This tells us we can have some confidence our results will continue to fall between our limits or 23.6 and 36.2.

Two key questions are worth raising:

- When calculating the control limits, how did we take into account the customer's needs?
- When calculating the control limits, how did we take into account the company's needs?

The correct answer to both questions is "We didn't." Control limits are calculated only from **data taken on the process**. They tell us what a process is **capable of achieving** in today's conditions. They bear no relationship either to our customers' needs or to our companies' needs. They care not at all about our wishes, hopes, and desires. They represent the Voice of the Process, providing guidance for action on the process, allowing us to answer the question "to make things better, should we use the special cause strategy or a common cause strategy?"

"I Don't Like Those Limits ..."

Look again at the data on customer satisfaction ratings that I showed earlier.

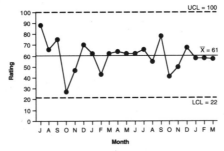

CUSTOMER SATISFACTION RATINGS

150

This chart tells us this process is stable, in statistical control, which means this company can expect the customer satisfaction ratings to continue to fall anywhere between 22 and 100. When managers see charts like these, I often have conversations that go something like this:

> *"Brian, I don't like those limits."*
>
> *"What do you mean?"*
>
> *"They're too wide. We can't afford to have scores that your limits tolerate. I think we should be getting much higher ratings. Let me redraw the limits ... right there ... between 65 and 100. That's what the company needs—ratings that mean our customers are getting the high-quality service they deserve!"*

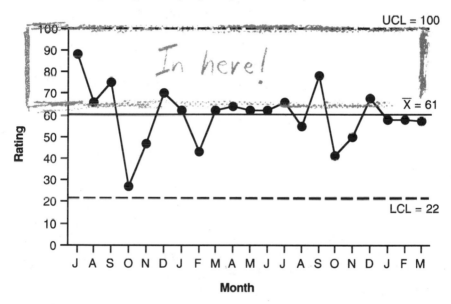

THE MANAGER'S PREFERRED LIMITS

We all want higher customer satisfaction—the question is *how*. Let's look at the consequences of arbitrarily redrawing these limits to where we'd like them to be.

Suppose any time a point went outside these "managerial" limits we asked questions: "what happened? what are you doing about it?" Would that be a high-yield strategy for improvement? The answer, alas, is no. We would just be tampering, having people look for special causes—what was different—when the undesirable results were all due to common causes. Such searches and the inevitable actions would make matters worse, not better. People learn false lessons and put in false solutions that increase variation and add costs. The common cause strategy of looking at all the data—stratifying, experimenting, and disaggregating—is far more effective at producing what customers need and what we want.

One manager said it so clearly:

> *"There's a major difference between whether you feel comfortable with this amount of variation and whether you feel comfortable with this approach to dealing with it."*

In the beginning, you probably won't feel comfortable with either the amount of variation *or* the way of dealing with it. As you'll discover, the biggest challenge for management is not deciding where we *want* the limits or the average. That's the easy part. The biggest challenge is how to get them there. Think back to the calculations. If we want tighter limits or a different average, how do we get them? Only by changing the process, reducing or changing the common causes acting on the system. When we reduce variation or change the level, the limits automatically change over time. To attempt to tighten them arbitrarily is costly and doesn't solve the underlying problems in the process.

Recall the three ways to get better figures: (1) Improve the system, (2) Distort the system, (3) Distort the figures. If we put enough pressure on people, they'll meet our demands with (2) and (3). But at what cost elsewhere? The best-known way to get the figures we want, in the way we want to get them, is to take advantage of the easy learning opportunity offered by special cause signals and bring a process under statistical control. Then we can work to further reduce the common cause variation around a better, more desirable level. The calculations we've just described are part of what it takes.

As a brief recap, statistical control limits:

- Are not based on what we would like a process to do. They are based on what the process is *capable* of doing. They are computed from data using statistical formulas.
- Provide guidance for action on the process. The limits help separate "common cause" from "special cause" variation. The appropriate actions are quite different for common and special causes.

- Indicate the width of the common cause highway and whether the process is stable or unstable.

Managers and Control Charts

Managers tend to think of such control charts as tools for operators and engineers—in short, as something low level that doesn't belong in *their* office. But the use of control charts should start in the CEO's office, not on the shop floor. Why? Because:

- Managers control the most important processes and systems in an organization, and the concepts of common causes and special causes are just as useful for those high-level processes as they are for any process deeper in the organization.
- Unless managers use the charts themselves, they will continue to overreact to variation, to tamper—which increases variation and costs and drives other people crazy.
- If managers do not understand common and special causes and the effective use of control charts, they (a) have a hard time coaching and guiding others who are applying these principles, and (b) inevitably send mixed messages to people lower in the organization who are using these tools.

NO HARD DATA

And what if we have no hard data—no counts or measurements or percentages that we can plot on a control chart? Does that mean the concepts of common causes and special causes cannot be used? At the very beginning of this book, I related the experience of a company that had just lost a flagship customer because of problems in developing a key new product (pgs. 3 and 53). They could not collect the kind of data they could plot on a control chart. But they were still able to apply these concepts.

Anna, the VP of marketing, looked around the room. Posted on the wall was a 30-foot, three-year timeline annotated with all the notable events that had happened during the product development.

153

"This is impressive," she remarked to the others in the room. "How did you get the information to construct this?"

"Well, we called together the 20 people who had done the most work on that product," someone answered. "We all wrote down everything important we could remember about the development effort and then posted them along this timeline."

"Then," another person chimed in, "we all took a step back and identified the problems we thought had led to the biggest delays. You can see the top five posted on the other wall."

Anna read the list. "Do you think those five problems will bite us again? Do they happen all the time or were they unique to this project?" she asked.

"That's easy," said Fred. "'Changes in key personnel'— No way that's an isolated problem! We have that in spades on every project. I've never been on a product development team where people weren't coming and going all the time."

"I was just going to say the same thing about 'changes in design requirements,'" said Marianne. "That's not unique, either. It seems we're always getting hit with new design requirements midstream."

The discussion continued along the same lines for all five problems. "So in summary," Anna said, checking with the group, "you believe that we've had problems like these many times before, but this is the first time they've actually cost us a major customer on a key new product launch?" Heads nodded around the room. "Maybe that's why we all thought at first there was something unusual going on this time," she added.

Whether or not you have hard data, you can still ask **"is what we're seeing something unique or is it an example of a larger class of problems we are having?"** If the problem is an example of a larger class of problems, and virtually all problems are, we can apply the common cause strategy. For example, with "changes in personnel" we might *stratify* by type of personnel: perhaps it's only marketing people who move in and out of projects. Our solutions would be different if: (1) the problem were unique to this project, or (2) was common cause and (a) true of all types of personnel or (b) true only for one type of personnel.

Another useful version of the same basic question helps support the principle of "blaming the process, not the person":

An executive described for me his frustration with the "concrete layer"—the upper-middle managers in his organization. No change he instituted ever got past that level, he said. He was ready to fire the whole bunch.

"Suppose you did fire them all and put in replacements," I asked. "How would the new ones behave a year from now?" He grumbled, but admitted they'd be no different.

"Surely," said the executive, "there are some times we can blame the employee. We had one who left a ladder inside a large vat and it cost us a million bucks to fix the damage! It wasn't anyone's fault but his."

I listened to his arguments then later in the conversation asked, "Suppose you'd gotten rid of that guy. Would it have prevented problems like that from recurring?" He admitted the same type of thing—though perhaps not so costly would probably have happened with other employees.

These managers were beginning to apply common cause/special cause *thinking* even though they couldn't chart data on the problems they faced. The generic form of this key question is: **if I replaced this set of employees with an entirely new set, could the same problem well have happened?** Most of the time, the answer will be yes because most problems are common cause—they arise from factors within the system. Disciplining or changing employees will do little good. New employees will be similarly constrained by the training, instructions, coaching, policies, measurements, methods, and equipment they receive.

Asking the right questions, based on knowledge of variation, takes a manager a long way toward developing effective actions. In the next chapter we'll examine a number of case studies to see how these principles and tools are applied in a variety of situations.

10
MANAGEMENT REACTIONS TO VARIATION

Although the concepts of common causes and special causes may sound logical when reading about them, their value doesn't really hit home until you see them in action. This chapter provides several case studies that will help you become more familiar with how these ideas are applied in practice. See if you can use what you've learned to anticipate my recommendations.

CASE STUDIES

Case #1: Unpaid Invoices

Camille, the manager of accounts payable, walked through the department, pleased by the hum of activity. She entered her own office and got settled at her desk. A few minutes later, Carlos entered, hesitating a bit at the door.

"What's up, Carlos?" she asked.

"Well, I just finished the figures for last month . . . " he said.

"And how do they look?"

"Uhhh, you're not going to like this . . . "

Camille steeled herself, then said, "Just give it to me straight. What's the news?"

Carlos checked the paper he was holding and said, "It seems

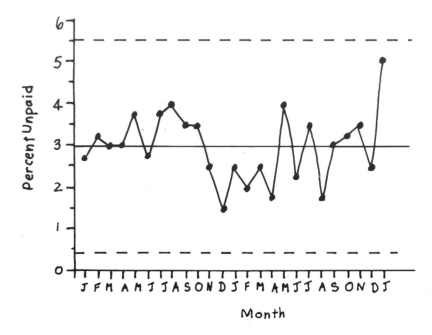

DATA ON UNPAID INVOICES

we're having a problem getting our suppliers paid on time. We had more than five percent of invoices unpaid last month."

"Over five percent! We haven't seen that in a long time. We used to hold invoices to help our own cash flow, but we're not doing that any more. What's going on out there? Let me look at those figures."

Look at the chart of Camille's figures on unpaid invoices. Here are the options she is considering. What would you recommend?

1. Look at each invoice that was not paid and find out who worked on that invoice. Have the employee involved go through further training.
2. Figure out what was different last month compared to other months. Were there more invoices? Were new or different services being paid for the first time? Were there new employees in the department?
3. Dig up all the invoices that had to be reprocessed in the past few months and categorize the causes of the problems. Look for patterns.

4. For several weeks, have people working on each major step in the process keep data on how many and what kinds of errors occur in their steps.

5. Change the account payables software.

The chart of Camille's data shows that this is a stable process, that there is no evidence of special causes. This means her best options are #3 and #4: they both represent common cause strategies. Option 1 is tampering: Camille needs to look for patterns across all the data. Training would be appropriate only if she found systematic differences between people who were trained differently. Option 2 is a special cause reaction: it assumes something was different or important about the last data point, which the control chart shows was not the case. Option 5 is a potential reaction but is premature at this point. Camille's available data do not show that the software is the cause of the problem.

Long-held beliefs are hard to overcome. Experience has shown that most people, when presented a situation like this, are tempted to hedge their bets. They'll use one of the common cause approaches, but *also* ask the special cause question, "What was different last month?" This is particularly tempting when data points get near the control limits. All our instincts scream: "DO SOMETHING! Things will get worse if we don't act!" On some occasions, a data point near the limits may indicate the presence of a special cause, but *far more often* these points are due to common causes, and subsequent data points fall back well within the limits.

Case #2: Increased Impurities

"Del, do you have a minute?"

"Sure, Aaron," said Del. "What can I do for you?"

Aaron handed Del a lab report.

"Eileen just finished measuring the impurities in the batch we're about to load into the trucks, and it doesn't look good. We've got an impurities measure of .23%. I know that we've got customers waiting for this shipment, but that's way above what we usually ship out."

"Let me think a minute," said Del. "That's more than one-and-a-half times what we had with the last batch. I thought we had been doing a good job lately of holding the impurities down."

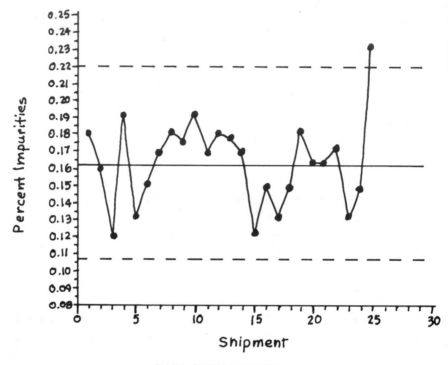

DATA ON IMPURITIES

Del paced the room several times then turned to Aaron. "Call the people waiting for this stuff and see if they can still use it. Otherwise we may have to scrap the whole batch. . . . I also want to see our data for the past few months so we can decide what else to do."

Look at Del's data in the chart. Here are the options he's considering. What would you recommend?

1. Blend material from this batch with material from a different batch that has a lower impurity level. The combined mixture will yield an acceptable level of impurities. This will save the material from being scrapped.

2. Look at the data by shifts, days, sampling machines, vessel types, and so on. See if there are patterns.

3. Send out a memo to all staff with information regarding the higher than normal impurity level. Note that there has been a bad batch, and that operators should be more careful in the

future. Post the control chart with the memo in the processing area so all employees can see what is being shipped and what is expected of them.

4. Make some educated guesses about possible causes, and change settings on the machines to see what happens. Have all pipes and vessels cleaned. Monitor the effect.

5. Have employees investigate what was different about this batch relative to other batches. Was this batch processed differently? Were the measurements taken differently? Is there a new supplier?

The best option for Del is #5, which represents the only special cause approach here. The control chart shows that the last impurity measure was well beyond the control limit: something had changed the system. Option 1 might be necessary but could be dangerous because that action alone will not solve the problem, and customers may suffer unintended side effects that you may or may not ever learn about. Options 2 and 4 represent common cause strategies (stratification and experimentation, respectively); they would help you find factors within the system, but would not show you what was different in the last batch. Option 3 is perhaps the worst option: improvement does not come from exhortations or slogans. Until we know what has happened in the process, employees are likely to end up tampering in an attempt to make improvements.

If you have looked carefully at the chart of Del's data, you may have also noticed that there was a special cause—a series of eight points above the centerline (points 7 to 14)—that appeared earlier and went undetected because no one was charting the data at the time. If Del is lucky, he may still be able to track down the source of that special cause, and if he's luckier, it may be related to the latest event. But his chances now are much slimmer than if he had known when the special cause appeared and been able to initiate an immediate search for the cause. The trail grows cold quickly.

It's useful to pause a moment and think about what our reactions might have been in these two cases had we not charted the data. Then think about the work environments throughout our organization. On how many processes do we have no data at all? How many times do people look at just the latest result, in isolation? Just the latest two results? Appropriate use of figures requires charts like these.

Case #3: Going Out of Business

The monthly report on the next page shows the projected and actual volume (pounds of product) and sales for seven different products, both for the current month and for the same month last year. If you focus on the two circled figures for Product Line A, you can see that there has been a drop in sales: volume went from about 1.9 million pounds ("1,891 thousand") down to 1.6 million pounds, representing a drop in dollars from $1.7 million to $1.45 million. Would you consider this drop serious, or do you think the figures are fairly steady?

One of my colleagues was asked to do some statistical wizardry to analyze sales of this product. Here's what he could do given the data on the report:

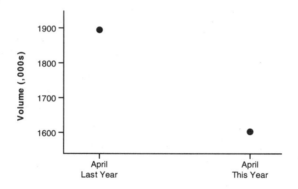

CHART OF SALES FIGURES FROM REPORT

The business director, Mr. B, was in a seminar when this chart was shown during a presentation. The dip in volume represented about a 15% drop. Would you be upset with a 15% drop? Being an astute manager, Mr. B decided to hedge his bet. He said: "Maybe I would, maybe I wouldn't."

"Well, tell me why you would or wouldn't," said my colleague.

"There are some things I know about the business that you don't," offered Mr. B. "This business has been declining over several years. I think we should sell it."

Do you believe Mr. B's assertion? What would you need to better understand the situation? Some history?

Report on Net Sales
(000's omitted)

	Actual Billings Current Mo./This Year		Estimated Billings Current Mo./This Year		Actual Billings Same Mo./Last Year		% of Estimate To date	
	Volume	Dollars	Volume	Dollars	Volume	Dollars	Volume	Dollars
Line A	(1,605)	$1,452	1,655	$1,483	(1,891)	$1,702	97%	98%
Line B	8,732	$3,111	8,906	$3,177	8,731	$3,198	98%	98%
Line C	11,875	$4,079	13,084	$4,457	13,676	$4,837	91%	92%
Line D	3,344	$1,467	3,330	$1,410	3,761	$1,672	100%	104%
Line E	26,929	$13,062	27,416	$13,253	31,387	$14,965	98%	99%
Line F	9,285	$7,068	9,087	$7,069	9,065	$7,149	102%	100%
Line G	10,486	$5,688	10,516	$5,754	10,298	$5,681	100%	99%
TOTAL	72,256	35,927	73,994	36,603	78,809	39,204	98%	98%

MONTH = APRIL   Billing Days = 21   Billing Days Last Year = 22

MANAGER'S REPORT ON SALES

By combing through the files, my colleague dug up additional historical data. The following chart includes figures from before, between, and after the two April figures that Mr. B was reacting to. The two original April figures are circled. What can you tell about the state of this business? Can you see the decline in sales that Mr. B was reacting to?

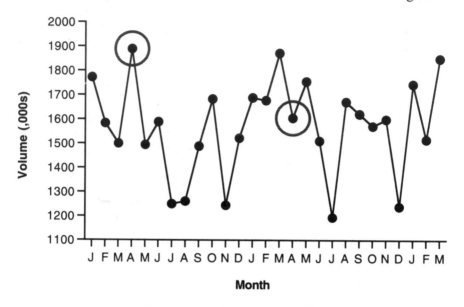

SALES DATA FOR TWO YEARS

How do you suppose Mr. B concluded it was a declining business? He, like all of us, formed a mental model of what was happening in the world around him. We all subconsciously pay attention to data points that seem to fit our model and ignore or explain away those that don't fit. We call those that don't fit "aberrations."

Mr. B's reaction to this chart when he first saw it was: "Where the hell did you get that data?" His experience just reinforces how easy it is for us to be misled by single data points delivered up one or a few at a time in a complex table of numbers.

Even without calculating the control limits, it appears that most of these data points fall within a band. (You could perform the calculations and draw the control limits and centerline and see that these initial perceptions are indeed correct.)

If the next month's volume was 1800, what would you think? If it were 1000, what would you think? Now you've got a basis for asking questions. Now you'd know it would be helpful to ask the question, "What happened? Why was May 1000?" but it would *not* be helpful to ask "Why was this May 1800 or 1600 or 1400 or even 1200?" All of those results fall within the band of common cause variation. In short, this business had been pretty stable for several years. It wasn't growing, it wasn't declining. But that conclusion would be much harder to reach using the traditional summary reports.

Case #4: Rising Sales

Any number of times I've heard managers describe seasonal patterns in sales or trends in other figures. In a big percentage of cases when we sat down and looked at the plots of the data, the trends and seasonality didn't materialize. Only common cause variation was evident. Our human tendency to see patterns and trends where there are none continues to amaze me. It reminds me of the Rorschach tests in which psychologists work with clients by analyzing images they see in ink blots. Plotting the dots changes a lot of perceptions.

But sometimes there is real seasonality or a real trend—real structural variation. Below is a chart shown earlier, now with control limits added.

This is a control chart for product sales. As discussed earlier (p. 116), these data have structural variation: an underlying trend that in this case is shown by an overall increase over time. The limits show

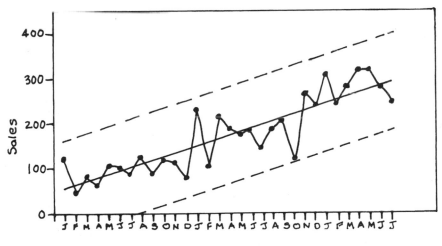

TREND IN SALES DATA

the width of common cause variation, as before, but this time they are not flat. These points require a slightly different calculation from the one we did earlier, but the interpretation is the same. There is a stable process on top of the structural variation, and therefore no reason to interpret the latest dot. There are no lessons to be learned from comparing high dots with low dots. We have some confidence in predicting the next few months' sales.

Without seeing this chart, a manager might react to the "steady drop in results" the last two months, or to the sharp drop several months earlier. The chart helps keep us from overreacting by reminding us this is most likely just common cause variation. No reason to tamper, to jerk the funnel—to put on a sales campaign or otherwise deviate from our basic strategy. This chart will also help us see if any of our initiatives really *change* the pattern; most do not.

Case #5: Construction Projects

"To control costs, project managers shall report on the costs of all projects that are 10% or more off from budget."

What are your reactions to this policy? Does your organization have policies like this? What are some of the effects?

Let's look at this policy from a 4th Generation perspective. To analyze the policy, it would be useful to have some data. Here are the cost variances that a company collected for 20 projects.

Project	% over or under	Project	% over or under
1	-12.5	11	-0.7
2	0.1	12	-7.8
3	-6.1	13	0.7
4	10.1	14	-5.7
5	10.1	15	3.5
6	9.5	16	-9.1
7	-12.5	17	-5.2
8	1.3	18	9.1
9	-0.7	19	0.7
10	30.0	20	-5.9

COST VARIANCES ON THE LAST 20 PROJECTS

Just having the data available changes our evaluation. You can see that five projects required explanations. Here's a better way to look at these numbers:

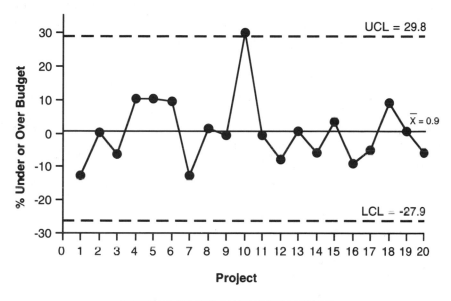

CONTROL CHART OF COST VARIANCES

For almost everyone, the control chart does a far better job facilitating understanding of these cost variances than does a simple list. As you can see, only one project was outside the limits, and therefore only one for which we would recommend the special cause strategy (p. 138):

- **Get timely data:** These data were only looked at eight months after that project was completed.
- **Take immediate action** (a Level 1 Fix): Not applicable; it's too late.
- **Search for what was different.** The project leader had written a report, but it didn't contain any information that helped them understand how this project was *different* from others. The only hope of discovery rests in people's memories (an unreliable source of accurate information!).
- **Find a long-term remedy:** Not possible here since "what was different" had been lost.

167

How about the rest of the projects? Should we be satisfied because the process is stable? Should we focus particular attention on those outside the 10% "action" limits? There are no other points beyond the control limits, no other signals of special causes—and therefore nothing special about the projects beyond the 10% limit. All the data points are relevant. It would not be effective to focus special attention (as had been done) on those outside the 10% managerial limits. Instead we should use the common cause strategy.

Potential stratification factors include type of construction, time of year, whether the project leader had certain training or not, size of project, number of design changes during construction, and many others. One company that looked at similar data discovered a relationship between the project size and the percent variance as illustrated in the following chart:

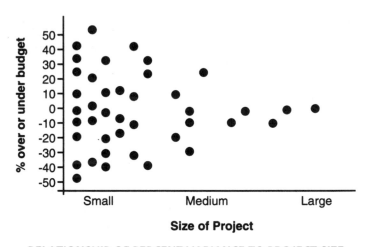

RELATIONSHIP OF PERCENT VARIANCE TO PROJECT SIZE

The chart shows that larger projects had smaller percent variances even though their dollar variances were larger. This provides important insight: a policy of explaining variances greater than 10% for all projects, no matter what the size, no longer seemed relevant. The company decided to keep three different control charts, one each on small, medium, and large projects (each of which naturally had different width control limits).

Still another organization found that the larger variances tended to show up primarily in one type of project, so they focused first on reducing the variances in those projects. As they went deeper they found they were chasing mice when tigers were loose. The big problems were not with cost variances. The trouble arose mainly from poorly planned projects, projects that had sloppy construction that cost millions over the years but came in "on budget": the discovery of these big problems had its roots in trying to understand the system. The company came to see that cost variances were an easy but not very useful indicator of project effectiveness. Part of the solution was to establish a "balanced scorecard" that relied on a variety of other indicators.

Should we manage to budget?

A key question arises: Do we want people to manage to budget? Most managers unhesitatingly say YES!—for some very good reasons. Among other things, managing to budget:

- Forces fiscal constraint
- Allows us to allocate resources
- Provides a basis for charging the customer
- Helps ensure we make a profit

In some cases, managing to budget can also encourage creativity, providing an impetus to "do more with less."

In practice, however, these "benefits" carry a heavy price. Suppose the project manager told you a project had encountered unexpected difficulties and was headed for a 35% overrun. Would you still want her to manage to budget? Some managers say, "Under those circumstances, of course I don't want her to stick with the original budget. I want people to tell me, give me early warning, and we'll adjust the budget." With such responses, I have a hard time understanding what people mean when they say "manage to budget."

But other managers say, "Yes, she must still come in on budget. We only have so much money. You can't overspend your bank account at home." What methods do these managers want the project leader to use to come in on budget? Improve the system, distort the system, or distort the figures? You know what happens. You've been there. You've lived in buildings where this has happened: windows left out; air conditioning system short-changed; hallways too narrow. Or, perhaps it was done just by distorting the figures—by charging expenses to other projects.

What does such behavior do to an organization? It produces substandard output, and perhaps even worse, **keeps executives from**

seeing the reality of things. They see the figures they want to see, and the consequences are carefully camouflaged. An organization that does not know its reality is like a ship sailing in a fog, headed for an iceberg. The figures will all look good until one day the holes below the waterline can no longer be concealed, and all of a sudden, one of our "most admired companies" sinks below the surface. This is not news. We've all seen it before; I've said it before. It's all around us.

One company charted the outcomes for its projects. Their chart looked like this:

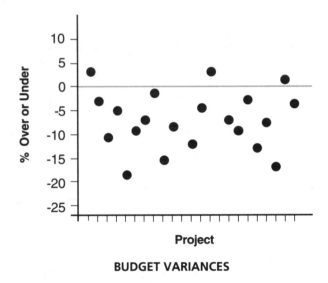

BUDGET VARIANCES

It's a stable process, centered at -8%, meaning that the projects come in an average of 8% under budget. Only three projects came in over budget, and then only slightly. Looks good, doesn't it. Don't you want projects to always come in under budget? But what's really happening in this company? Managers make conservative estimates, sacrificing opportunities to invest the capital elsewhere, year after year . . . a good way to go out of business. That company had made it clear to people that they should come in under budget. Promotions depended on it. So they distorted systems and figures and came in under budget.

The disadvantages of managing to budget are numerous:

1. Promotes short-term business decisions; optimizes the piece, the cost of the individual project, at the expense of the whole (the company's overall performance)

2. Customers, quality, and perhaps even safety receive short shrift
3. Stifles creativity (except in encouraging people to find creative ways to meet their figures)
4. People spend whether they need to or not
5. Leads to tampering

A good first step is to stop doing counterproductive things. So suppose you were the manager in charge of construction projects, and the chart on page 167 was your chart. Would you go back to your staff and say: "I have read this wonderful book and I now understand that all the variation in our project costs is due to common causes. So from here on out, you only have to investigate and identify the causes of the cost variances when the variances are more than 29%"? Would you feel happy about that statement? Would you feel nervous about issuing such a policy? Why does it make you feel nervous? Because it seems like you're giving your employees permission to be off by 29%, endorsing sloppy estimation and work. As the manager I quoted before said:

> *"There's a major difference between whether you feel comfortable with that amount of variation as opposed to being comfortable with that approach to dealing with it."*

He was unhappy with the amount of variation he found in his processes and wanted less; but he realized that plotting the data, and using the common cause and special cause strategies was the best way to go about reducing that variation.

VARIATION AND PERFORMANCE

Occasionally, following a good day or a good month, you may get a little note:

And more often, after a bad day or a bad month, you'll get a different note:

What does getting notes like these do to a person's sense of control? Some days, some months, try as hard as we might, things go well and we get praised. Other days, other months, try as hard as we might, things don't go so well and we get blamed. We search for clues about what to do differently. Something has changed, obviously! We need to be on top of it, but we don't know what it could be. So we find *something*. Our search turns up what seems to be a special cause "culprit," even though most of the time the difference is due to common causes that we did not appreciate or understand. And that leads to superstitious learning:

> *On that really good day, we had a special 7:00 A.M. meeting to get everyone fired up. I'm going to keep doing that.*

Such common, well-meaning reactions to variation in performance destroy people's sense of control. They stimulate false learning and lead employees to adjust, or worse yet, to "freeze," both of which add cost and hobble improvement.

This is bad enough, but even worse can happen. The manager that sent the note, "Good job," almost always finds that after one of those pats on the back, things get worse. But when you go out there and kick tush, things get better. Look at the chart on the next page:

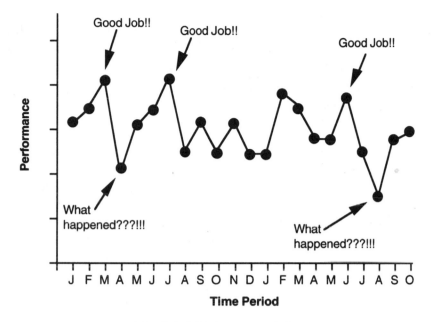

Time Period

WHY IT DOESN'T PAY TO BE NICE

Usually we only notice a "good" performance when it is near the upper edges of the highway. When it is that high, chances are the next figure will be lower. In our eyes, when we give praise, things get worse. When there are low dots and we kick tush, almost every time, the results get better ... and we fool ourselves into thinking our actions had an effect. What lesson do we learn? Don't give praise—kick tush and things will get better. So we quit giving praise and get tough: superstitious learning based on a misunderstanding of the inherent behavior of a stable process. The recipients of this managerial behavior develop ways to stay out of the low zone, thereby distorting systems, distorting figures, and increasing costs.

Many high-level managers believe that being tough is what got them where they are. Lloyd Nelson is right.

"Failure to understand variation is a central problem of management."

Comparing High and Low Performers

Any time we have more than one person, department, or facility doing the same or related work, we have a natural tendency to compare their performance: "Greg has twice as many sales as Betsy"; "Jake's division is first in safety, with less than half as many serious incidents as any other division." Such comparisons occur for one or both of the following reasons:

- To spark competition between employees
- To encourage the low performers to learn something from the high performers

The question is whether it is worthwhile to compare high and low performers for either of these reasons.

The answer for the first reason—to spark competition—is an obvious no. A recurring theme in this book, introduced back in Chapter 3, is that the elements of a system must cooperate if we are to optimize the system as a whole. We all have a lot of competitiveness in us. Adding to those natural tendencies only tears a system apart. One area needs to be eager to take a $50 hit so another can gain $100.

The answer relative to the second reason—encouraging learning—is a qualified maybe. When we compare high and low performers to facilitate learning, we are assuming the "highs" have a better method that others can learn. In reality, though, this assumption will be true only if we rule out two other reasons why they might have ended up on top:

1. We could be comparing apples with oranges.
2. It could be common cause variation.

Let's look at each of the issues in turn.

Comparing apples with apples

Consider two employees, working side by side, each doing the same work, using the same equipment and materials. One gets consistently better results than the other. There is some chance in this situation that we will learn something valuable by comparing how they do their jobs because one of them seems to have consistently better performance under "identical" conditions. The difference, however, may be simply in their natural capabilities, not in their methods. Methods can be transferred, but capabilities cannot.

Now consider two other employees, both doing similar work, one of them consistently outperforming the other. Only this time they work in facilities in different parts of the country. Here, the odds of learning by looking at high versus low performers have slipped. Why? The two situations aren't as comparable any more. One facility may have newer equipment, or use different suppliers, or have a different customer base with different requirements. The greater the differences, the more likely that we will only discover false lessons if we copy techniques from the higher performer.

Two hotels in a large chain often found themselves being compared because they were located close to each other. One was a new facility near a major airport; the other was an older facility downtown. The clientele that used these facilities were different: guests at the older city hotel were primarily business travelers who spent many nights per year on the road and were much more severe critics. The airport hotel got a broader mix of guests, many of whom were vacationers just staying for a night. In customer satisfaction ratings, the newer airport hotel almost always received higher scores than the downtown hotel. Almost every month, it was praised and the other criticized.

What was gained by constantly comparing these two facilities? Little or nothing. But a lot of damage was done. The lion's share of the difference in ratings was due to factors that neither hotel could do much about; the differences didn't lie in training, motivation, skill, intelligence, materials, or working methods. Continued pushes for the "weaker" facility to learn lessons from the "better" facility were counterproductive. If the "weaker" facility ever got over its resentment and tried to match what the "better" facility was doing, it'd be more likely to learn false lessons than effective ones. A much better course would be to have the facilities work together as peers, not "one up, one down."

Before comparing high and low performers, our first challenge is to make sure we are comparing apples with apples, and oranges with oranges. This leads us to stratify performance data on factors such as type of location (airport, downtown), customer base (business, leisure), type of facility (new, aged), or any other factor that seems appropriate. Doing so helps us find apples we can compare with apples.

Performance and common cause variation

Suppose we've found apples to compare with apples and now find that one person or group or facility has better performance than another. We must still ask: "Does that difference mean anything?"

175

For example, one manager had 11 engineers who did similar work. In the past year the "best" had made only 1 "serious error" while the "worst" had made 11 such errors. Perhaps you've anticipated the question: "Is the system that produced the 11 failures different from the system that produced the single failure?" That's the important managerial question. The answer turned out to be no. Common cause variation could lead to 1 failure one year and 11 the next, from the same system. There is no evidence of special causes. *Even if we change nothing in the system, the 11 engineers could end up in a completely different order next year.* Thus the odds are low that we would learn anything of value by looking at the "best" to find out what he or she was doing differently.

In a common cause situation *all* the data are relevant. We use the data from *all* 11 employees, work with all of them, to raise the performance of all. We don't pick out the "worst" engineer and focus our effort only on him or her. We don't pick out the "best" and try to copy his or her techniques. Instead, we help them all to work together. We stratify, experiment, and disaggregate and seek better methods so that *all* will get better results. Again, the major point is not WHO did the work, but rather "what, how, when" questions related to everybody's work.

The final answer to the question of whether it pays to compare high and lower performers? ... If we find a consistent pattern over time when comparing apples with apples, then we *are* likely to learn from the better performers. Our challenge is to do this in a win-win way so we can retain the enthusiasm and cooperation of all.

Getting Started

Rather than give a summary of topics discussed in this chapter, I've found it more helpful to provide some guidelines for applying the principles of variation to management work:

- **Plot data on high blood pressure items:** Don't try to do too much at once. Choose one to three measures that are the most important to you, figures you find yourself reacting to the most. Remember, a major reason to plot our data points is to moderate our human tendency to overreact.

- **Plot data on a more balanced scorecard:** Most managers currently rely most on financial data. Get data on customer satisfaction, outgoing quality, safety, and cycle time (how long it takes for key processes to respond to customers).

- **Plot the data in time order by hand:** The best plots are hand-drawn, posted on your wall where you can add a dot as soon as the figure is available. Even if you are skilled with computers, resist the temptation to do this work electronically. In many years of working with these concepts with people from all walks of life, the difference in understanding that comes when people take pencils in hand and draw dots on their graphs has never ceased to amaze me. It's such a simple act, but it has such a profound influence on people's gut-level understanding and appreciation for the data. Plotting three or four data points every month, or even every day, takes virtually no time, and it gives you an appreciation for the data and the ability to recall past events that you just can't get using technology.

- **Make notes on charts by hand:** When something happens that you think might have a significant impact, jot down notes—you had a major sale campaign, violent weather shut down three facilities, the air traffic controllers went on strike, materials changed. Human memory is frail; these notes will help you to interpret possible patterns in the data and also help you to remember things that you thought would have a major effect, but didn't.

- **Don't overreact to variation:** Once again, most of the time, a given dot will be the result of common cause variation. Reacting to those individual dots just creates havoc in the organization. Overreaction does nothing to improve quality, increase customer satisfaction, or reduce the causes of costs.

- **Apply common cause and special cause strategies:** If a special cause appears, act quickly to find out what was different and to develop short- and long-term responses. In common cause situations look at all the data and use stratification, experimentation, and disaggregation to create lasting improvements.

- **Apply these principles even when you have no hard data:** Ask, "Was this an isolated event or is it an example of a larger class of problems we are having?" and "If I replaced this set of employees with a new set, might I well have the same problems?" Most often, the answers to these questions will lead you to work on the larger class of problems using the common cause approach.

EPILOGUE

Throughout this book, I have resisted the temptation to name companies in the examples. Doing so encourages people to adopt a special cause mentality: "Those companies must be unusually stupid," or "They can't be that great, look at. . . . " I have seen almost every problem described in this book many times in many companies. The problems are not unique to any single company. They result from common causes: behavior, actions, and beliefs that are endemic to current approaches to management. Without having been in your organization, I'd be willing to bet that many if not all of the problems I've described are happening in your own organization. Here is another example in which it's more difficult to conceal the company's identity. But think about your own company, even if you can guess this company's name. Watch how the story unfolds. Could this have happened to your company?

Front page, *The New York Times*, 19 September (the emphasis is added by me):

Company X Employees Missed Breakdown [and paralyzed Air Traffic Control]

Long-distance telephone service failed in New York City on Tuesday night because Company X *technicians* did not notice for six hours that a generator had stopped working and that a key switching station was therefore running on batteries, the company said. . . . It was in the end a *failure by employees to follow routine procedures.* . . .

So far so good—sounds like they've already found the *who*—those faulty workers! Now let's look at the next day's paper.

First page, business section, *The New York Times*, 20 September:

Company X Admits Alarms Failed in Cutoff

After union officials charged that Company X had falsely blamed technicians for the breakdown of long-distance service in New York City on Tuesday, company executives yesterday admitted that some alarms were not working and that *managers* had not followed proper procedures. But they

179

declined to be specific and their statements appeared to be inconsistent. . . . [Company officials] said that no technician had made any errors. . . . "If all appropriate operating procedures had been followed by *supervisory personnel*, it may have been possible to avert the disruption." . . . [The lead investigator] said, "We don't know *who* is to blame."

Hmm, the *who* seems to have shifted a bit higher. Now from the **first page of the business section,** *The New York Times,* the next day, 21 September:

More Errors Disclosed by Company X

In a further admission of management error resulting in Tuesday's disruption of telephone service, Company X said yesterday that *a key supervisor* assumed that crucial alarms would work and that the alarms would alert other workers capable of monitoring a critical power supply for long-distance service. . . . In a letter to employees yesterday . . . the chairman of Company X said the company had explained the accident poorly. . . . "Lapses in *management* practices in an area where we have decades of experience . . . allowed what should have been an easily resolved problem to get out of hand."

The problem has risen a bit higher yet, but we've still got a *who*. From inside the **business section** the same day, 21 September:

Many Other Phone Failures Affected Air Traffic Control

Major telephone failures that significantly degrade air traffic control services are far more common that is generally recognized, according to a Congressional subcommittee . . . there were *114 episodes of "major" telephone failure*s that disrupted air traffic control in the [past year].

What does this imply? Does each of these 114 have the same who? Is each a special cause? Or are there some deep underlying causes at work?

Then, from page 2b, *USA Today,* 7 November the same year:

Company X Error Caused Outage

Human error caused a malfunction in Boston-area telephone equipment that knocked out most long-distance calling. . . . "The preliminary assessment is that a step was missed in what should have been a standard operating procedure," [Company X] said. . . .

These are examples of what we see every day. They reflect a belief that *people* are the causes of most problems, and we search for a *who* to blame. Think about these news stories using the lessons from this section. How would you answer these managerial questions:

- Was the problem unique or an example of a larger class of problems they were having?
- If the company replaced all its employees with a new set, could the same outcomes well have occurred?

What actions would you recommend to Company X as a strategy for reducing such problems? Would you want to look at all the data? Or would you look at just the data from the big New York outage? Should we look for what was different about the New York outage from our regular day to day operations? Or should we stratify all 114? Or better yet, get data on *all* the outages—minor, major, and near-misses?

I commonly ask managers to raise their hands and take an oath that in the future they will "get the dots and plot the dots." It sounds simple. But it continues to amaze me what a powerful effect getting and plotting dots has on the management of an organization. The questions managers ask of each other change dramatically: instead of just discussing the latest result, people much more appropriately focus on how to reduce the variation in a process and how to improve its level—much higher-yield approaches. They do less tampering; they stop asking "Why was that result high, why was that result low, and what are you doing about it?" Instead, they ask "Why has this process continued to operate at the same level for the last two years in spite of all the things we've tried?" And they're often asking this of themselves as much as of anyone else!

If managers don't make this change, if they continue reacting to only the latest result or two, or comparing this result with the result from a year ago, without knowing whether the variation they are seeing is due to common causes or special causes, they are almost surely underreacting or overreacting, and both are deadly. They see trends where there are no trends and miss trends when there are trends. The consequences of failing to identify and react appropriately to variation are severe:

- Wasted time and energy
- Diverted attention
- More variation in the system

- Loss of productivity
- Loss of morale
- Loss of confidence in manager
- Jobs put in jeopardy
- Careers put in jeopardy
- Problems go on

Take a moment to reread the newspaper stories and think about your own organization. Could someone have written essentially the same stories about your company merely by switching the name?

We learn much more from investigating the *how*, but are far more interested in the *whos:* I doubt, for instance, that I'll ever see *People* magazine replaced on the newsstands by *Process* magazine. Yet the who is rarely the point. The opportunity for rapid improvement is ours if we will go against the grain and learn to get the dots, plot the dots, and focus on the process. It's not glamorous, but it is effective. It's dealing with the world the way it *really* is.

Part Four

Creating and Maintaining Gains

PROLOGUE

One month, a company started finding metal particles in the powder it purchased to line plastic molds. The particles caused defects in the molded parts, and naturally the company wanted the supplier to get rid of the particles ... and soon!

The supplier was dismayed that such a severe problem had arisen despite its effort to get every employee involved in improving processes. A task force set to work to find the cause, searching for days, examining every inch of the production process: all the equipment, the vats, the chemical storage tanks, the pipes. But to no avail.

Then one day a longtime employee came forward and said, "I think I may know where those particles are coming from. It may be me." When asked for details, the employee explained that several months earlier, he had gotten fed up with the way the powder kept caking up and jamming the machines.

"I got the idea that a wire brush I had at home would do a great job of cleaning off the caked powder," said the employee. "So I brought in the brush, and it really works well. The machines run beautifully and we have far fewer shutdowns. ... But I think maybe the metal particles might be coming from that brush." Subsequent tests showed that, indeed, the metal brush was the likely source of the particles.

The managers were pleased that the problem had been found and proud that they had not even considered firing the employee. In fact, they boasted to the customer that they had instilled such a level of trust in their organization that the man felt comfortable coming forward instead of hiding the truth.

The managers at the customer company weren't so impressed. "We can't believe you allow such chaos to go on in your organization that somebody would even conceive of making such a change without checking first on what it might do. You people had better get your act together."

A major paper company, early on in its improvement efforts, shut down a huge paper machine for preventive maintenance. Different groups of employees, each enthusiastically embracing the notion of continuous improvement, took advantage of this downtime to make a number of "improvements" to the machine. When it was time to bring the machine up again, it wouldn't work. While any one or two ideas might have been good, having different groups make uncoordinated changes was too much for the machine to handle. It took months to get this machine's performance back to the where it had been.

Once we make a commitment to improvement, ideas on how to make things better start coming at us from every direction. And, in general, the more ideas the better! But as these examples show, we can't simply act on every idea that comes along. Unless change happens in a systematic way, we will do more harm than good. So, though all managers and other employees have a responsibility to be on the lookout for improvement ideas and opportunities, **management has a particular responsibility to customers and to shareholders to manage those improvements.** The following chapters look at several key ingredients of managing improvement: paying attention to the way that work gets done, using data and a process focus to identify improvement opportunities, and using a common improvement framework to make improvement more rapid.

11
BETTER METHODS, BETTER RESULTS

The brightly painted car streaks around the racetrack under the blazing sun. It's late in the race. The driver pulls off for the crucial last pit stop before the final push for the checkered flag. Time is of the essence. Hands fly in a blur of precision as all four tires are changed, the engine checked, gas added, the windshield cleaned, and the driver given fluids. In about 16 seconds the car is ready and the driver pulls out to rejoin the race.

Nearly everyone has witnessed the preceding scene, even if only in a commercial for automotive products. The only way that pit crews can achieve their high levels of performance day in and day out is because they develop and adhere to **best-known methods.** They know exactly what equipment they need, where it should be placed, what sequence of steps they need to go through, and what each person's role is. They repeat key tasks in the exact same way, time and time again, until they find a better way. It's a capability we take for granted in that context, yet we demand nearly the opposite in our own lives: "I want the freedom to do my job my own way."

The questions facing us today are whether our organizations can really afford that kind of freedom, and, if not, what alternatives we have. To answer those questions, let's look at another example.

I found myself standing in a hotel hallway waiting for a colleague. By chance, I had stopped outside the open door of a room that was being cleaned. My idle glance caught sight of the housekeeper moving about the room, and soon I was transfixed. With precise movements, she worked quickly and efficiently: dusting every surface, checking every lightbulb and TV channel, cleaning every ashtray, replacing any item that needed replacing, straight-ening everything that was out of place ... all without hesitation or pause, never retracing her steps. Every potential source of dis-comfort or irritation to a guest was checked and eliminated.

Many people watching this housekeeper might have thought that she was just an unusually competent person. But anyone who has tried to develop and preserve highly effective methods would probably share my suspicion, which I later confirmed: she was not the exception in this hotel—all the housekeepers cleaned that way. The outstanding performance I witnessed was made possible because everyone who came in contact with this job—this employee, her managers, coworkers, and predecessors—paid close attention to every problem that guests experienced. They all then participated in developing and documenting methods for counteracting these problems, taught them to current employees, and used them to train all new people. Equally importantly, they focused on *productivity,* ruthlessly searching out and eliminating *every* wasted motion. **The results were standard methods that created exceptional service with maximum efficiency.**

PROS AND CONS OF STANDARD METHODS

I was having lunch with Earl, a friend and the president of a bank holding company. In the conversation, he said, "This new bank I've inherited is filled with problems. They have standards coming out of their ears. People can't focus on the customer. I'm going to throw out all the standards."

Though surprised by his statement, I decided the best course was to ask for more details before reacting. "Earl," I said, "can you give me an example of how a standard is getting in the way of a customer focus?"

"The problem is mostly that there are standards on every-thing," he said, mentioning a few examples. "People end up pay-ing more attention to where the $20 bills should be placed in the drawer than on the customer."

Earl's priority was making sure his customers got the best possible service. And to him it looked as if standards stood in the way of accomplishing that goal. Most managers I've worked with share Earl's views.

In fact, they have risen to the top because of their ability to work *around* systems and standards—to get the job done no matter what. They've seen many cases where standards

- stifled creativity and led to stagnation;
- interfered with a customer focus;
- added bureaucracy and red tape;
- made work inflexible, boring;
- only described the minimal acceptable output; and
- wasted time.

These are powerful arguments against using standard methods.

Few managers seem able to make as strong a case *for* standardization. Oddly, one of the strongest champions I know is a sales manager—a minor miracle, since sales is widely viewed as an art form.

> *"Everyone was pretty skeptical at first about standardizing our sales process," said John. "But we went ahead anyway. We looked into how we had trained salespeople in the past few years . . . and then got people to talk about what they were* really *doing. We asked them to describe what worked well and what tricks they'd developed. Then a group of sales managers and sales staff put together a flowchart and some other documents describing the major steps of a 'new' sales process that captured the best ideas. We had to struggle a bit to not get too detailed—we didn't want to totally restrict people's creativity."*
>
> *"And what did all this do for you?" I asked.*
>
> *In the first campaign in which the new standard methods were used, he said, they closed 12 of 13 targeted new accounts, lost none, and gained over a half-million dollars in increased sales—dramatically better results than they had ever achieved before! And these results came without the usual headaches: no special deals cut, no customers made angry, no old customers lost, less rushing around, less winging it.*

When I pressed for details, this manager, without hesitation, rattled off specific ways in which standardization contributed to these impressive results. I jotted down notes as he spoke. Having standard methods that everyone shared and bought into, he said, allowed them to do the following:

- Make progress with a customer more visible and make it easier to track that progress over time

- Keep *all* customers in the loop
- Decide how many sales targets to work at once (because everything was visible, they knew exactly how many prospects or customers were in which stages of the selling process)
- Capture and share lessons
- Evaluate points of weakness in selling capabilities
- Identify different individual strengths and weaknesses, and thus develop methods for playing to different salespeople's strengths and bolstering their weaknesses (in short, use team selling to better use their resources)
- Evaluate *how* and *by how much* new initiatives helped sales (new training, new warranty package, for example)
- Cooperate with distributors in selling to the end customer
- Create a basis for personal performance development
- Communicate more effectively with other functional areas, such as product development and customer service
- Communicate more effectively among themselves

By having *shared* methods, this manager and his staff were in a better position to evaluate the effect of changes in their process because they had a firm baseline of performance. They achieved consistently high levels of performance by doing critical aspects of every job in the current best-known way: "Once we saw the difference, it just didn't make sense to do anything less," he said.

Finding a balance

The difficulty we face is that **the arguments for and against standardization are both true**. If you go out today and tour a dozen organizations, you'll find some where resentment against standardization runs high because people are feeling trapped in straitjackets, or because they worked hard to develop standards that were subsequently put on a shelf and never used. In other organizations, employees will say that because of standards, their workplace has never run so smoothly nor been such a good place to work.

How is it that standardization can be reviled in one organization and revered in another? The answer lies in how the standards are administered, how we go about developing, maintaining, and upgrading standard methods. Carving standards into granite blocks, creating standards where there needn't be any, or imposing them from outside interferes with a customer focus, adds bureaucracy, and stifles creativity—had high jumper Dick Fosbury never been allowed to experiment with a new method, he never would have invented the Flop. To achieve a balance, we must develop standards judiciously—where it matters most—and treat them as living, breathing guidelines that can and **must be** constantly improved. When effectively managed, standards provide the kind of **foundation for improvement** demanded in today's marketplace.

CREATING ORDER FROM CHAOS

Companies that decide to make standard methods a key element of their management practices face many questions. Among them is how to approach the issue without creating undue alarm. For that reason, some companies prefer to avoid the emotional reaction against the terms "standard" and "standardization" by using the terms "best-known method" or "best practice." The name is relatively unimportant; it's the principle that is critical.

But there are many other more practical questions: What level should they work on first? Start small or big? Whom should they involve? What needs to be standardized? How do we make sure people use standards once we have them? These are difficult but important questions. Let me frame some answers by drawing a harsh but, I believe, realistic picture of where most organizations are today:

- Management has never effectively emphasized the use of documented standards.

- Few employees have experienced the benefits of effective standardization; many have been subject to rigid implementation of arbitrary rules. Virtually no one sees the need for standards.

- Most employees receive little training on how to do their jobs Instead, the majority are left to learn by watching a more-experienced employee.

- Most employees have developed their own unique versions of any general procedures they witnessed or were taught. They think, "my way is the best way."

- Changes to procedures happen haphazardly; individuals constantly change details to counteract problems that arise or in hopes of discovering a better method. Tampering is rampant.

Companies that use standardization effectively operate very differently:

- The company knows why it is developing standards; how standard methods contribute to achieving its overall purpose.
- Management uses best-known methods themselves and strongly supports and checks on the use and ongoing improvement of standards. Managers have personal experience with developing, using, and improving standards in their own jobs.
- Employees understand how different facets of their work affect the products and services delivered to customers; they know which elements are most critical to producing high-quality output with minimal waste, and they consistently perform those tasks the same way.

Going from wherever you are today to the point of having effective standards will not be easy, partly due to the widespread resistance to standardization. Part of the conversion will depend on people experiencing the benefits of standardization for themselves. Companies that *have* made the transition and are reaping the rewards typically

- Create standards judiciously
- Involve many people
- Begin with Check
- Build an organizational memory
- Train and retrain

Each of these guidelines is discussed next. Used together, they can smooth the transition to standardization by making sure that creating and using best-known methods are more likely to add value to the organization and its customers than to become roadblocks to creativity and improvement.

Create Standards Judiciously

In the summers of 1957 and 1958, I made money for college selling sets of cookware door to door. Due to turmoil in the company, I worked alone the first month and received no coaching beyond the initial training course. And I sold nothing. A third of the summer was gone and I had no sales, only expenses! The impetus to do better was strong.

One day, I got a new manager who came out on the road with me to watch me in action. Afterwards, he said I should be giving the price before *I described the "first call special," the wonderful bonus that customers got if they placed an order that day. I changed that sequence and began to sell immediately.*

This experience taught me about a **leverage point**: a place where a little change has a great impact. I talked about this concept back in Chapter 3 because it is a key notion in understanding how to achieve major gains in any system. In this context, it captures the idea that every job, every process, has within it high-leverage points that we *must* standardize if we want to achieve consistently high performance, and low-leverage points where standardization is superfluous, serving only to restrict flexibility. Our challenge is to find places where variable methods seriously hinder our ability to provide consistently high value to customers, then standardize only those. For example:

A pastry chef's favorite confection was popovers. On a good day, he made the best popovers in the Midwest. But not every day was a good day. In desperation, he had tried all manner of things to improve his performance: He rigorously stirred the batter by hand rather than using an electric mixer. He preheated the oven to just the right temperature. He made sure the eggs were at the proper temperature, the flour of the highest quality. But no matter what he did, not every day was a good day.

Then at a class he was taking, he learned about how to efficiently run experiments to find out which of the factors that might affect the quality of popovers really did. He tested the temperature and size of the eggs, the temperature of the batter, the quality of the flour, whether he stirred the batter by hand or with a mixer, the temperature of the oven, and so on. He found that only one factor really made a difference: having the batter at room temperature before putting the popovers in the oven. When that factor was controlled properly, his popovers came out perfectly time after time.

By virtue of his careful experimentation, this pastry chef identified the most critical aspects in creating perfect popovers. And, at the same time, he also discovered what was *not* important. Now he didn't have to wait for the eggs to warm up when he took them out of the refrigerator ... and all those years he had wasted time stirring the batter by hand when a mixer would have worked equally well! Now he also knew that he could revert to manual mixing if the mixer ever broke down, with no effect on the quality of the popovers.

Knowledge about what is *not* important is almost as valuable as knowledge about what *is* important. It helps us save time and money, and frees our attention so we can better focus on the few things that make a difference. This kind of flexibility shows up in every kind of job. It allows us to diligently manage what's really important and to use the cheapest or easiest approach elsewhere. As a rule of thumb, keep the degree of standardization as low as possible consistent with needed results.

Involve Many People

The new superintendent was eager to make an impact in his department. He had noticed that three of the four senior operators carried around little black books. Knowing that all of them were married, he discreetly inquired about those books and discovered with some relief that each kept track of the important machine settings that made the machines run best. They took such pride in this knowledge that they shared it with no one, not their counterparts on other shifts, not even their vacation relief. Not surprisingly, each black book had different settings.

Though there were no financial incentives for getting the best results, production and quality results were tracked by shift, and the shift with the best results was always publicly recognized. The new superintendent made several changes, beginning with tracking daily output rather than shift output. He also convinced the senior operators to come together for a series of "black book meetings." They'd each bring their books and work to reach consensus on a standardized "black book" that was thereafter kept in the control room, open to all. Even after the initial work was done, the senior operators came together every three months to discuss and verify updates to the methods described in the common black book.

This department subsequently achieved the best results the company had ever seen, setting company records in quality, safety, unit cost, and machine efficiency. Those results were not only maintained over subsequent months, they were constantly improved.

The idea of identifying the most effective and efficient way to perform a task has been around for decades. Indeed, there is a strong connection between best-known methods and the principles of efficiency that have been known to industrial engineers since the time of Frederick Taylor and the Gilbreths. In an important sense, Taylor's work can be thought of as industrializing the "master-apprentice" relationship of 2nd Generation Management. In the Taylor system, white-collar experts studied the work; blue-collar workers just did as they were told: "Check your brains at the door; you can pick them up as you leave." This division of labor had some advantages in the late 1800s and early 1900s but inevitably led to adversarial relationships and failed to capitalize on the experience and knowledge of the people doing the job every day.

The key difference today in 4th Generation Management lies in *who* develops, maintains, and improves standards: now the primary responsibility lies with the people who actually do the work. In practical terms, this means we must

- Involve those who do the work as leaders in developing better and better ways to do the job.
- Make sure they understand customer needs.
- Involve (as partners) specialists or other knowledgeable people who understand how the process does or should work—people who can teach you and other employees about the underlying theory or principles that guide the work.
- Designate an "owner," a person responsible for keeping visible the documentation, for updating the standard and its documentation as improvements are identified, and for assuring that newcomers and others are trained.

Unfortunately, when an organization starts its standardization efforts, employees often distrust management's motives. They may think that management doesn't believe they know how to do their jobs or that sharing their knowledge will make them vulnerable. They may also fear rigid implementation of strict rules that have little bearing on customers' needs. Experienced employees, in particular, typically feel that they don't need any documentation to do their work. In fact, they may have honed their skills to a level where they are not even aware of what procedures or techniques help them achieve their high levels of proficiency. There is no simple way around such resistance. The best approach is to let people experience the benefits for themselves: less waste, less rework, higher customer satisfaction, and saner lives!

Begin With Check

The executives of a company that makes refrigerators and other large home appliances toured another company that had

195

greatly reduced its inventory levels. The plant floor was clean and orderly, work flowed smoothly, and there weren't big stacks of parts waiting to be processed. Assets that had been tied up in inventory were being used for other purposes. The executives were greatly impressed. They went back to their own company and ordered every manager to get rid of inventory. To their dismay, production plummeted, stores ran out of products, and customers became angry and switched to other alternatives. The executives hastened to order the inventory put back in.

Another company read Dr. Deming's 14 Points, and saw Point 3: "Eliminate dependence on inspection." So they moved all inspectors to other jobs. Total chaos ensued. The problems that had been caught by the inspectors now passed right on to the next work station or to the customer. That mistake cost them millions.

These companies ran into trouble because they changed their methods before they understood why those methods were there in the first place. They eliminated safety nets in their processes without eliminating the factors that made those safety nets absolutely essential. After returning to its old levels of inventory, the first company described began to systematically identify and remove the problems that made the inventory necessary. The second company followed much the same route: they reinstated the inspectors and then systematically worked on process improvements until inspection was no longer needed (except as a way to gather data for further improvement). As they started to realize the gains from their efforts, they began to redeploy the inspectors.

The temptation to "make changes" is great once we start asking people for improvement ideas. But it is a temptation we have to resist: in the beginning we simply don't know what really is a good way to do a job. Are the documented standards best? The methods people are actually using? New ideas being recommended? Can we eliminate certain steps or inventory or inspection, or are they there for a reason? To answer these questions, its best to use CAP-Do:

- **Check**: Make sure we know *why* the work is being done. See if this **purpose** is clearly documented. Locate any existing documentation of methods. Compare **actual practice** with the **documented methods**. If there are no documented standards, compare different practices among the people doing the work.

Compare how the effectiveness of the work is supposed to be checked with how it is actually checked.

- **Act:** Reconcile the actual practices and the documentation, changing whichever we decide to change (that is, change the actual practices to match the documentation, or change the documentation to match the actual practice). Do this for both how the work is supposed to be done and how it is supposed to be checked. If no standard methods are in place and no one can show with data which methods are really "best-known," a practical alternative at this stage is simply to agree on *a* method they all will use. This will at least establish a consistent framework upon which improvements can be built.
- **Plan:** Develop a plan for upgrading the documentation, for making it more useful. Develop a plan for encouraging the use of the documented standard. Determine how to detect flaws and potential improvements in the standard.
- **Do:** Train to the new documented standard. Use the new standard.
- **Check:** Once again compare actual practice with documented standards to determine inconsistencies. Investigate those inconsistencies. If the standards are not being followed, for instance, is it because the documentation is too difficult to use? Because people don't appreciate the need for using the standard? Because the standard doesn't allow people to keep up, or prevents them from doing quality work? Because people have found a better way?
- **Act:** Again, reconcile the actual practice with the documentation, changing whichever the data shows we should change.
- **Continue cycling the PDCA wheel.**

Build An Organizational Memory

A reformulation team in a petrochemical additives business had discovered that changes in several ingredients of a major product would save the company over $750,000 a year without affecting the quality of the final product. The team made its recommendations to management and offered new purchasing guidelines. Everyone was pleased.

A year later, this company was shocked to find that none of the promised savings had appeared. An investigation revealed the purchasing department had not used the new guidelines. Why?

Because several key people in the purchasing department had been reassigned and many people on the reformulation team had been moved to other areas of the company and no longer came in contact with that particular product. More importantly, no one had bothered to adequately document the new guidelines. So the old materials were still being purchased.

This company is not alone. Like many others, it thought it was doing a good job of getting employees involved in improving the way the work gets done. But, in a more critical sense, it had abandoned new employees to the whims of fate by failing to provide effective mechanisms for retaining the lessons their predecessors had learned.

This company paid a stiff price for having an **eyelash learning curve**. Employees come into a job, spend a lot of energy and time learning how to do the work well, then move on, taking all their knowledge with them. The cost to the organization should be apparent in this curve: it repeatedly pays the price of having individuals learn how to do the job. There is no **organizational memory** to allow people to start where their predecessors left off, nothing that captures new methods that produce better results. The individuals learn, but the organization does not.

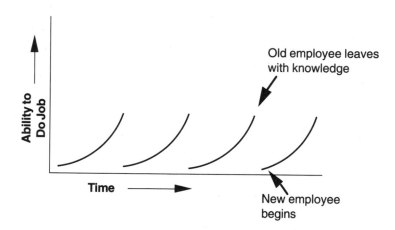

EYELASH LEARNING CURVE

A much better learning curve is shown on the next page. Organizations with this type of learning curve continue to advance their knowledge by preserving the lessons each individual learns. These companies far outshine ones that keep repeating history month after month, year after year, employee after employee. They have more rapid learning, less waste, less complexity—in short, higher customer value with lower costs.

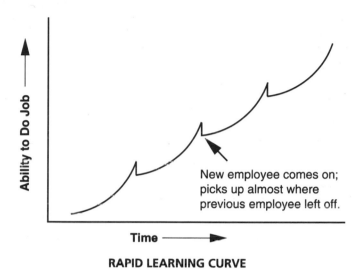

RAPID LEARNING CURVE

How do we create a **rapid learning curve**? There are two key ingredients: having best-known methods documented, and training people on what those methods are.

Train and retrain

Once we have developed and documented best-known methods, we face the issue of how to make sure they are used. Education and training play a key role, but the question is whom do we train? The need to train new employees and new managers is obvious. Training experienced employees, however, is a subject that usually meets with resistance. For many years, I was one of the skeptics. After all, experienced employees usually have a lot of knowledge about how to do their jobs: what could they possibly gain from more training?

Several factors caused me to change my mind. When discussing best-known methods, employees end up sharing their ideas with each other and with technical experts. Inevitably, the method chosen for the standard combines good ideas from many sources. Even experienced employees learn subtle, and not so subtle, differences between the new standards and the techniques with which they are familiar. Second, people naturally forget. It's part of our biology. Methods, unless they are scrupulously reinforced and maintained, deteriorate over time. Everyone can use a reminder now and then about the standard they are supposed to be using. For those reasons, I've come to believe that training and retraining experienced employees is just as necessary as training novices if we are to make sure that our standards are followed. This lesson extends as well to training supervisors and other managers: they can't coach others or help to monitor and improve a standard if they don't know it themselves.

Training and standardization create a nice positive spiral. A high degree of standardization is needed to make training possible. Without standardization, training is cumbersome, inefficient, and generally ineffective. And without effective training, any standard is soon lost.

STRATEGIC REDESIGN

The general principles described here apply at all levels of the organization. In recent years, for instance, the concepts of **reengineering** and **business process redesign** have been gaining popularity as ways to radically redesign large-scale systems and processes to eliminate waste and rework. Many companies, for instance, are learning to live without purchase orders and confirmatory paperwork, instead creating automatic systems that alert suppliers when stocks are low, thus eliminating paperwork and bureaucracy that adds no value to their products and services.

These two approaches stem from a common question: *"Should we improve what we have, or start over from scratch, with a clean sheet of paper?"* Many companies have discovered that it's one thing to completely redesign a process . . . on paper . . . and another task entirely to implement the proposed changes. Though in theory we may want to take out a clean sheet and design a new process from scratch, in practice this often leads to great hassle for relatively little additional benefit—or, as in the examples described previously, even greater chaos than what we started with. Progress is generally faster if the *concepts* of reengineering are borne in mind but we take an alternative approach: With CAP-Do we can better understand the current process, then treat as "given" as many of the major process blocks as possible, changing only those components that promise major benefits. We then work to reduce waste within and between the major blocks. I call this approach **strategic redesign.**

As always, we must bear in mind that *all change is ultimately social change.* What seems to us to be minor changes may well feel like radical changes to someone else. Any change requires changes in behavior and in interactions within and between groups, changes that do not happen overnight. The more we preserve the components of the existing process, and the more localized or focused the changes we ask for, through strategic redesign, the less disruption employees incur in their daily work—giving us the results we need far faster and cheaper than if we undertake a radical, "clean sheet" approach.

The Check in this use of CAP-Do is driven by questions such as:

- Why do we need this *process* at all? How does it help us better serve customers?
- What need is met by doing this *step?*
- Why do we do this step now?
- Why do we do this step in this way?

Starting with Check allows us to understand any existing process steps and documentation and how they are used or not used. It helps us understand why people do their jobs the way they do and prevents us from repeating past mistakes. It also capitalizes on process knowledge that employees have developed over the years.

THE LINK BETWEEN METHODS AND RESULTS

To those unfamiliar with or perhaps even hostile to the idea of standardization, it may seem that I have strayed far afield from the topic of improvement. I hope, however, that the many examples cited in this chapter make it clear that standardization and improvement are two sides of the same coin. The sales manager described earlier, for instance, did not suddenly decide one day that his company needed better methods. He knew it needed better results. It just so happened that standardizing on key aspects of the sales process was the way to get better results.

This kind of experience is common. At first, you will find that people have little energy for "standardization" and great energy for "improvement." But standardization—or, more generally, a focus on methods—is often an easy path to improvement, especially early on

201

when there is great variation in how work is done. Similarly, maintaining the gains from improvement eventually boils down to a focus on methods—what we will do differently to maintain the gains, to prevent recurrence of a problem, and to achieve new, consistently higher levels of performance.

When all the ingredients of effective standardization are in place, we have the capability for real improvement. Employees will know what pieces of their work are most critical to delivering high value to customers. And they will be able to use PDCA to do and constantly upgrade their work:

- There is a Plan they helped to create for how the work will be done and how they will know if it is effective.
- They Do the work according to the plan.
- They Check how well the work is going, using indicators they helped to create.
- They take Action to put in place immediate remedies and participate in developing ways to prevent problems from recurring.

Equipping employees with the power and ability to use PDCA to develop and improve methods, and managers with the ability to find and fix faults with the system truly is the basis for continuous, rapid improvement. Better methods are fundamental to better results.

12

IMPROVING OUR ABILITY TO IMPROVE

"One of our biggest problems here is safety," Kevin said to Lynn, a statistician his company had retained to help them out. "Serious incidents are rare, but people still get hurt far too often. None of our efforts in the past few years have paid off."

"What have you tried?"

"A lot of different things. Gordon, the VP of Operations, sent a memo to all employees reminding them how important safety was. Then I met with each department head and personally asked them to make safety a priority. It's been the first item on every manager's agenda for 18 months now. You might have also seen the safety posters we put up in June with our new slogan: 'Safety and Common Sense: Partners for Life.' I like it. A guy over in maintenance came up with that idea and won $1500 in the contest we ran to raise safety awareness."

"And you say none of this has done any good?" asked Lynn.

"I'm afraid not. Our records have never been great, and the number of incidents have gone up three months running. What do you think we should do?"

"Let me look into it a little more, Kevin. I'll get back to you with some initial thoughts next week."

Despite an obvious concern and commitment to improve safety, this company had accomplished nothing significant in several years. A *commitment* to improvement was insufficient to bring actual improvement; the commitment had not brought with it the *ability* to improve. In this chapter, we'll look at several key factors that not only give us that ability but also make us capable of *improving how we improve*— the hallmark of an organization that is improving rapidly. To begin, we'll pick up the rest of Lynn's story.

203

PATHWAYS TO IMPROVEMENT

Lynn began her investigation by looking at the safety figures. She found they were stable over the past two years. By stratifying the data, she discovered that the most frequent type of injury was sprained fingers. With that in mind, she toured the facility, closely observing many employees at work. She noticed machine operators in one area moved heavy metal blocks in and out of the machines by inserting their fingers into small holes near the tops of the blocks. Conversations confirmed that most sprained fingers happened in this way.

"Have you ever considered getting rods to put in those holes so it would be easier to lift the blocks?" she asked the operators.

"Oh, yes," they answered. "We even had some once. And they worked great. But there were never quite enough, so we all started borrowing them from each other . . . and then began hiding our own so nobody would take ours. Now we usually can't find them when we need them."

Lynn's recommendation to management was obvious at that point: purchase more sets of lifting rods and paint outlines on the wall in the shape of the rod sets to show where they should always hang. This simple change dramatically reduced the number of sprained fingers.

The company just described was sincerely devoted to improvement, yet it had taken them years to uncover even a simple solution like purchasing additional rods. Why? The trouble was that they had been taking broad measures to address a vague problem: "too many safety incidents." Putting up posters and holding meetings to encourage people to focus on safety did little to reduce the number of injuries. Real progress came only when they used data, combined with direct observation in the workplace, to isolate a specific problem and develop a remedy targeted at that specific problem.

Vague solutions to vague problems generally add cost and bureaucracy, and create little if any improvement. Focused solutions to focused problems bring rapid improvement. Effective use of data, especially when coupled with on-site observation, allows us to develop the kind of focus needed to create real, lasting improvement.

But we can develop focus in other ways.

Tom and Kim worked for a utility company. Tom's office was right next to Kim's. Several times a day, Tom would get up, go to a file cabinet out in the hall between the offices, extract a piece of paper, insert it into a folder, and add the folder to the stack in his outbox. From time to time, Kim would pick up the folders from Tom's outbox, go through them, pull out all the sheets of paper that Tom had added, and put them right back into their original spots in the hallway file cabinets.

These mysterious pieces of paper were official forms from the regulatory authorities giving the company approval to do a particular type of job. Tom put them in the folders so that the people going out to do the job would have their permits with them. Kim took them out of the folders because she knew that no employee out in the field had ever been asked to show a permit, and that management was concerned the forms might get lost if sent to the field.

One day, Tom and Kim were asked to diagram the process used to provide paperwork to the field staff. In the course of their analysis, they discovered the short, circular route taken by the permits and immediately stopped their wasted efforts.

Years earlier, when this process had started, Tom's and Kim's predecessors had worked in different buildings miles apart. Eventually, the offices were moved to the same building, and then more recently put side by side, to the point where Kim and Tom now shared file cabinets. Their situation would have been lamentable had their offices still been miles apart. Having offices next to each other and sharing a file cabinet made it ludicrous. Their situation is not uncommon, because few of us have been taught to view our work as part of a process, as just one step in a series of steps that link suppliers with customers. Only when Tom and Kim examined their work as a series of steps did the waste become obvious. This brings us back to the issues discussed in the preceding chapter and to a second principle for improving faster: look at the process, focus on *how* the work gets done.

Start with data or process?

These examples make improvement seem simpler than it usually is in practice, but they do illustrate two basic approaches to improvement. In the first, Lynn started with *data*. In the second, Tom and Kim started by understanding the *process*. Which of these two approaches is better? The simple answer is that we need both.

For example, there was no obvious process associated with "safety incidents" that Lynn could have flowcharted even if she had wanted to.

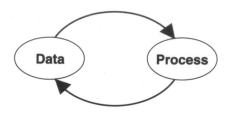

DATA OR PROCESS?

In contrast, Kim and Tom didn't know there was a problem until they tried to understand the process. These people began at points that were best for their situations. Either starting point sets in motion an upward spiral in quality and productivity: useful data help us identify better processes; a deeper understanding of a process leads us to better data. Both help us "improve the system," the only *reliable* way to get better and better results, day in and day out. Many organizations have found it helpful to have a common framework for improvement that helps link the various components together.

A FRAMEWORK FOR IMPROVEMENT

Charlie is the CEO and Chairman of the Board of a service company and also participates on the boards of three subsidiaries. For years, he felt like his life was one long meeting. He had to attend four board meetings each month and multiple subcommittees. Of course, he also had regularly scheduled meetings with his own staff, with the budget team, with the operations staff.... What he resented most was the lack of time to visit customers or walk through the facilities and talk with his employees.

He raised the issue at a board meeting one day and was surprised at how much the experience of other board members mirrored his own. They were all frustrated with what seemed to be interminable meetings and repetitive decision making. They decided they needed to do something about it.

If you were on this board, where would you start? Would you just cancel some of your regular meetings? How would you know what impact that had on the organization? Charlie and the other directors decided to practice what they had been preaching and use logic and data to address their problem.

Their first step was getting a clear purpose: increase the efficiency and effectiveness of board operations and decision making. Their next step was getting a handle on exactly how big the problem was. So they all looked through their calendars for the past six months and counted how many hours they had each spent on board work. The data showed that the CEO alone had spent 190 hours on board-related work in just 31 weeks, nearly 13% of his time. He and other directors also helped to create flowcharts depicting the process used to make several recent major decisions. To say it was convoluted would be too polite. The intricate maze of loops from committee to committee was mind-boggling. Furthermore, many decisions addressed by the parent board had also been tackled by one or more of the subsidiary boards. Obviously, there was great room for improvement.

Further investigation allowed Charlie and the other board members to pinpoint financial issues as the main source of complexity and waste, and to identify exactly how that waste manifested itself (what committees discussed which issues for how long, etc.). They ended up by better defining the focus of each board (strategic vs. operational, for example) and restructuring the board (such as combining different committees). As a result of these changes, Charlie and each of the directors were able to cut in half the amount time they needed to spend on board work, and, moreover, decisions flowed much more quickly and smoothly through the organization.

These board members not only used data to help them achieve their improvement goal, more specifically they used a framework called the **7 Step Method**, which will be described in more detail shortly. This framework helped them identify a key contributor to complexity and time in the board operations—in other words, to *focus* on a specific problem and develop specific countermeasures. This leads to a third principle of rapid improvement: having an improvement framework increases the chances that we'll ask the right questions, make the right links, and find the deep causes of problems.

The 7 Step Method

The table on page 208 provides an overview of the 7 Step Method. Each of the seven steps has a clearly defined aim and a set of questions that helps us achieve that aim.

7 Step Method for Improvement

Step	1. Project	2. Current Situation	3. Cause Analysis	4. Solutions	5. Results	6. Standardization	7. Future Plans
Goal	To define the project's purpose and scope.	To further focus the improvement effort by gathering data on the current situation.	To identify and verify deep causes with data; to pave the way for effective solutions.	To develop, try out, and implement solutions that address deep causes.	To evaluate both the solutions and the plans used to implement them.	To maintain the gains by standardizing work methods or products.	To anticipate future improvements and to preserve the lessons from this effort.
Questions to be answered	• What is the project's purpose? What problem or "gap" are you addressing? • What impact will closing this gap have on customers? • What other reasons exist for addressing this gap? • How will you know if things are better? • What is your plan for this project?	• What is the history? • Can the problem or situation be depicted in a sketch or flowchart? • What happens now when the problem appears? What are the symptoms? • Where do symptoms appear? Where don't they appear? • When do symptoms appear? When don't they appear? • Who is involved? Who isn't?	• What are the possible causes of the symptoms? Which of these are verified with data? • What are possible deeper causes of the verified causes? • How does the verification of causes affect decisions about who should be working on this effort?	• What solutions could address the deep causes? • What criteria are useful for comparing potential solutions? • What are the pros and cons of each solution? How do they relate to the gaps and causes? • Which solutions seem best? Which will you select for testing? • How will you try them on a small scale? What data will you collect? • Which trial solution turned out to be most effective? • What are the plans for implementing it full scale?	• How well do results meet the targets? • How well was the plan executed? What can this tell you about planning for improvement?	• What is the new standard method or product? • How will all employees who do this work be trained? • What's in place to assure the gains are maintained? To prevent backsliding? • How will methods, procedures, and results be monitored? How will anyone know if things are working the way they should work? • What means are in place to foster ongoing improvement?	• What remaining needs were not addressed by this project? • What are your recommendations for investigating these remaining needs? • What did you learn from this project? How can these lessons be communicated? • How will the documentation be completed? What happens to it when it's finished? • How will this project be brought to a close? How will you celebrate?

THE 7 STEP METHOD

The next page gives a quick overview of how the CEO and board used the 7 Step Method to help them (this was the first effort in which any of them had used the 7 Step Method, so their application was far from perfect, but they did stick within the general framework):

- **Step 1: Purpose.** The essential question of purpose is "what are we trying to do?" Answering that question helped the board members focus their improvement effort at a specific target ("increase effectiveness of boards by reducing decision-making redundancy").

- **Step 2: Current Situation.** This step made them answer the question "what have we been doing and what has it produced?" This meant developing a deep understanding of the **history** and the current state of each board, including what issues each board tackled. They also developed several flowcharts that visually showed how decisions flowed within the organization; as a result, they realized that financial issues were by far the trickiest and most time-consuming.

- **Step 3: Cause Analysis.** The board members investigated what factors had contributed to the current situation, that is, why the path followed by financial issues was so convoluted. Part of the trouble, they discovered, was a high degree of overlap between the interests of the various boards.

- **Step 4: Solutions.** The board members discussed ways in which the boards could be reconfigured to provide a better match with the needs of the corporation and its subsidiaries and with each board member's interests and capabilities. To try out their ideas on a small scale (an essential aspect of PDCA), they created sketches of the options available to them and "walked through" several typical decisions. They also created a chart where they recorded the pros and cons of each option. They put into practice the approach that seemed best.

- **Step 5: Results.** They continued tracking the amount of time that members spent on board issues (it was cut by a third) and how decisions flowed through the organization.

- **Step 6: Standardization.** They used the new board configurations and followed the new processes. At the end of two months they did a check of how things were working, leading to several minor but useful changes. They scheduled a repeat of this check and update at the end of each quarter.

- **Step 7: Future Plans.** The CEO and board members realized they could have been more rigorous about their data collection. They also identified other board issues that should be addressed in a comparable manner.

The logic behind the 7 Step Method has taken shape over the past decades based on the experiences of companies from around the world. If you look at its structure, you'll see that it is a close relative of PDCA, or rather CAP-Do. The questions in the early steps provide specific recommendations on what to Check, and the remaining steps link that knowledge with plans and actions for developing countermeasures. By using these questions to develop specific plans tailored to our own improvement needs, we can avoid some of the most common improvement pitfalls and traps.

To further illustrate the value of the 7 Step Method, I'll discuss another example, and, as we go, point out where each of the seven steps fits in.

> *A major customer of a chemical company complained that surface blemishes on the products they purchased were getting worse. The surfaces were unusually pitted, the customer said, and other surface defects were also increasing. "You'd better fix the problem," they said, "or we'll take our business elsewhere next year." . . .*

It was relatively easy for this company to get through **Step 1: Purpose**, since everyone knew they had a big problem that was affecting a major customer. The objective: sharply reduce the number of surface defects so the customer would keep doing business with them. The importance and relevance of the project was clear to all from the very beginning.

> *. . . Earlier efforts to correct these surface blemishes had failed, so the company brought in an outsider to help guide this key improvement effort. He first asked the production technicians and workers what they thought was causing the problem. The consensus echoed beliefs widely held in the industry: several well-known contaminants were obviously to blame.*
>
> *The outsider, however, asked them to be their own devil's advocates and not accept any ideas they could not support with data. In response, they used specialized equipment to look at samples of different types of blemishes at a microscopic level. To their surprise, they discovered that the two biggest problems were really only one "problem"—one contaminant that looked very different depending on the severity of its effect. . . .*

All of the elements of the 7 Step Method are important for achieving true improvement, but none perhaps more so than **Step 2:**

210

Current Situation. It is in this step that we develop the focus that will allow us to put in effective remedies. How well we do this step is thus critical to the final outcome. So far, this company had developed a deeper understanding of the problem, but their localization efforts weren't done yet.

> *. . . The customer had sent this company time plots showing the rate of the surface blemishes on several products over the past several months. Upon close inspection, the employees saw that one set of products had virtually no increase in blemishes, while another set clearly showed an upward trend, a special cause signal! . . .*

Look at how far this company's understanding of the problem had come: from "lots of surface defects" to "one type of blemish that has different magnitudes and is increasing on one particular product type." Better still, they had identified a special cause, which means they were presented with an easy learning opportunity. In their case, they could move on to **Step 3: Cause Analysis** to see if they could understand what was different about that particular product type that would cause blemishes to appear there and not on other products.

> *. . . What could explain the difference? They generated a lot of ideas. "Show me the data," the outsider said. They kept digging deeper and deeper into the problem until, eventually, they pinpointed the source of the problem. At that point, the needed change was quite obvious: it was a solution that no one would have thought of before they started the investigation, however!*
>
> *Failure rates for the surface blemishes, measured on a standard industry scale, had been running as high as 15 defects per unit at the start of this effort, far worse than the industry norm of 1 defect per unit. . . .*

Doing a thorough job in Step 2 and Step 3 allowed this company to move quickly through **Step 4: Solutions** and **Step 5: Results**. The solutions aren't always obvious or simple to implement, as this company discovered, but careful detective work does at least make it likely that the solutions put in place will actually work! But this company's effort wasn't done yet.

> *. . . All too aware of how quickly such gains can be lost, the employees who did this work made sure that they captured and preserved the new methods that made this lower defect rate*

*possible (**Step 6: Standardization**). The standard methods and associated training were piloted, improved, then made part of daily work.*

*The celebration of the success of this effort didn't last long because the customer asked if they could get the defect rate down to 1 per every 3 units within a year. After a quick celebration and time to reflect on what they had learned (**Step 7: Future Plans**), the employees continued working on further improvements. By relentlessly going after data and focusing further and further on the causes of the defects—continued cycling of Steps 2 to 6—the company exceeded this expectation by a factor of ten: within 18 months they had passed the customer's target and reached a level of 1 defect per 30 units.*

By using data to better understand its processes, this company achieved the best quality levels ever achieved in its industry. It was able to keep this customer, and, better yet, to get even more of its business. Getting the improvement, however, was not its only emphasis: by continuing to capture and upgrade the methods they used (Step 6), people never slid back into the old ways of doing business. They continued moving *forward!* The achievement and the delighted customers created interest and enthusiasm within the company for similar improvements in other areas. Success was contagious . . . and brought with it an unexpected benefit: the new standards they developed for a U.S. facility were so effective that they were adopted by a new facility in Europe, saving the company months of start-up pains.

Every employee needs to understand the three principles of rapid improvement covered so far in this chapter—using **data** to develop focus, understanding **how** work gets done, and using a **framework.** The component that's still missing, however, is how managers can actively increase the rate of improvement across the organization. Let's take a look at how the managers in one company addressed this issue.

Improvement As a System

Several years ago, a large company became committed to rapid improvement. Management set a goal of doubling its "first-pass quality" (a measure of how often they had to resort to rework, repair, restarts, and so on to produce quality output). They wanted to reach this goal within three years.

As they came closer and closer to the end of that period, the executives began to realize they hadn't seen nearly the gains they were expecting. To understand why, they performed a Check of the improvement efforts started during the three-year period. They discovered that three categories of officially sanctioned projects had evolved:

1. *"Quality Task Forces," each composed of a cross section of managers and technical experts, used to solve technical problems.*
2. *"Customer Number One Teams," each composed of managers and professional staff, used to address primary concerns of customers.*
3. *"I-Teams" (Improvement Teams) composed of first-line employees, used to solve problems in their daily work.*

Within each of these categories, some groups had achieved significant gains: One task force, for instance, improved first-pass quality fourfold, twice the stated objective, with an associated savings of millions of dollars per year. Similarly, a customer team succeeded in cutting the cycle time for a key process by more than half: it took them less than half the original time to fulfill a customer request for service.

Unfortunately, many other projects had shown few signs of progress for more than a year.

Results like these are not uncommon. Most organizations find that when they first get started, some improvement efforts bring spectacular results and others fail miserably. Many factors contribute to such outcomes: the link to customer needs, clarity of direction, availability of resources, knowledge of the participants, degree of guidance and support, ability to develop focus, and so on. Most of these causes lie within the system, which means they are ultimately management's responsibility. It is management's responsibility to make sure that improvement is not merely the hit-or-miss outcome of good fortune, but the reliable outcome of effective *improvement systems:* effective systems for identifying leverage points to target for improvement, for identifying appropriate employees for selected priorities, for clarifying objectives, for removing barriers, and so on. By working on such systems, management can **improve their organization's ability to improve**.

These managers realized they could drive more rapid improvement if they could figure out what factors increased the chances of a project's success. Was it the composition of the group working on the project? The guidance they received? Training? Resources? Ability to use data? The information they had gathered in the first round of checking did not provide answers to these questions, so they decided to probe deeper.

In a second round of information gathering, the managers reviewed documentation from many projects. They interviewed the leaders of several successful projects within each category. Then they prepared overviews of all three categories of projects: how many projects were started, if and when projects concluded, what the results were, how many people were involved, what kind of guidance and support each project received, what types of problems each project experienced, and so on.

Here are some things these managers learned from this check.

- All the Quality Task Forces used PDCA explicitly. Each one was required to develop specific criteria for "success" and plans to achieve stated goals, to regularly evaluate progress against the criteria, to develop and test countermeasures, and so on. *Neither of the other project categories had a consistent framework*; some projects in the other categories used PDCA or the 7 Step Method, but many did not follow any particular pattern.

- There were obvious successes and failures within each category, but it was difficult to judge the progress of most projects.

- Members of several projects explicitly commented on the need to have standardized work practices, as well as standard methods for creating and updating those practices, so the gains they had made could be preserved.

- Supervisors in several areas were frustrated in trying to communicate both with their managers and with the improvement groups. They found it difficult to discuss progress, support needs, results, and so on. The improvement groups reported similar frustrations, particularly in dealing with people who were affected by the outcome of a project but not involved directly with the improvement work.

- The leadership of the Quality Task Forces had specific criteria for choosing projects that were important to the company. The other categories did not have such criteria. The management group for the I-Teams met weekly; they spent most of their time discussing team support issues.

- The use of data tools was sporadic.

- It was particularly difficult to gather information on the Customer Number One projects because few records were available.

- Many projects experienced problems with cross-functional needs (even something seemingly as simple as moving a machine).
- Many projects requested budget authorization to implement recommended changes but there was no policy in place about how such requests should be handled.

All this information was valuable . . . but the key question for management was which of these factors made a difference, which were the leverage points. As these managers came to realize, they still couldn't answer that question *because the information simply wasn't available*; there were too many gaps in the records. For many projects there were no clear measure of success, no easy way to figure out what the people had actually done, nothing that documented the results. Thus, though there were many things the managers *suspected* as contributing to success—having clear criteria and following an improvement framework, for instance—they did not have the data to support those theories. Nevertheless, they decided to take the following actions based on their hunches and the general impressions they were able to glean.

- They identified criteria for selecting projects.
- They established core requirements for every sanctioned improvement effort:
  –must have a clear, written aim
  –must establish performance measures ("how will we know if things are better?")
  –must establish a baseline of performance and at least a rough target for amount of improvement expected
  –must establish at least a rough-order plan that includes a schedule
  –must schedule regular reviews
- They adopted a standard improvement framework for projects to use in planning their efforts and reporting their results.

This analysis and the subsequent actions proved to be a turning point in this company's improvement efforts. Managers now understood at a much deeper level that to drive rapid improvement throughout the company, they needed not only to better support *individual* projects but also to find ways to understand what was happening in the *set* of projects—ways to analyze the improvement process across projects. Only by addressing both of these issues could they hope to improve their organization's ability to improve.

Six months later, they were able to do another Check and this time not only were the projects better, but so were the data they could collect—data that was much different from the data used *within* the projects. The participants in the projects needed data on the process being studied: quality and productivity measures, indicators of customer satisfaction, and so on. The managers needed data that reflected the problems and successes within the projects and information on the improvement processes being used. For example, they collected data on how long projects spent in different phases of improvement and what problems they ran into in the different phases. That kind of data is often softer than we would like, but it is the sort that is most useful to senior managers. With this new data, these managers were in a much better position to understand why some projects were successful and others weren't. They were now able to make targeted changes such as training to meet specific needs of those doing certain jobs or of those involved in particular aspects of improvement. They were also in a good position to plan for even better data collection on future projects.

The benefits that this company and others gain from this kind of systematic approach to improvement are similar to those described by the sales manager on pages 189–190:

- More projects are completed; few drop out of sight or flounder for any length of time.
- Most projects reach or exceed desired targets. Those that don't bring the predicted progress are still rich sources of learning.
- It is easier to capture and share lessons about how to make improvements.
- Managers find it much easier to track the progress of all improvement efforts over time. They find it easier to look across improvement efforts to evaluate points of weakness and strength. They can evaluate *how* and *by how much* new initiatives (such as training, guidance, added resources) help improvement efforts.
- Managers, supervisors, and project participants find it much easier to communicate with each other.

Doing a one-time Check will bring some improvement if you take action, but bigger gains come when we begin to take responsibility for improvement as a system and begin to regularly review improvement efforts. Just as good data are central to rapid improvement in more-focused situations, so too are **good data across projects essential to improving our ability to improve.**

216

Summary

Every employee has a responsibility to keep seeking ways to improve the work they do. But management has a larger responsibility to customers, shareholders, and other stakeholders to manage those improvements. This means encouraging the development of best-known methods to improve results and to establish a solid base on which further improvement can be built. It also means using data and process thinking to focus on specific sources of problems and develop specific countermeasures. And it means adopting a shared framework for improvement throughout the organization, which both increases the odds of success for each project individually and makes it easier for managers to find ways to improve the organization's ability to improve.

EPILOGUE

A small nonprofit group decided that one way to raise money would be to hold a conference that would draw people from around the country into their city. A steering committee of five volunteers did all the work needed to organize and run this conference. They worked day and night for months to make all the arrangements. The week of the conference went by in a blur; the volunteers probably got 20 hours of sleep among them during those five days. The night before the conference they were frantically stuffing binders and creating name tags. Almost 500 people came, and it was a smashing success. The volunteers were elated . . . but they were also zombies.

The revenue from this conference allowed the organization to hire its first paid staff person. Having learned their lesson, the steering committee members roped other organization members into helping out with a second conference. Both that year and the following year, 40 volunteers, divided into five teams, helped the paid staff member organize and run the conference. They were charged not only with doing the work but also documenting what issues they addressed, decisions they reached, and methods they developed for doing the work. The conferences were again successful. Revenues flowed in. Afterwards, each team met to discuss what did and didn't work well, and to capture possible improvements for the next conference.

The organization kept growing. And the now-annual conference continued to be the main source of revenue. Its success was critical. With each conference, the staff and volunteers used and improved even further the methods and lessons learned from previous conferences. And with each conference, the level of frenzy dropped even further.

By the fourth year, so many effective methods were in place that far fewer people were needed to do the work, even though conference attendance had reached 600 or more people. By the fifth year, all the preparations were done a full week in advance *of the conference date. A handful of volunteers had helped with a few key tasks, but most of the work was done by three paid staff, all of whom worked regular hours and didn't even have to work weekends. The staff members were elated ... and though pleasantly exhausted, were not the zombies their predecessors had become.*

The efficiency with which this annual conference is now run is the envy of many organizations. The conference organizers have always delivered quality to their customers: detailed notes, easy registration, clear directions, well-organized meetings, outstanding sessions. At first, though, they had to achieve this quality through brute force: long hours, checking and rechecking, heroic efforts. Now, by identifying best-known methods and eliminating waste, they do it with finesse.

There is some fraction of people to whom this is bad news. They thrive on the adrenaline rush that derives from disorder and chaos. To them, the thought of eliminating waste and developing standards leaves them cold.

"You know," said the newly reelected state representative, "I hardly felt like I was having a campaign this year. My staff had documented the key processes they use to do their work. And those processes worked. So I got plenty of sleep, and they seldom had to put in overtime. I kind of missed all the scrambling around, the excitement of realizing we had only 24 hours to do something that normally would take a week or more."

Having standardized, low-waste processes does not mean that our workplaces have to become dull and lifeless. The new challenge is to create a new excitement, one that is based on rapid improvement and delighted customers—not one that is based on heroic brute-force efforts.

We must make our standards *vital*, living. They must live and evolve with new ideas and changing conditions in the workplace and the marketplace. Brute force efforts are too wasteful, too error prone, and too stressful on our employees, on our organizations, and, most importantly, on our customers.

Part Five

Creating the Environment

PROLOGUE

The name sewn over the left pocket of the worn blue shirt said "Marta." The woman looked as if she were in her 80s though she must have been much younger. Her voice was soft and shaped by a heavy East European accent. She spoke to the others around the table, some dressed like her, others in dark suits or fashionable dresses.

"The data and the charts ... they let the process speak to us," she said. *"Before, I never knew how to tell my supervisors what was happening. Now I can. Now they will listen to me when I have data. Now I can make better product."*

Marta spoke with simple eloquence about how excited she was after all these years to have new knowledge and tools for doing her job...for *improving* her job. Her words had a powerful effect on the executives in the group. Few employees, themselves included, had worked for the company as long as she had. Her experience reassured them that they were taking the company in the right direction.

Marta was struggling to find ways to help her company be more successful. Luckily, her organization was working hard at improving its ability to focus on customers, to share across boundaries, to understand variation, to push for data and search for deeper causes, to work toward optimizing the organization as a whole. These changes, aimed at making the *business* better, also changed the culture—what it felt like to come to work day in and day out, what was looked upon as "business as usual."

But leading organizations are not waiting for cultural changes to come along: they are anticipating and making the needed changes up front so they can move ahead more strongly, unencumbered by cultural baggage. The foundation for these cultural changes is described by the last corner of the Joiner Triangle: **All One Team**. That's my shorthand for treating all employees as if we are in the same lifeboat, adrift at sea, knowing that our best chance of survival rests in working together, rowing in the same direction. It means believing in people and treating each other with dignity, trust, and respect. When we believe in people, we operate from the assumption that they come to work wanting to do a good job and that our role as managers is to remove the barriers that get in their way. **We come to focus not on motivating people but on removing the demotivators,** the things that get in the way of doing higher-quality work with higher and higher productivity.

Many organizations are now experimenting with new ideas in human resource management and are discovering they can make significant progress by analyzing current and planned policies and practices, using some now-familiar questions as a guide:

- Does this encourage or discourage a customer focus?
- Does this work for or against optimization of the system as a whole?
- Does this encourage people to work together?
- Does this reflect process thinking?
- Does this reflect an understanding of variation?
- Does this reflect a belief in people?
- Does this promote rapid learning?
- Is this a win-win approach?
- Will this help us create rapid, sustained progress?

Using these criteria, we can find alternative practices that create greater energy for rapid learning and rapid improvement and a greater commitment toward optimizing our ability to serve customers.

13
ALL ONE TEAM

Whenever I talk about "All One Team," some people get the impression that I'm referring to individual teams of some sort: work teams, project teams, cross-functional teams, quality circles, and so on. Although formal teams play a key role in 4th Generation Management, the intent here is much broader. What I mean is an organizational environment where everyone from the front lines to the executive suites understands and acts like they are all on the same team, working together to continually enhance customer satisfaction.

The topic is closely related to "optimizing a system." For people to treat each other as teammates, they have to believe it is in their best interests to cooperate; they must be more concerned with how the system as a whole operates than with optimizing their own little piece. You might recall the crew team described earlier in Chapter 3. We asked each crew member to think only of his or her own performance, to row at his or her individual best—mimicking the situation many employees now face. The result was utter chaos. The scull lost forward momentum and the rowers floundered amid splashes and lost oars.

This crew team's experience demonstrates the need to eliminate policies and practices that *destroy* a sense of teamwork, that prevent employees from working together on behalf of the organization as a whole. Many such forces exist in most organizations today. In this chapter, we'll look at what some of those forces are and at new approaches that can help shape effective alternatives.

Competition or Cooperation?

Many of the examples in this book, including that of the crew team, have pointed to the need for us to start relying less on competition and more on cooperation. To many people this sounds heretical. We all

225

know that there will always be some competition. People naturally compete to some degree whenever something is scarce: for instance, when there is only one job position open and many candidates who could fill it, or when capital expenditures can only be stretched so far.

No one can do much about such "natural" scarcity and a certain amount of competition that inevitably comes with it. But many organizations have gone out of their way to create additional competition where there need not be any, to create what Alfie Kohn calls "artificial scarcity." These organizations have policies in place that effectively limit the number of "winners" for no reason other than to create competition. In some companies, business units and their leaders are ranked from top to bottom with the top names in "get ahead" green and those at the bottom in "near death" red. The company recognizes only one person as "employee of the month"; it gives raises according to a forced distribution in which there has to be a loser for every winner. Top management tells the heads of units: "Resources are scarce. You're in competition with those other departments, those other business units. You've got to fight for your share." The executives don't say it, but they imply that other units in the organization are the enemy.

The question we must address is whether such manufactured competition among managers and other employees helps or hurts an organization.

The Light and Dark Sides of Competition

All of us have competed for something at some point in our lives and know the positive side of competition. It can, in the right circumstances, raise excitement, feed the fires of creativity, and motivate us to try harder.

But all of us have probably experienced the downside of competition, too:

> Joel picked up the phone when it rang. It was Bill.
> "The figures are in for last month," said Bill. "Did you know that Frank's facility came in way ahead of yours in productivity? What are your people doing over there?"

> Sarah got a similar call. "Scott's location has less than half the on-time delivery problems you had," said Bill. "He's shown it is possible to be customer focused. See what you can do to get your group up to his level."

Alonzo was third on Bill's list. "Congratulations," said Bill. "Your safety record was the worst of the eight facilities this past month! Don't you care about people? Don't you think it's about time you took some action? Why don't you see if you can at least get out of last place!"

Joel, Sarah, and Alonzo were three of the eight facility managers in Bill's division. Every month, all eight got phone calls pointing out where their figures were weak compared to the other facilities. As Joel told me one day, "The competition among us was terrible. We hated each other's guts. None of us wanted anything to do with the others." But, he added, there is a lot more to the story:

"About a year ago," Joel said, "Bill began to see what all this competition was costing the company. He stopped pitting us against each other and instead encouraged us to get together to share lessons, to help each others. We did what he asked...reluctantly at first! We were all suspicious. . . .

"That's why we were all surprised at how much we got out of those sessions," he continued. "In fact, they went so well that we started organizing them ourselves. Now we meet a full day every month, rotating among the eight facilities. . . . I learned how Sarah was handling some materials we'd had trouble with. Alonzo shared a dynamite new training program he'd found. . . . We're all improving much faster by working together on common problems."

This company achieved far better business results by changing policies and practices to encourage cooperation among these managers than it ever did when they were pitted against each other. And why?

- When they cooperated, the managers were better able to focus on the customer; under competition, they had to focus on *each other*, and the customer got lost.
- Cooperation speeded up learning. Under competition, nobody wanted to share learnings or be seen as copying what others did. The NIH syndrome (Not Invented Here) had been very strong, greatly inhibiting progress.
- Optimizing the separate facilities did not optimize the whole. Products and services from the different facilities were different in subtle ways that cost them customer satisfaction. Cooperation let them identify differences, evaluate their relative merits,

227

and begin to identify best-known methods. They began to realize the benefits of improvement and standardization.

Though a chain of hotels all bore the same name and served the same customer base, little else linked them. Differences were large and small. Some hotels had a free breakfast, others none. Some included a free local newspaper in the morning, others a choice of several newspapers, others a free national newspaper. Some had express checkout, others didn't. Travelers never knew what to expect: even if they liked one hotel in the chain, they were never certain what they'd get the next night at one of its sister facilities. There was a great deal of variation that cost the organization customers.

Sorting out such differences requires a focus on customers and cooperation; cooperation requires a win-win approach. Competition is win-lose. For every winner, there must be a loser. And virtually all of us, under competition, become reluctant to share our best ideas. If I do, then somebody else might come out ahead. I might wind up a loser. But if I keep the idea to myself, I can be the winner ... I can move on ... get the promotion.

But let's stop to think: don't we want all employees to be willing to share ideas, to help each other on behalf of our customers? Don't we want our organizations to be so successful that all of us "get ahead"?

Such emphasis on cooperation is essential to creating an environment where rapid, continuous improvement can happen. Another key element is reflecting a belief in people.

RADIATING A BELIEF IN PEOPLE

Do you believe in people?

Though almost everyone answers yes to this question, a noticeable gap usually exists between theory and practice. Pull out your human resource policy manual. Odds are it's a thick binder filled with statements that read like legal contracts, describing in detail what is or is not acceptable behavior:

"All employees shall receive time off with pay up to a maximum of three (3) days for working time lost if there is a death in the immediate family.... These days must fall within a seven

calendar day period ... one must be the day of the funeral. ... The following relationships are considered immediate family: father, mother, brother, sister, spouse, child, stepfather, stepmother, stepchildren, stepbrother, stepsister, grandparents, grandchild, aunt, uncle. ... The personnel department may require verification of death and relationship to the employee."

"Allowable travel expenses will not include laundry unless the employee is gone for more than four (4) days. ... Reimbursement for meals will be made at the following rates. ... Breakfast and dinner expenses can only be claimed when the employee is away overnight."

When looked at objectively, such policies reflect an attitude that given an inch, people will take a mile. They will attend funerals of people they barely know just to get out of work; they will dine at the fanciest restaurants in town as long as "the company" is paying. That is not what believing in people means. And it's not how people act, either. One company had a bereavement policy that read like the preceding one. But as its management began to understand the principles of 4th Generation Management, they changed it to a simple sentence:

"If you need time off due to the death of a close relative or friend, please notify your supervisor."

Notice that employees are now considered to have close friends as well as close relatives. But even so, after this change, time taken off for bereavement *dropped by 36%.* Why? Not because there were fewer deaths. Rather, employees were treated with trust and respect and started treating the company the same way.

Before the change, the average amount of time taken off for bereavement was a full 2.98 days per incident—people were skating as close to the three-day limit as possible. After the change, the time per incident dropped to 1.57 days, only half of the former prescribed limits.

Where Policies Go Wrong

Organizations, their customers, their investors, and other stakeholders suffer severe losses when the working environment

- reflects a mistrust of people,
- treats special causes like common causes,

229

- focuses on limits to allowable behavior instead of targets of desired behavior, and
- emphasizes win-lose.

These issues are intimately connected. For instance, some years ago a company had an employee (I'll call him Ted) who was, in all eyes but his, abusing the company's travel policies. Company management was sorely tempted to rewrite the policies so that each of Ted's infractions were explicitly listed and prohibited. But then they stopped to examine the consequences of that reaction:

- Ted was not a malicious person out to rob the company in subtle ways. His own internal boundaries were just different from most other people's. They could have written pages and pages of rules on travel and reimbursement, and still Ted would have slid into new ways to go beyond what most people would think reasonable.
- Pages of rules convey the message that the company doesn't trust people to make intelligent, adult decisions; that they will only understand what the right choices are if we spell them out in detail.
- Ted's behavior was far beyond the norm in the company. It was a special cause—outside the normal system. But rules written to "control" Ted would have been applied to all. They'd have changed the system in response to a special cause.

For these reasons, Ted's behavior needed to be treated separately. After several discussions between Ted and his managers, they became convinced that Ted just had a different sense of morality when it came to travel: to him, anything that was not immoral or illegal (outside the limits) must be just fine. He had many questions, some of which were common to most travelers, but some of which defied imagination:

- I missed my flight. Can I claim the extra meal I had to buy?
- My flight was delayed and I had to call home to let them know I'd be late. Can I charge that long-distance phone call to the company?
- If I spill something on my suit, can I get reimbursed for dry cleaning?
- I really find the luxury suites more comfortable. If I stay there, I'll be better rested and have more stamina during the trip.
- If I stay over a Saturday night, the airfare will be cheaper, so can I use the savings to rent a car to go visit my aunt?

- Can I get reimbursed for the extra charge for a massage to relieve the stress of travel?

In all other ways, Ted was a model employee. He worked long hours, studied everything he could about his field of work, and went out of his way to help customers. The managers ultimately assigned a "travel coordinator" to Ted who made these decisions for him. He never quite understood the need but learned to live with the system.

For everyone else, however, management constructed a simple policy:

- Travel decisions should be made in terms of what will work best for our customers, the employee, and the company.
- Employees will be reimbursed for all reasonable business expenses incurred when they are traveling on company business. Employees should act as if they were spending their own money.

The full policy contains some other details since there are reporting requirements for tax purposes, but the basics are easy to grasp and to remember. With this approach, individuals can make appropriate judgment calls themselves. Most employees, given these two guidelines, include many of the reimbursement requests listed above under "reasonable expenses"—such as meals when flights are delayed. They generally do not include expenses that most would consider frills.

Close the loophole?

Anyone who has written a policy that tried to spell out what is and is not acceptable and then witnessed the implementation of that policy, has undoubtedly been surprised by how many different loopholes arise. Try as hard as we might, life's situations are too complex and varied to be captured on a piece of paper. **"Close the loophole" thinking is inherently flawed,** a dead end. It adds cost and bureaucracy to no avail. The manuals just get thicker and thicker, the bureaucracy heavier and heavier. We add cost and complexity, work that is useful to no one. And we all suffer—employees, customers, investors, and our communities.

What alternatives are there? Think back to the Taguchi Loss Function (p. 72). This model describes the difference between thinking in terms of *goal posts* versus *targets*. "Just get it between the goal posts" is fine in football and soccer, but as a management strategy it is very costly. We can manage more effectively, achieve higher quality and less waste, if our mindset is "get closer and closer to the target."

231

The same notion holds true for human resource policies: we're better off describing a target or an ideal than defining limits. For instance, some years ago in my company, we spent several months investigating how other companies handle issues such as harassment and other types of undesirable employee conduct. The potential list of behaviors to forbid would have covered numerous pages and still not have begun to capture everything. Instead, we asked ourselves what it was we wanted to accomplish, what our goal was. The answer: a work environment where people feel safe and can devote their energies to serving customers. To communicate this goal to our employees, we came up with one statement:

> It is the policy of Joiner Associates that every employee will be treated with dignity, trust, and respect.

When I show this policy to other executives they often say, "That leaves a lot open to interpretation." And they're right. With this approach, the company's job does not stop with writing the policy. We have to work with employees, *all* employees, to develop a common understanding of what the statement means.

Yet, for all its brevity, this statement is very robust. It can be applied to a wide range of situations, everything from posting cartoons to making jokes to office gossip. When someone asks whether a certain behavior is acceptable, the response they get is, "You tell me. Will it get you closer to the goal or further away from it?" It's a question we all try to keep in our consciousness as a way to check our own behavior. We recognize that no one is perfect. We all have departures from the ideal behavior. The bigger the departure, the bigger the loss: while a slightly off-color joke might cause some people a few uncomfortable moments, an overtly racist or sexist action might cause serious anxiety among many employees. Our challenge is to reduce these departures—and the loss.

One role of managers, then, is to coordinate the education and communication needed to develop a common understanding of our policies throughout the company. The communication occurs in hiring interviews, new employee orientations, open discussions at staff meetings, one-on-one discussions with employees who have questions, and in the counseling of employees who have problems straying from the target.

The payoffs of replacing a goal-post mentality with being clear about the aim are numerous. One wonderful aspect of this approach is the flexibility it gives to employees and the organization. "Reasonable travel expenses," for instance, has at times included a celebratory dinner at a nice restaurant, but more often, an inexpensive breakfast special for $2.99. In addition, we don't need to waste time trying to develop rules for every conceivable situation. Instead, each Associate need only remember a handful of guidelines to help make decisions: "Will it help me better serve my customers?" . . . "Am I treating this customer, or this person, with dignity, trust, and respect?"

Trusting People

A few years ago, the police department in my home city of Madison, Wisconsin, needed new police cars. In most organizations, standard practice would have been to have the Purchasing department work out a deal with a car manufacturer, looking for the best price among "equally qualified" suppliers. But instead this department let the police officers make the decision. Would you be willing to take that step or would you be afraid they'd get gold-plated Mercedes-Benzes?

The answer starts with other questions: "Do you believe in people? Do you trust them to act in the best interests of the company?" If you do, then you won't be surprised by the outcome of this story. The chief of police trusted the police officers to make the decision, and they bought a reasonable vehicle that's worked out very well. What do you think being trusted by the department does to the morale of the police force? What do you think it does to their work with the people in the neighborhoods? How would you like to risk your life in a car somebody bought on price tag?

These leaps of faith are not easy, but they send a powerful message to employees about management's commitment to change. Trust is a small word with huge implications for how you manage your company and how employees feel about working there. Years ago, a manager said to me, "I've discovered that most employees, given the same information that I have, would make the same decision I'd make." Such an eloquent statement—and so true.

Dealing with the exceptions

The great majority of people live up to the trust we place in them, but inevitably a small percentage repeatedly violate our trust. If we don't work with these "special causes" separately (as I described for Ted) or terminate them, we risk damage to the remainder. In my experience, the key is still to focus on achieving a win-win solution. This may mean spending time working with an employee to help figure out what type of work he or she really enjoys or providing an outplacement service for a terminated employee.

SUPPORTING A CUSTOMER FOCUS

Many benefits derive from working toward an All One Team environment, for putting more emphasis on cooperation, for radiating a belief in people, for treating employees with trust and respect. The most important of these benefits may very well be the lessons from the two housekeepers whose stories I told at the end of Part Two. One told me how awful it was to work at her hotel: she often lacked the supplies needed to do her job, was blamed for every problem, and got the impression that management hated her. At the other hotel, the housekeeper said how much she liked working there, how her supervisors and managers would help her solve problems and prevent them from recurring, and how she received extensive training on how to do her job. At each of these hotels, the quality of the service I received was a direct reflection of how managers treated employees. **Our employees will not treat customers any better than we treat our employees.**

Being sensitive to how we treat our employees is thus central to having a customer focus. And no issue has a greater impact on the treatment of employees than the issue of performance appraisal, the subject of the next chapter.

14
THE CHALLENGES OF PERFORMANCE APPRAISAL

Darlene entered her boss's office apprehensively. The time had come for her annual performance review. Though she felt she had done well this year, she knew that management didn't always see things the same way she did.

After getting the pleasantries out of the way, Pete got down to business. "Let's see here . . . out of the 33 people in your group, your performance was just slightly below average," he said. "While that's certainly satisfactory as far as the company is concerned, there's obviously room for improvement. And that means your increase for the year, based on your performance, will be 3%."

"Three percent?! That's not even cost of living," said Darlene. "I don't understand. Most people have told me how much they enjoy working with me. I always complete my assignments on time. . . . I think I work as hard as anyone else in the group. How did I end up with a below average rating?"

"I'm not saying we're unhappy with your work. It's just that our new tracking measures show that you had slightly more 'serious errors' than others in your group. . . . Look, I can see that you're disappointed. But this new system gives you control over the size of your next raise. All you have to do is try a little harder. Perhaps we could get you into some classes. . . . "

Every organization that wants to develop and compensate its employees needs to have some systems for determining where they are doing well, where they need help, and what their job is "worth." Darlene's company, like many others, used a system of performance appraisal, or performance evaluation, and, unfortunately for her, she ended up on the low side of the evaluation that year.

Put aside for a moment the question of whether Darlene really was "below average" or not. The most important questions for a 4th Generation company are clear. Did the meeting Darlene just had

- encourage a customer focus?
- work toward optimizing the system as a whole?
- encourage Darlene and others to work together?
- reflect process thinking?
- reflect an understanding of variation?
- reflect a belief in people?
- promote rapid learning?
- help the company create rapid, sustained progress?

Unfortunately for her and for the company, the answer to all of these questions is no. Her manager had little understanding of the process factors that might have contributed to Darlene's "below average" performance. He also did not know whether Darlene was truly a special cause or whether her performance was well within the common cause system for the work she did. He did not appear to understand the extent to which he and other managers were largely responsible for the major factors that determined Darlene's performance.

Using questions like these to guide decisions about performance appraisal or evaluation is still largely unexplored territory. Though many companies have come to realize that their traditional systems are inadequate to meet the demands of a more complex marketplace, they aren't sure where to look for more effective answers. The lessons of 4th Generation Management provide some partial answers. Let's begin by clarifying just what the problems are with current systems.

TYPICAL PERFORMANCE APPRAISAL SYSTEMS

Performance appraisal systems typically involve:

- Standards of performance that may be either subjective or objective; they are commonly negotiated between manager and employee or imposed by the manager

- A period of performance during which the employee is observed (usually a year)
- An assessment by the manager of the employee's performance, based on observations and perceptions; sometimes the employee contributes his/her perceptions as well
- A meeting in which the employee's performance is discussed and evaluated

Performance appraisals are quite common, and although few people I've ever talked to *like* them, odds are you have been on either the giving or receiving end, and more likely both. Organizations tend to load a lot onto their performance appraisal systems. Some typical uses include:

- giving feedback to employees
- giving direction to employees
- identifying training needs
- fostering communication between manager and employee
- providing evidence for promotion decisions
- providing a basis for compensation decisions
- serving as a defense in legal cases associated with promotions or terminations

How well do performance appraisals meet these important needs? The list alone provides a clue: no single system is ever likely to do a first rate job on all these disparate needs. When we look carefully, it's evident that performance appraisals conflict with several 4th Generation lessons:

- The implicit assumption is that an individual's performance can be judged in isolation of the system within which he or she functions, something we now know misses the point. The evidence is clear. Most problems lie in the system—relatively few are due to the individual. (See p. 33).
- They fail to recognize *variation in perceptions* of performance. Have you ever gotten a new manager and overnight your rating dropped from "great" to "not so hot"? Did your performance change that much or was it mostly a difference in perceptions?
- And, most deadly of all, performance appraisal systems fail to recognize the extreme importance of cooperation. Many performance appraisal systems actually structure in competition among employees by creating a win-lose environment.

These failings have led to three components of performance appraisal systems that are so deadly that I've come to call them the **Three Great Demoralizers**.

- **Ranking**: Somebody is given rank #1, somebody else is ranked #2, somebody else #3, ... somebody else last.
- **Rating**: Many companies establish a hierarchy of ratings that managers use to label employees. Some people will be rated as "outstanding high," some as "outstanding," some as "outstanding low," others as "satisfactory" or "satisfactory low," and still others as "barely here" and so on. Virtually always there are formal or informal quotas on how many employees can be in each category. The quotas are there to avoid the "grade creep" that inevitably results as managers try to maintain morale in their areas. Managers are told, "Not everybody in your group can be 'outstanding high!'" (One manager defied the system but was told he'd used up his quota of "outstanding high" for the next ten years.)
- **Forced distributions**: People are put into groups based on perceived performance, with each group receiving a different raise. A certain percentage will get the top raise, another percentage the next highest raise, and so on. Typically the distribution of these raises is forced into a bell-shaped curve. For someone to get the top raise, someone else must get the bottom raise.

In company after company I've asked large groups of employees, "Is there anything about your performance appraisal system that you find demotivating?" The hands go up and ranking, rating, and forced distributions are mentioned time after time. They all create artificial scarcity. All require that there are only a few winners and that we find losers to have winners. All have the net effect of discouraging cooperation: why help someone else be a winner when that might only force *you* lower on the scale? Having losers in your group is an asset!

My advice on these Three Great Demoralizers is simple: "Abolish them tomorrow!" These three do much harm and no good; the remedy is simple and swift.

ALTERNATIVES TO PERFORMANCE APPRAISAL

Some other aspects of performance appraisal are also harmful but can't be changed as easily as the Three Great Demoralizers. You may find it helpful to devise separate systems using the strategic redesign principles described earlier (p. 200) to meet the different demands currently placed on performance appraisal. For example: What kinds of feedback will most help employees and how can we get it to them? How could we best identify and meet employee development needs? How should we compensate employees?

The answers are not simple; you may need to explore many alternatives. As always, however, keep in mind the aim of the now-separate systems and the key criteria listed previously. Some elements of alternative systems are discussed next, drawing from the experiences of my own and other companies.

1. Provide Ongoing Feedback and Development

Once a year, every employee of a leading nonprofit membership organization has a one-on-one "employee development meeting" with the executive director. To prepare for that meeting, the employee compiles information gathered throughout the year. He or she also sends questionnaires to several immediate customers and does follow-up interviews to discuss all the answers. The customers are asked to identify skills or services the employee provides that they like, areas they'd like to see improved, and any general comments about what it is like to have contact with that person. The employee compiles the results and brings his or her analysis to the annual meeting as a backdrop for discussions on educational needs and development opportunities.

This type of formal annual review, which is only one element in that organization's employee feedback and development efforts, differs from a performance appraisal review in several key ways:

- The feedback comes from the employee's customers, not the boss; the employee thus truly gets feed*back*, not feed*down*.
- The employee is responsible for gathering the information used in the meeting.
- Pay and other compensation issues are not linked to these feedback and development discussions.

This annual development meeting is the culmination of ongoing efforts to assess customer needs and satisfaction throughout the year. The executive director's role in this system is helping employees determine who their customers are, specifically which customers should be contacted for the annual review feedback, and how and when other customer information and feedback should be gathered throughout the year. The director also helps the employee interpret the results, identify areas for improvement, and prepare and implement development plans.

A companion to this organization's employee development efforts is an annual **systems review meeting**. In this meeting, all employees come together for a half day to discuss how well the processes used by the organization are working. The executive director thus hears about common roadbumps encountered by employees and helps set priorities for improving those systems. She also, coincidentally, discovers ways in which perceived employee performance is shaped by systems issues.

Another much larger organization uses a similar feedback system, with a twist. Each *area* is asked to evaluate each other area and to comment on a number of issues such as "helpfulness," "timeliness," "accuracy," "innovativeness," and so on. In addition, each area is also asked, "Is there any individual who stands out in the other area, either favorably or unfavorably?" This system reflects the understanding that most performance issues are not due to the individual, but that occasionally there are special causes. Finding an individual with outstanding performance gives the organization a chance to identify ways to improve the methods used by all. Finding an individual who is outside the system on the low side is a signal for special attention. For all others, the emphasis is on improving the system as a whole (reflecting the understanding of variation developed in Part Three).

An important component of feedback in a number of organizations is data on *process measures*. Such data provide a solid basis for timely discussions with employees about the process and replace most of the need for individual performance reviews. These organizations have developed their systems by working with employees to determine what kind of feedback will help them know how well they and their processes are doing. Discussions also include how and when that feedback should be gathered and analyzed (activities that are generally performed by the employee, not the manager). The emphasis has shifted toward *feedback from customers* and *problem solving with employees* rather than evaluation by bosses. Such changes greatly reinforce a customer focus.

2. Rewards and Recognition

A company had invited me for a visit. As I entered the office of the Vice President of Marketing, I saw, off to one side, a "transit," a large instrument used by surveyors.

"Why do you have that?" I asked out of curiosity.

"Oh, the transit . . . Our CEO, Mac, gave one to each of us who were involved in a big customer survey last year," he replied. "Survey . . . surveyor's tool. We though it was pretty clever of him."

"Hmm," I replied, inviting him to continue.

He obligingly went on. "All six vice presidents went out and interviewed a range of people at our biggest customers. We talked to all the key players in depth, finding out what they liked and didn't like about doing business with us. We'd never done anything like that before. It was a lot of work, flying all over the country . . . but we learned a tremendous amount from those face-to-face conversations, not the least of which was how we could increase sales! Mac gave us these transits to remind us how much he appreciated the extra effort we put in. It was a big success."

The executive walked over to the transit. "Few people know what these are, so nearly everyone who comes into my office asks me about it. And I get to retell this story over and over again. I know it sounds corny, but I get to relive the sense of pride and energy we all had back then. I'm very proud of the work we did. This transit is a constant reminder that the company—and our customers—values the work we're doing."

Everyone likes to be recognized for a job well done, for contributions that add to a company's success. This company had found a clever way to reinforce the intrinsic motivation that each of us has. Having people feel good about the work they do is a key point in 4th Generation Management, because it's through that work that we delight customers and create win-win for all.

Spontaneous recognition of a job well done, in a way that extends the memories, tends to work much better in practice than do traditional bonuses or commissions paid for attaining numerical objectives. The former keeps the emphasis on customers instead of on the rewards and helps to optimize the whole. I've seen many such examples of spontaneous recognition and celebrations: baseball caps with the title of a project or milestone, custom T-shirts, designer self-stick notes with a favorite logo or saying printed on each page.

My own company also encourages team celebrations. For example, employees within a work group typically go out for breakfast or lunch to celebrate small successes, and larger groups get together for afternoon breaks or noontime pizza parties every few months to celebrate major milestones. These celebrations bring people together in a relaxed environment, build camaraderie, and reinforce the idea that we are all working together to create success for the company, its customers, and ourselves.

3. Organizational Measurement System

Performance appraisal, or better, its replacements, constitute a major component of what I call an **organizational measurement system**. Often, our measures and our strategy are at odds. If our strategy says "Let's go north!" but the way we measure performance sends the message "Let's go south!," where will people head? Answer: "Somewhere between south and nowhere." What we measure and pay attention to largely determines what gets done. Most often when we see illogical behavior, the fault is in the measurement system, not in the employees. As one manager told me:

> We now measure "System Reliability," an indicator that reflects overall performance by including all errors and downtime no matter where they occur. This has helped us enormously. Before, we measured each area's reliability separately and suboptimization was rampant. One area's results would look better if that area ignored defects and merely passed them along to the next process. We ended up arguing about who should be blamed for some problems while other problems fell through the cracks, and the company as a whole suffered. Now, by measuring overall system reliability, our measures constantly remind us that we are All One Team."

There are no universally effective performance indicators, but three systemwide measures that often seem to help are **overall customer satisfaction**, **total cycle time**, and **first pass quality** (a measure of how often we must resort to rework, repair, restarts, and so on to produce quality output). Knowledge of the overall measures you select needs to be communicated clearly throughout the company so that all employees understand what they are and why they were selected. But, as mentioned several times in this book, that alone is not enough. We must do the hard work of identifying the leverage points, the points where a relatively small change has a major impact on how the organization as a whole performs. Putting indicators on leverage points gives faster feedback to the people in those areas as they seek to move the levers in the desired direction *and* helps us evaluate our theory that moving those levers will indeed improve the performance of the whole.

Throughout this work on measurements and indicators, we must keep in close touch with people and remind them (and us!) of our overall aim of enhancing customer satisfaction. Otherwise, we are likely to lose sight of the whole and focus solely on the indicator, a sure path to destruction:

> An airline that I used to fly with regularly had a very customer-focused goal: being "Number 1 in on-time arrival." But actions based on that goal had some unexpected consequences. One day, I got caught in a traffic jam going to the airport and arrived at the gate one minute late. The doors had just been closed, and, as I watched, the ground crew retracted the jetway. The next flight was four hours later. I asked (politely) if the attendants could please open the doors, extend the jetway, and let me on the plane. They politely declined.
>
> So I sat there. And so did the plane.
>
> I tried explaining my exalted frequent flyer status (I was one of their top few customers; I flew so often with them that I got a free, automatic upgrade to first class on every flight). The attendants were unimpressed.
>
> So I kept sitting there. And so did the plane.
>
> I asked again (still politely) to be allowed to board. Again they refused. I simmered. The plane finally left the gate more than an hour late. This and a series of comparable encounters cost them a customer. I now fly this airline only when absolutely necessary. And I tell this story to others.

Why would this company's employees treat a top customer this way? It was certainly well within their capability, and perhaps was even their inclination, to extend the jetway and let me board the plane. But something stopped them. The problem was far beyond their sphere of control, for it lay deep within the company's basic management system. These employees worked under 3rd Generation Management, and their objective—their measurement—was to make sure flights had on-time departures. They were judged on whether they met that goal, not how they got there.

Thus what began at the top as a sound decision to enhance revenues by making customers happier by having on-time arrivals ended up having the exact opposite effect. Management had done well in identifying on-time departures as a leverage point and had therefore set out to improve timeliness of departures. But then they made a common mistake. They judged and rewarded people based on their on-time departure numbers (defined as a closed door and retracted jetway), and thus, ironically, sent a clear message to employees: meeting the goal is more important than serving the customer. And the employees quite understandably made the "illogical" mistake of falling in love with the indicator and ignoring entirely the purpose it was meant to serve—increasing customer satisfaction.

Revising measurement systems is not easy work and research is underway to find better approaches. But even now we can increase the odds of success and reduce the chances of making things drastically worse if, as in everything else we do, we involve people and use PDCA and CAP-Do—trying changes on a small scale and studying and improving any system we devise.

4. Compensation

A manager at one of the big three U.S. automakers said one day in a meeting, "You know, I think that if we doubled the pay of everyone here, it wouldn't have any impact on our overall performance." After some discussion, everyone in the room agreed ... though they also agreed it was an experiment they wouldn't mind participating in! Of all the sticky issues surrounding employee performance, compensation is perhaps the stickiest. But there are steps we can take, short of doubling everyone's pay, that will help our organization's overall performance.

Like many other management practices already discussed, current approaches to determining compensation stem from the assumptions that people need rewards and punishment to do a good job and that individual contributions are the biggest factors in determining success. In contrast, the 4th Generation approach is based on the assumption that intrinsic motivation is a far more effective motivator than financial rewards or punishments, and that organizational performance is greatly influenced by how well people cooperate.

The first step, as I said before, is to eliminate any vestiges of the Three Great Demoralizers lingering in your compensation system. Their win-lose focus causes many problems. Get rid of them tomorrow. Second, acknowledge that compensation, particularly *relative* compensation (how much one employee makes compared to someone else), is much more likely to be a demotivator than a motivator. In this sense, fair compensation is like a "Must Be" feature, like the customer perceptions discussed back in Part Two: compensation that is perceived to be unfair will certainly leave people dissatisfied, and even if it is perceived to be fair, people are likely to be neutral at best during the bulk of the year.

I don't think there is any compensation system that everyone will think is fair, but we can still strive to eliminate problems that current systems create. It's far more fruitful, therefore, to focus on creating as little demotivation as possible with your compensation system rather than to focus on using it to motivate employees. Does it sound odd to talk about pay as a demotivator rather than as a source of motivation? Take a moment to think about techniques companies have used that link pay with motivation: bonuses, commissions, incentives, piece rates, merit pay. Almost no company uses piece rates anymore; that form of incentive pay has been largely abandoned because it was obvious that quality and other key ingredients of company success were too often sacrificed.

A farm equipment company contacted us about helping them improve one of their major facilities. In our early discussions it came out that their employees refused to attend meetings to discuss how to improve their work: it took time away from today's production and would adversely affect the formula used for next year's incentives.

Similar problems also plague companies that use bonuses and commissions to motivate employees, though the linkage is not quite as obvious:

- Team selling, strategic selling, and customer research are sorely neglected in companies that pay on commission. Each sales person acts as a separate profit center, largely unconnected to the rest of the organization. Organizations that eliminate commissions can, with effective management, achieve the kind of sales results summarized earlier: "$500,000 in new business, 12 of 13 targeted accounts closed, ..." (p. 189).

- Individual incentives are a major source of barriers among functional areas and business units. Why help another area if it takes your time and thus comes out of your bonus? The organization becomes a set of loosely connected systems, each seeking its own maximum, to the neglect of the whole.

The arguments against incentives such as commissions or bonuses

245

probably go against the grain for many managers. If you put a carrot in front of most people (such as a raise or bonus), or offer them the stick (do this or get fired), they will do more of what you ask. They'll try harder for the reward; they'll reduce the number of things you see that were getting them in trouble. These benefits, in this sense, are very real. Unfortunately, the downsides of such practices are not so visible. They are often widely separated in time and space from the spurt in performance. The farm equipment company, for instance, did not see the link between the spur that its incentive formula provided and the overall slow rate of improvement in that facility. The sales manager didn't realize until after the fact that, although commissions did undoubtedly get increased sales from some people (at least in the short run), they stood in the way of getting far better sales from *all* representatives in the months ahead. That's why it's so important for us to keep our eyes on the big picture, on the effect of policies and practices on the system as a whole and not just on individual performances.

When employees seek individual reward, they begin to chase the indicator that triggers the reward. But chasing indicators is a major source of problems: all the pieces look good in their own right, but somehow fail to add up to organizational success.

To optimize the organization as a whole, intrinsic motivation works far better than financial rewards or punishment. Our job is not to get each member of the crew team to row at his or her individual best. It is to optimize the speed of the racing shell as a whole. As discussed in Chapter 3, doing so will require that *none* of the individuals rows at his or her own individual best!

Joiner Associates' compensation system

Compensation is a very sticky issue and many people ask me what we do about it at my company, Joiner Associates. As I've indicated, there are no recipes to follow: I offer this discussion to illustrate the decisions that one group of managers decided was best in their circumstances. We've been using this approach for seven years now and have found it works surprisingly well. That doesn't mean that every employee is happy with their compensation; it means that most employees believe the approach we follow is basically sound and that management has a reasonable basis for supporting its decisions.

In conversations with employees and in our corporate documentation, pay is always discussed in the context of total compensation. It is only one component of a package that includes a 401(k) plan, vacations, health insurance, life and disability insurance, and the total experience of working at Joiner Associates—the intangibles that contribute to the "quality of life" here: a casual, informal, open, supportive atmosphere where we seek to treat employees with dignity, trust, and respect.

Four components determine the monetary portion of a person's total compensation:

- **Salary**—We try to set salaries roughly at market when we hire people. We research pay rates for similar jobs in our geographical area and elsewhere in the country. That allows us to set levels that are generally in the ballpark of market rates for that job: we don't want to be significantly above or below market.
- **Salary increases**—Once a year, in the fall, everyone in the company receives the same *percentage increase* in salary. This percentage is selected to keep the bulk of Associates' salaries in line with market. This increase accounts for factors such as cost of living and the personal growth and development of all Associates. It is *not* influenced by corporate profitability.
- **Prosperity sharing**—When the company is in a financial position that allows it, every employee who has been with the company two years or longer receives the same *number of weeks of pay* in prosperity sharing (that number is prorated for those who have been with the company for less than two years). This element of compensation depends on the company's financial success. Every year we set a target of being able to give employees several weeks of pay in prosperity sharing, but there have been years when there was nothing to share and others where unexpected successes allowed us to be more generous. (Like everyone else, we experience variation around our financial forecasts.) Managers ask me all the time if we use prosperity sharing to motivate people. The answer is no. We use it as a component in our compensation system to help prevent compensation from becoming a demotivator.
- **Special adjustments**—Our aim is to have the three factors above keep compensation in line with the market. However, there have been cases when a special adjustment was necessary. In some of these cases, an individual had taken on new responsibilities, and a special adjustment upward was necessary to keep compensation for that job in line with the market. In other cases, longer-term employees' pay has neared the ceiling for a

given position. In these cases, we give a partial increase instead of a full percentage increase.

A lot of effort goes into making this system work: year-round we receive data on pay rates for various jobs, every spring we reexamine the definitions for every position in the company, every fall we look in depth at what has happened to salaries and where they seem to be headed.

The basic model for this compensation system is simple: we seek to have the work itself be the source of motivation and to avoid having compensation be a demotivator. To do this, we attempt to pay market rates and use a simple across-the-board percent increase to handle the bulk of changes due to cost of living and normal growth and development. This keeps most people "within the system." We occasionally have special causes ("outside the system") that require special adjustment when we find a pay rate that is out of line with market.

Will this system work for you? Some of the approaches we're using may be useful to you, but the details will surely differ. I'm not about to say that everyone should follow our path. But I am saying that you should think about developing alternative compensation systems that incorporate the principles discussed in this book and move away from viewing pay as a motivator and instead focus on making sure it is not a demotivator.

Summary

Deciding to focus on customers, understand data and variation, and develop better and better methods won't bring the needed improvement in results until we also incorporate the elements of All One Team. This means changing all policies and practices to recognize the importance of cooperation, win-win, and a belief in people. One way to change is to move from defining limits of permissable behavior to defining the desired behavior. "Close the loophole" thinking, always defining more and more limits, is inherently flawed and will only drain our organization's energy. Trust and working toward the ideal is far better. Key systems that contribute to an organization's environment include performance appraisal and organizational measurements. We should eliminate, tomorrow, the Three Great Demoralizers: ranking, rating, and forced distributions. New approaches to employee growth and development begin by debundling appraisal systems into separate systems for separate needs, then developing more targeted ways to meet those separate needs—for instance, developing ways for employees to get customer feedback directly. Rewards, recognition, and compensation take on new patterns as we recognize that they can easily be turned into demotivators—forces that destroy our internal motivation. Making sure our organizational measurement system is aligned with our strategies is fundamental.

EPILOGUE

"The way I see it," said Larry, "in the mid-80s everyone started jumping on the employee 'empowerment' bandwagon. So we managers went out and shouted down from our mountaintops, 'You're empowered.' And the reply from the work force echoed back faintly: 'What does that mean?' Unfortunately, we couldn't answer them because we didn't know ourselves what it meant.

"But," Larry continued, "things have started to change. Last week one of our long-term employees came up to me and said, 'Now I know who my customers are and how what I do affects them. I've been trained in how to do my job, and when there's a problem, I can get and analyze data that help me know what action to take. I can use the data and our process documents to communicate better with my managers and other employees. People listen when I have problems or suggestions. We take action. We try out things. Together, we're improving our work .... Is that what you meant by empowerment?'"

Larry's company had achieved what many companies hope to achieve: a work force that is not only committed to serving customers but also able to act on that commitment. In doing so, they had stumbled on the secret of 4th Generation Management: We need *all* the elements for *any* of them to be fully effective. We can't just tell employees to get involved in improving their work. We have to teach them about customers, about data, about variation, about processes; and we as managers have to learn all of this ourselves. Then we can create systems that allow them to share ideas and take action on behalf of customers without getting penalized. It is by this path that we delight all our stakeholders: customers, employees, shareholders, suppliers, and communities.

POSTSCRIPT

"What about Phil?" I suggested when a CEO asked my opinion about a key promotion. "He'd be the one I'd most want to have as my executive vice president."

The answer was one that I'd heard before: "Phil's got a lot of capability—no doubt about it. But these top jobs are filled with crises, and Phil hasn't had much experience dealing with major crises. He just hasn't had many major problems in his area. It's too bad in a way ..."

Encounters like these have been some of the most frustrating of my career. There was nothing I could say to this CEO that would have changed his mind, nothing that would have made him realize that Phil was being passed over for promotion because he'd gotten rid of all the moles in his area. Phil could no longer add "expert at whack-a-mole" to his résumé ... so another manager, one who had moles coming out the woodwork, who regularly had to handle several crises before lunch (many of his own making!), got the promotion. An opportunity to reduce waste and speed up improvement had been missed *and* a message had been sent to the organization as to what was really valued and what was not.

This CEO had not yet come to fully appreciate the benefits of viewing the world using the lenses of 4th Generation Management. Many managers still have not experienced the value of placing customer needs above all others even though the potential benefits are enormous. They do not understand that their organizations are systems, each part affecting all other parts. They do not see the messages in the variation in the figures they see every day, every week, every month. They have not come to recognize the downsides of internal competition even though it is slowly sapping the enthusiasm and energy of their employees.

When we first start to use these new lenses, what we see is not always pretty.

Desks crammed the large room, each occupied by a telephone operator. Every minute of every day calls poured in. The company's intent was to provide customers with prompt service; the

253

goal in this area was to answer 95% of the calls within 15 seconds. A large dial in the center of the wall showed the operators what percentage of calls were meeting the 15-second goal.

In a smaller room in the corporate tower, 16 people sat around a table: half were telephone operators, the others, senior executives. The operators had just finished a nice presentation on work they had recently completed. Everyone was pleased. Having heard about their goal, I decided to see what effect it had on their performance.

"Is it always easy to meet that 15-second goal?" I asked. The operators' answer confirmed what I already knew: of course not. Otherwise, it wouldn't be a goal.

"What happens when that dial starts to slip a bit?" I asked.

"We start rushing calls," the operators answered. "We're not as courteous as we should be."

"And what if the dial drops even further?"

"We try to cut off calls as quickly as possible," came the cautious reply.

"Any effect of that?"

"Sometimes customers have to call back two or three times to get all their questions answered. And we don't always get all the information we should, so when the technicians go out to do the job, they don't have all the information they need."

I could see the executives starting to blanch, though I suspected things were likely even worse. After the meeting, I probed a little farther. "What happens when the dial goes down further still?"

They got quiet, then someone answered, "We sometimes get the supervisor to call in. We answer the phone, he says 'Hi, this is Joe' and hangs up. We get credit for a quick call and the dial goes up."

"Anything else, when things get really bad?"

"Well . . . ," one blushed, "sometimes we just disconnect. Push another button. We get credit for the call, but the customer has to call back again."

Using the traditional measures, these operators seemed to be doing a fine job. Their customer service indicator was very high: 95% of the calls answered in 15 seconds. But with new lenses in place, we can see clearly that in striving to achieve their goal, these operators were quite likely increasing the number of angry customers who would show up at rate hearings as well as contributing to low productivity among technicians, who often lacked information needed for their jobs.

No executive *wants* to increase inefficiency and waste, cost and bureaucracy. Yet without a dedication to customers, without an understanding of systems thinking and variation, without an appreciation for cooperation and the use of data, that is unfortunately what we end up doing.

Taking the new path is seldom easy. It takes knowledge, wisdom, tenacity, and patience. A turning point for yet another company came when they had to cancel a product that had been in development for some time.

> *A group of 15 upper-middle managers agreed to spend a day doing a postmortem following the product cancellation. In the past, meetings to analyze major problems had always been heated with accusations flying around the room, each department blaming the others for problems. But this time, some understanding of these principles led them to try a new approach, like the company I described at the very beginning of this book. The tone of the meeting quickly became one of mutual learning. Together, these managers began to understand and acknowledge the problems with the New Product Development process and take action to make real improvements. There was a real crisis and they knew that to do otherwise could possibly be a fatal mistake, jeopardizing the future viability of their entire business.*
>
> *At the end of the day, the managers emerged from the room feeling better than they had in months. They had accomplished what none of them thought was possible: examining key elements leading to the cancellation—without blame. They openly looked at mistakes, missed milestones, and all major actions and decisions involved with the development effort. They identified common issues and discussed specific actions to address these problems. One such action was to adopt joint program planning across the entire development process.*

The managers in this meeting emerged seeing the world in a new way. They experienced for themselves the power of looking at the data together to understand the story and their parts in it, of blaming processes not people. In doing so, they came to see that they were each part of a larger system, and each had a vested interest in how that system as a whole operates. They freed themselves to see their organization the way it really operates, and thus to begin making real progress, real improvement.

This meeting was just the beginning of ongoing efforts to continually review and improve their product development process. It was a major priority given constant and continual focus by this group of upper middle managers. As a result, 16 months later a key potential customer of the previous canceled product was so impressed with the tremendous improvements in the next product that the customer awarded this facility a new contract worth hundreds of millions of dollars.

Changes like these take time, and, more importantly trust. Trust is not a commodity we can buy in a day; it is a gift we must earn over time. A colleague who is a former union representative told me about the following experience:

> *"As a union representative," he said, "you get used to win-lose relationships. You get used to hearing management say 'We'll consider it' in response to a request or suggestion for addressing a problem." In his heart, he knew that meant "we'll write it on this sheet of paper then crumple it up and shoot it into the trash as soon as you leave the room."*
>
> *When one of the facilities he represented got new leadership, he did not at first hold out any hope of real change. He presented an idea to management and heard the same response, "We'll consider it." A week later, he returned to the meeting room and was astonished at what he saw. To these managers, "We'll consider it" meant serious work analyzing what would happen if the idea was implemented: identifying objectives, analyzing potential cause-and-effect relationships, looking at positive and negative side effects. Over time, he saw that this same pattern repeated again and again. He would come with an idea or suggestion and their response was always a thorough consideration. Sometimes they would say the idea looked great. Other times, they'd say that it didn't quite meet the objectives, but that he could do more analysis if he wanted to. Eventually, he got to a point where if he heard the words "we considered it, and it didn't look good," he trusted their analysis and didn't even ask to see the supporting documentation.*
>
> *"I realized that our ability to move forward all boiled down to an issue of trust," he said. "Once there was trust, we started to*

work together using the principles you advocate. Over the next four years, we moved this facility from the 'endangered species list' to the best that company had ever had. And we saved 5000 jobs along the way."

The principles I've described in this book are helping companies around the world become stronger and more responsive to a rapidly changing marketplace. And, as more and more people are discovering, they work just as well in other aspects of our lives: in relationships with family members, in church and civic groups, in working with governments or with schools. Fourth Generation Management is not a panacea, it does not provide instant answers to long-standing problems. But it can open our eyes to new ways to think about and approach problems and opportunities.

The decision to use these principles on the job or at home is ultimately a very personal one. I don't ask that you take what I've said on faith, but I do urge you to give it a try. The future belongs to those who see the challenges and grasp the opportunities. Choose something that is important to you—a major opportunity you're facing or a problem you must address or a situation where the path is unclear. Plan a test. Figure out ahead of time how you will know if things are better. Then put these ideas to work and see what they can do for your organization—and for you. As you begin to take action, you'll discover the need for new knowledge, new skills. Continue to integrate and learn. You'll be amazed at what you can do.

Appendix
MORE ON CONTROL CHARTS

A. DETECTING SPECIAL CAUSES

In Part Three, I described one way to detect a special cause: one or more points outside the limits to the common cause highway. There are three other basic techniques that are useful even when no points are outside the common cause highway:

- **6 or more points in a row steadily increasing or steadily decreasing (a "trend").**[1] If we see six points in a row going up (or going down), we sense a movement of the funnel up (or down) incrementally between data points. In practice, we seldom detect a special cause with this test; it is included primarily so people won't suspect a special cause when there are only two or three dots in a "trend." The test reminds us that we don't have significant evidence of a trend until we get six dots in a row trending up or trending down.

- **8 or more points in a row on the same side of the centerline.**[2] When we see eight points in a row all above or all below the centerline, it usually signals that the funnel was bumped and has stayed bumped; less often, it may signal the beginning of a trend.

- **14 or more points alternating up and down**. This pattern could cause us to sense movement of the funnel back and forth after each point. In real life, this can arise from two alternating sources, such as two shifts ($_{day}$-^{night}-$_{day}$-^{night}-$_{day}$-^{night}) or two heads on a machine (^{A}-$_B$-^{A}-$_B$-^{A}-$_B$). Another source is made-up data. Why do people make up

---

[1] If there are ties—two data points in a row with the same value—do not count the second data point as part of the trend.
[2] Do not count points that fall on the centerline as part of the pattern.

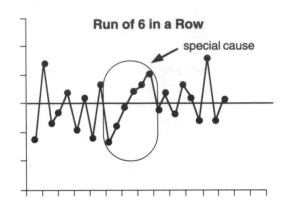

Run of 6 in a Row

special cause

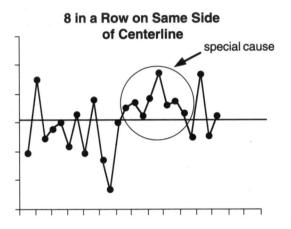

**8 in a Row on Same Side
of Centerline**

special cause

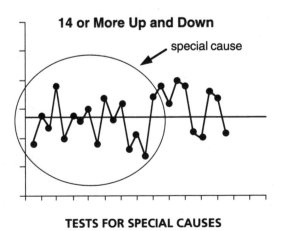

14 or More Up and Down

special cause

TESTS FOR SPECIAL CAUSES

data? Fear. They're fearful of what management will do if the figures don't look like they are supposed to look. Or it could be indifference: they've come to believe that nobody looks at the data anyway so why bother taking measurements.

These tests for special causes help us decide whether to use the special cause strategy or common cause strategy. They are not infallible. We may miss an occasional special cause, or we may react to a special cause signal that ends up being only common cause variation. But even though these tests are not perfect, they greatly enhance our chances of reacting appropriately, especially when compared to any known alternatives such as using our intuition, or looking at traditional managerial reports. The control limits and tests help us avoid overreacting (treating a common cause like a special cause) while still not missing special causes when they do appear. They provide effective guidance for **action on the process.** And, only by taking effective action on the process will we have better results tomorrow.

B. STRUCTURAL VARIATION

Sometimes there is a distinct trend, a definite seasonal pattern, or some other specific structure to our data. For example, the chart on sales presented on pages 116 and 165 had a definite trend (we've reproduced the control chart of the sales data below). Finding the control

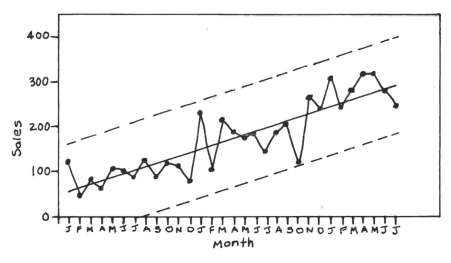

SALES CONTROL CHART

limits in cases where there is structural variation is a matter of separating structural variation from the remainder. We can then use the regular control chart calculations on the differences, the values that remain after we subtract out the structural component.

Determining the control limits is relatively easy once we've done the hard part of estimating the structural component. For a straight line, such as the upward trend in this example, we can get fairly good results simply by placing a clear plastic ruler on a chart of the data and drawing in a trend line. Determining the structural component for more complex patterns (such as seasonal variation) is more difficult and requires greater expertise.

The following table shows how the control limits for the sales control chart were calculated. The second column has the data on sales. The third column reflects the structural component of that data, the underlying upward trend. This trend becomes the centerline of the common cause highway. The fourth column shows the difference between the second and third columns—we have subtracted the structural variation from the sales figures and exposed the residual variation. The fifth column shows the ranges of these differences. These were computed just as we did on pages 148–149. So too were the median range, $\tilde{R}$ and the distance from the centerline to the edges of the common cause highway, $3.14\tilde{R}$. We add this distance to the structural component (column 3) to get the Upper Control Limit (column 6), and subtract to get the Lower Control Limit (column 7).

Control Limit Calculations
with a Structural Trend

(1) Month	(2) Sales (in 000s)	(3) Trend Line	(4) Diff. (2) − (3)	(5) Range of Diff.	(6) UCL	(7) LCL
Jan	122	57.5	64.5		164.9	0 *
Feb	48	65.3	-17.3	81.8	172.7	0
Mar	84	73.1	10.9	28.2	180.5	0
Apr	65	80.9	-15.9	26.8	188.3	0
May	107	88.7	18.3	34.2	196.1	0
June	102	96.5	5.5	12.8	203.9	0
July	88	104.3	-16.3	21.8	211.7	0
Aug	127	112.1	14.9	31.2	219.5	4.7
Sept	92	119.9	-27.9	42.8	227.3	12.5
Oct	119	127.7	-8.7	19.2	235.1	20.3
Nov	116	135.5	-19.5	10.8	242.9	28.1
Dec	82	143.3	-61.3	41.8	250.7	35.9
Jan	232	151.1	80.9	142.2	258.5	43.7
Feb	106	158.9	-52.9	133.8	266.3	51.5
Mar	215	166.7	48.3	101.2	274.1	59.3
Apr	188	174.5	13.5	34.8	281.9	67.1
May	175	182.3	-7.3	20.8	289.7	74.9
June	185	190.1	-5.1	2.2	297.5	82.7
July	145	197.9	-52.9	47.8	305.3	90.5
Aug	187	205.7	-18.7	34.2	313.1	98.3
Sept	205	213.5	-8.5	10.2	320.9	106.1
Oct	122	221.3	-99.3	90.8	328.7	113.9
Nov	264	229.1	34.9	134.2	336.5	121.7
Dec	240	236.9	3.1	31.8	344.3	129.5
Jan	307	244.7	62.3	59.2	352.1	137.3
Feb	244	252.5	-8.5	70.8	359.9	145.1
Mar	282	260.3	21.7	30.2	367.7	152.9
Apr	315	268.1	46.9	25.2	375.5	160.7
May	320	275.9	44.1	2.8	383.3	168.5
June	279	283.7	-4.7	48.8	391.1	176.3
July	247	291.5	-44.5	39.8	398.9	184.1

$\widetilde{R} = 34.2$ **Centerline** = Trend line

$3.14\,\widetilde{R} = 107.4$ **Control Limits** = Trend $\pm 3.14\widetilde{R}$ = Trend ± 107.4

---

* Mathematically these figures are negative, but in practice sales figures generally do not go below zero.

FIGURE B.2

C. SKEWED DATA

The formula $\overline{X} \pm 3.14\tilde{R}$ given on pages 148–149 for calculating the control limits applies when the common cause variation is roughly symmetric. This may not always be the case; data on time-to-failure, for example, often has skewed common cause variation.

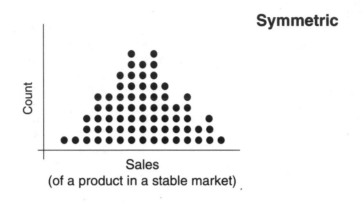

Symmetric

Count

Sales
(of a product in a stable market)

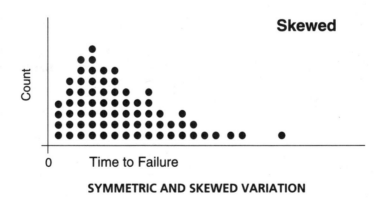

Skewed

Count

0   Time to Failure

SYMMETRIC AND SKEWED VARIATION

In practice, it is not always easy to tell the difference between skewed data with no special causes, and symmetric data with special causes all on one side. When in doubt, I look to see if there is a natural boundary the data seem to pile up against; for example, the failure times piling up against a natural lower boundary of "zero time" to failure. In such cases, I suspect skewness. I draw a line on the control chart if there is a natural boundary inside or very near either of the control limits. For example, the customer satisfaction data on page 130 had a natural upper boundary at 100%—the figures could never go beyond that limit. When the Upper Control Limit (UCL) is mathematically over 100, I still draw the limit at 100 and use that in interpreting the chart noting there can never be a special cause signal on the high side because no value can ever be over 100%.

In some cases, it is helpful to sketch a frequency plot of the data such as those shown on the previous page. Frequency plots can help with detecting skewness and some other features of the data (such as digit preferences), but they are *never* a substitute for plotting the data over time. Once you've lost the time order in data, you've lost most of the useful information. Why? Because special causes are virtually undetectable once time order is lost.

When the data are quite skewed, interpretation is difficult. In some cases, a transformation of the data aids appropriate interpretation. Try computing the square roots, logarithms, or reciprocals of the measurements and analyzing these just as you would ordinary symmetric data.

D. DIFFERENT CHARTS FOR DIFFERENT DATA

The following tables give a brief overview of some of the different kinds of data you may encounter and the type of control chart that is appropriate for that data.

Situation	Chart Used	Calculations	Comments
Number of defects, accidents, or flaws # of accidents/month, # of times the phone is not answered within three rings, # of breakdowns/week, # of flaws on an automobile	c chart	$\bar{c} \pm 3\sqrt{\bar{c}}$	Always plot data in time order if there is a natural chronological sequence; but may also use a c or u chart on non-time-ordered data such as when comparing facilities. **Notation:** c is the count of occurrences; $\bar{c}$ is the average.
	u chart	$\bar{u} \pm 3\sqrt{\dfrac{\bar{u}}{a}}$ Limits move in and out as *a* varies.	Use when area of opportunity varies, that is, if the size of the area or population at risk changes. Examples: reorganization doubles the # of employees in one division, doubling the area of risk; different automobiles have different-sized hoods. **Notation**: same as above, plus *a* is the area of opportunity, and *u = c/a*.
Fraction of "defectives" fraction of requests not processed within 15 minutes; fraction of orders not processed perfectly the first time through (first-pass quality)	p chart	$\bar{p} \pm 3\sqrt{\dfrac{\bar{p}(1-\bar{p})}{n}}$ Limits move in and out as *n* varies.	**Notation:** n is the number of units per subgroup x is the number found defective p is the proportion of "defective" ($p = x/n$)
	np chart	$\bar{x} \pm 3\sqrt{\bar{x}(1-\bar{p})}$	The **np chart** is usable only when n is roughly constant. For p or np charts, the fraction must be based on **counts**, not measurements; for proportion of measurements, use an individuals chart. E.g., for proportion of labor cost to total cost (which are measurements, not counts) use an individuals chart.

TYPES OF CONTROL CHARTS

Situation	Chart Used	Calculations	Comments
Variables data, one figure at a time *sales, cost variances, customer satisfaction score, total cycle time per order, average cycle time per month*	**Individuals Charts**	$\overline{X} \pm 3.14\ \tilde{R}$ or $\overline{X} \pm 2.66\ \overline{R}$	Usable with any data over time but not as powerful in detecting special causes as the other more specialized charts. **Note: Do not use $\overline{X} \pm 3\ \hat{\sigma}$ where:** $$\hat{\sigma} = \sqrt{\Sigma(X - \overline{X})^2/(n-1)}$$ since special causes would be masked. **Notation:** X = individual measurement; $\overline{X}$ = average $\tilde{R}$ = median of the ranges; $\overline{R}$ = average of the ranges
Variables data, sets of measurements	**X-bar and R charts**	$\overline{\overline{X}} \pm A_2\ \overline{R}$ For R chart: $UCL = D_3\overline{R}$ $LCL = D_4\overline{R}$ See table on next page for values of A₂ and D	Useful in, e.g., measurement laboratories when the same "unknown" is measured several times per day to check measurement stability. May also be used, with care, for charts of moving averages (such as a chart of running three-month averages of customer satisfaction scores). **Notation:** n = # of items in subgroup (e.g., n = 3 msmt/day) X = individual measurement $\overline{X}$ = average of the measurements in the subgroup $\overline{\overline{X}}$ = average of the averages R = range of values in subgroup (largest minus smallest)

TYPES OF CONTROL CHARTS, CONT.

Factors for Determining the Control Limits
for $\overline{X}$ and R Charts from $\overline{\overline{X}}$ and $\overline{R}$

Number of Obs. in subgroup (n)	Factors for $\overline{X}$ Charts		Factors for R Charts	
		Control Limits:	Lower Control Limit:	Upper Control Limit:
	$\hat{\sigma} = \overline{R}/d_2$	$\overline{\overline{X}} \pm A_2 \overline{R}$	$D_3 \overline{R}$	$D_4 \overline{R}$
	d_2	A_2	D_3	D_4
2	1.128	1.880	0	3.267
3	1.693	1.023	0	2.575
4	2.059	0.729	0	2.282
5	2.326	0.577	0	2.115
6	2.534	0.483	0	2.004
7	2.704	0.419	0.076	1.924
8	2.847	0.373	0.136	1.864
9	2.970	0.337	0.184	1.816
10	3.078	0.308	0.223	1.777

TYPES OF CONTROL CHARTS, CONT.

E. USE OF MEDIAN RANGE

We often get asked about our use of "3.14 times the median range" (3.14R̃) in control chart calculations instead of the more common 2.66 times the average (2.66R̄), or (unfortunately), 3 times the standard deviation (3σ̂). We started using 3.14R̃ about 1984 because we found that an occasional special cause tended to distort the average range much more than it distorted the median range. So a special cause is less likely to be hidden by 3.14 times the median range than it would be by using 2.66 times the average range.

The factor 3.14 (instead of 2.66) is readily derived from mathematical statistical theory. The mathematical equivalent to 3.14R̃ had been around since at least 1953 (E.B. Ferrel, "Control Charts Using Midranges and Medians," *Industrial Quality Control,* Vol. IX, No. 5, pp. 30–34). The difference between 2.66R̄ and 3.14R̃ is minor in most cases. Not so for 3σ̂, which will mask most special causes. We know of no situation in which 3σ̂ should be used to calculate control limits. The 3.14 and 2.66 are derived from mathematical statistical theory to give the same limits in the long run as 3σ̂ when we have pure common cause variation from an exactly bell-shaped normal distribution.

Note: $\hat{\sigma} = \sqrt{\Sigma(X - \bar{X})^2/(n-1)}$

FURTHER REFERENCES

Other useful information on the use of control charts is in:

Fundamental Statistical Process Control: Reference Manual (adopted by Ford, Chrylser, and GM); available through the Automotive Industry Action Group (313-358-3580), 1991.

Wheeler, Donald J. *Understanding Variation: The Key to Managing Chaos.* Knoxville, TN: SPC Press Inc., 1993.

Wheeler, Donald J., and David S. Chambers. *Understanding Statistical Process Control.* Knoxville, TN: SPC Press Inc., 1986.

Kume, Hitoshi. *Statistical Methods for Quality Improvement.* Tokyo: The Association for Overseas Technical Scholarship, 1985.

Notes

PART ONE

p. 5   W. Edwards Deming, *Out of the Crisis* (Cambridge, MA: MIT Center For Advanced Engineering Study, 1986). Background on Dr. Deming can be found in Mary Walton, *The Deming Management Method* (New York: Putnam, 1986).

p. 5   A useful summary of some of this background is in Marvin R. Weisbord, *Productive Workplaces: Organizing and Managing for Dignity, Meaning, and Community* (San Francisco: Jossey-Bass, 1987). There is a useful compilation of some of the benefits of these principles of management in James P. Womack, Daniel T. Jones, and Daniel Roos, *The Machine That Changed the World.* (New York: Rawson Associates, 1990).

p. 5   Ironically, the Japanese were stimulated to listen to Dr. Deming and Dr. Juran in the 1950s because they erroneously thought the Americans were practicing these concepts. See Ryuji Fukuda, *Managerial Engineering: Techniques for Improving Quality and Productivity in the Workplace.* (Cambridge, MA: Productivity Press, 1983), p. 163.

p. 9   Most people know aspects of 3rd Generation Management as "Management by Objective," or MBO. As originally crafted by Peter Drucker, MBO did not have many of the dysfunctional characteristics manifested in practice. That's why I prefer the terms "3rd Generation Management" or "management by results" to describe current management practices.

p. 17   See F. Timothy Fuller, "Eliminating Complexity from Work: Improving Productivity by Enhancing Quality," *National Productivity Review*, Autumn 1985, pp. 327–344. Tim later told me that the manager of the area that supplied components to Tim's area was not pleased because the incomplete kits stacked up in *his* area. Tim had to work hard to assure him that he was not trying to assign blame, he was trying to improve the overall process and localize the occurrence of problems. In fact, overall inventory dropped immediately because there was less work-in-process: fewer partial assemblies sitting around.

p. 20   The power of using cycle time reduction to drive improvement is described in George Stalk, Jr. and Thomas M Hout, *Competing against Time: How Time Based Competition Is Reshaping Global Markets* (New York: The Free Press [Macmillan], 1990).

p. 20   The whack-a-mole analogy was suggested to me by Charles W. Ashing III of General Electric Aircraft Engines. Many people identify with this caricature as representing much of their own work.

p. 23   The Deming Chain Reaction can be found in W. Edwards Deming, *Out of the Crisis* (Cambridge, MA: MIT Center for Advanced Engineering Study, 1986), p. 3.

p. 23   I first heard from Dr. Gipsie Ranney the concise statement, "Costs are not causes, costs come from causes."

p. 26   We based our sketch of the organization as a system on the version Dr. Deming presented in *Out of the Crisis* (Cambridge, MA: MIT Center For Advanced Engineering Study, 1986), p.4. For other information on system thinking, see W. Edwards Deming, *The New Economics: For Industry, Government, Education* (Cambridge, MA: MIT Center for Advanced Engineering Study, 1993) Chapter 3; Russell L. Ackoff, *The Art of Problem Solving* (New York: John Wiley & Sons, 1978); Peter Senge, *The Fifth Discipline: The Art and Practice of the Learning Organization* (New York: Doubleday/Currency, 1990); and Geary A. Rummler and Alan P. Brache, *Improving Performance: How to Manage the White Space on the Organization Chart* (San Francisco: Jossey-Bass, 1990).

p. 26   When preparing a video-based instructional program on 4th Generation Management, we dramatized the lesson of system optimization by filming a crew team rowing as they normally would, then asking each person to row at his or her individual best. The scull sliced easily through the water when the crew members were pacing themselves to each other; it moved sporadically at best when they were only out for themselves. (See *Fundamentals of Fourth Generation Management*, Joiner Associates Inc., 1993.)

p. 28   Several useful references on the effective use of cooperation are Alfie Kohn, *No Contest: The Case against Competition* (Boston, MA: Houghton Mifflin, 1986); John H. Carlisle and Robert C. Parker, *Beyond Negotiation: Redeeming Customer-*

Supplier Relationships (New York: John Wiley & Sons, 1989); and Roger Fisher and William Ury, *Getting to Yes: Negotiating Agreement without Giving In* (New York: Penguin Books, 1981).

p. 30 The newspaper example comes from Myron Tribus, *Quality First: Selected Papers on Quality and Productivity Improvement*. Washington, D.C.: National Society for Professional Engineers, 1987. (NSPE Publication No. 1459)

p. 34 Many years ago, Dr. Joseph M. Juran developed the notion that most problems lie within the system. See, for instance, Joseph M. Juran, "Quality Problems, Remedies, and Nostrums," *Industrial Quality Control*, June 1966, pp. 647–653. Other books of interest include Joseph M. Juran, *Juran on Leadership for Quality: An Executive Handbook* (New York: The Free Press [Macmillan, Inc.], 1989), and *Juran on Planning for Quality* (New York: The Free Press [Macmillan], 1988). At times, other writers and I have referred to this phenomenon as the 85/15 rule, since in our experience it seems like even more than 80% of the problems are beyond the control of the individual employee. Dr. Deming now says that in his experience it's more like 96/4.

p. 35 The notion of Levels of Fix arose one evening in a conversation with Robert Stiber.

p. 38 For background information about the Pareto principle, see Joseph M. Juran, *Juran's Quality Control Handbook* (New York: McGraw-Hill, 1974).

p. 40 The concepts of bottlenecks and leverage points are discussed in Eliyahu M. Goldratt and Jeff Cox, *The Goal: Excellence in Manufacturing* (Croton-on-Hudson, NY: North River Press, 1984).

p. 41 For a good perspective on the benefits of cooperation in business, see William G. Ouchi, *The M-Form Society: How American Teamwork Can Recapture the Competitive Edge* (Reading, MA: Addison-Wesley, 1984).

p. 44 For more information on PDCA, see Kaoru Ishikawa, *Introduction to Quality Control* (Tokyo: 3A Corporation, 1990), pp. 20, 37–55), and Paul Lillrank and Noriaki Kano, *Continuous Improvement: Quality Control Circles in Japanese Industries* (Ann Arbor, MI: Center for Japanese Studies, University of Michigan, 1989), pp. 21–23.

p. 48 For an excellent summary of what has been done to assess the effect of social programs, see John P. Gilbert, Richard J. Light, and Frederick Mosteller, "Assessing Social Innovations: An Empirical Base for Policy," in *Evaluation and Experiment: Some Critical Issues in Assessing Social Programs*, Carl A. Bennet and Arthur A. Lumsdaine, eds. (New York: Academic Press, 1975) pp. 39–193.

p. 51 See Gerald M. Nadler and Shozo Hibino, *Breakthrough Thinking: Why We Must Change the Way We Solve Problems and the Seven Principles to Achieve This* (Rocklin, CA: Prima Publishing & Communications, 1990).

p. 51 For more on creativity and rapid learning, see Ellen Langer, *Mindfulness* (New York: Addison-Wesley, 1989); Philip Goldberg, *The Intuitive Edge: Understanding and Developing Intuition*, (Los Angeles: Tarcher, 1983); and Roger von Oech, *A Whack on the Side of the Head: How to Unlock Your Mind for Innovation* (New York: Warner Books, 1983).

p. 54 Using the Fosbury Flop as a model of a paradigm shift was suggested to me by Ed Purdy of the Philadelphia Electric Company. Ed wanted to make sure people understood that the old method wasn't "wrong"—it was the best we knew at the time. But it would be wrong to persist in using the older method now that we know a better way.

p. 55 Harry V. Roberts and Bernard F. Sergesketter, *Quality Is Personal: A Foundation for Total Quality Management* (New York: The Free Press [Macmillan], 1993).

PART TWO

p. 63 The example of customer-focused innovation by the camera company came from Dr. Noriaki Kano.

p. 68 See David A. Garvin, "Competing on the Eight Dimensions of Quality," *Harvard Business Review*, Nov-Dec 1987, pp. 101–109.

p. 69 Dr. Noriaki Kano's model of customer perceptions is described (in Japanese) in a 1984 article "Attractive Quality and Must-Be Quality," *Journal of Japanese Society for Quality Control*, 14(2), pp. 39–48 (N. Kano, N. Seraku, F. Takahashi and S. Tsuji). See also Shane J. Schvaneveldt, Takao Enkawa and Masami Miyakawa, "Consumer Evaluation Perspectives of Service

Quality: Evaluation Factors and Two-way Model of Quality," *Total Quality Management*, Vol. 2, No. 2, 1991, pp. 149–161.

p. 72   A paper that does a nice job of showing how to use data to link customer perceptions of quality with product and service characteristics is William H. Lawton, "Design, Marketing and Quality Management" in *A Practical Guide to Quality* (Madison, WI: Joiner Associates Inc., 1993). See also John R. Hauser and Don Clausing, "The House of Quality," *Harvard Business Review*, May-June 1988.

p. 74   We refer to "reactive sources" of customer information, since in many cases the customer initiates the contact. Though sales contact is often initiated by the seller, we include it in this category because, like the other three basic sources, information about customers can be collected rather easily as a by-product of another job.

p. 84   For more information on increasing customer complaints see Kaoru Ishikawa, *Introduction to Quality Control* (Tokyo: 3A Corporation, 1990) pp. 213–215.

p. 86   This data on the effect of proper handling of complaints comes from *Increasing Customer Satisfaction through Effective Corporate Complaint Handling* (Detroit, MI: Technical Assistance Research Program [TARP], Chevrolet Motor Division, 1987).

p. 97   For more information on creating a customer focus see Carl J. Sewell and Paul B. Brown, *Customers for Life: How to Turn that One Time Buyer into a Lifetime Customer* (New York: Doubleday, 1990).

PART THREE

p. 108   Lloyd Nelson's statement can be found in W. Edwards Deming, *Out of the Crisis* (Cambridge, MA: MIT Center for Advanced Engineering Study, 1986) p. 20.

p. 111   The chart shown on page 111 is based on a simulation of Patrick Nolan's experience that we developed for instructional purposes. Patrick's actual chart is shown on the next page. As you can see, there are even more lessons; real life is always more interesting than simulations! For instance, like Patrick, you often have gaps in your data, and have to figure out how to deal with them. Also, there is a run of nine points below the

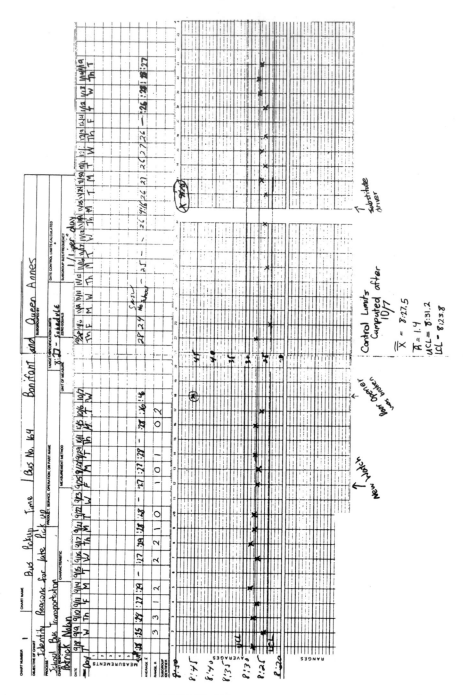

PATRICK NOLAN'S CHART

centerline near the end of Patrick's chart, an additional signal of a special cause that would have to be investigated (see the Appendix for descriptions of "tests for special causes"). In addition, Patrick calculated his control limits midway through the data collection and used a slightly different formula based on $\bar{R}$ rather than $\tilde{R}$ (again, see the Appendix for more description of how to calculate control limits).

p. 118 The rules of the funnel were developed by Dr. Lloyd S. Nelson, and popularized by W. Edwards Deming. The huge problems caused by executives asking "Why was that dot low? Why was that dot high?" were driven home to me by Dr. Deming.

p. 127 The comment "Don't just do something, stand there!" came from Dr. Edward M. Baker.

p. 128 The medication example was pointed out to me by Heero Hacquebord.

p. 141 My own thinking on the common cause strategy has been greatly aided by discussions with colleagues Rob Stiratelli and Kevin Little.

p. 153 The development of the questions that promote common cause/special cause thinking even when you can't get hard data was stimulated by conversations with Dr. Deming as he described the origin of the terms "common cause" and "special cause." Dr. Walter A. Shewhart had developed the technique of statistical control charts and the basic concepts of process capability in the 1920s. He used the terms "chance causes" and "assignable causes" to distinguish between the two major types of variation he found in processes. During the time that Dr. Deming was collaborating with Dr. Shewhart, a prison riot occurred in New York state. The public, naturally upset by the incident, kept asking why a riot had happened at that prison—what was different there? (A special cause question.) But the evidence seemed compelling to Dr. Deming. There was nothing unique or special about that prison. Rather, the factors that led to the riot were common to many prisons. Put another way, the question they asked was, "Is there something special about that prison that led to the riot, or were the conditions that produced riots common to many prisons, with the one being merely the place where it happened to occur?" This conversation with Dr. Deming led me to the question, "Is this an isolated problem or is it an example of a larger class of problems we could be having?" That question later evolved into, "Is this an isolated event or is it merely an example of a larger class of problems we are having?" This latter question has proven useful in many contexts when hard data are not available.

p. 155 The question, "Would it make any difference if we replaced these employees with an entirely new set of employees?" had some of the same origins. It arose in part from discussions concerning the Exxon Valdez disaster in which millions of gallons of oil spilled into an Alaskan sound. Dr. Deming pointed out a long time ago that:

> A fault in the interpretation of observations, seen everywhere, is to suppose that every event (defect, mistake, accident) is attributable to someone (usually the one nearest at hand), or is related to some special event. The fact is that most troubles with service and production lie in the system. (See Out of the Crisis, p. 314.)

The captain of this ship was the one nearest at hand, and, therefore, was the brunt of much of the blame initially. But subsequent investigations revealed many problems that were built into the system. A disaster was inevitable . . . eventually. This stimulated the thought that we so often blame our current problems on the employees we currently have. What would happen if we exchanged them for a different lot, produced by the same system that delivered this lot to us, and managed in the same way that this lot was managed? Might we well have the same problems again? Put another way, if a company replaced its set of sea captains with a different set—produced by the same system, managed in the same way—might that company still experience many of the same problems? The answer, in almost all cases, is yes! "Most problems with service and production lie in the system." Much more progress will be made by working on the system than by assigning blame.

p. 166 The case concerning the policy of explaining cost variances was provided to me by Dr. Thomas W. Nolan.

p. 173 The ideas inherent in the "good job" chart were called to my attention by Associate Kevin Little and apparently originates in the work of Daniel Kahneman and Amos Tversky, who have worked in the area of perception and judgment. In one study, they found that experienced flight instructors noted that "praise for an exceptionally smooth landing is typically followed by a poorer landing on the next try." As they conclude, "the failure to understand the effect of regression [variation] leads one to overestimate the effectiveness of punishment and to underestimate the effectiveness of reward." (See *Judgment under Uncertainty: Heuristics and Biases*, Daniel J. Kahneman, Paul Slovic, and Amos Tversky (eds.), [New York: Cambridge University Press, 1982] pp. 10–11, 67–68.)

PART FOUR

p. 193 The chef discovered the key elements in making popovers when taking a class on designed experiments under the late William G. Hunter. Professor Hunter documented examples from this class in "Some Ideas about Teaching Design of Experiments with 2^5 Examples of Experiments Conducted by Students," *The American Statistician*, 31:1, 1977, pp. 2–5. Two other useful sources on experimentation are George E. P. Box, William G. Hunter, and J. Stuart Hunter, *Statistics for Experimenters* (New York: John Wiley & Sons, 1978) and Ronald D. Moen, Thomas W. Nolan, and Lloyd P. Provost, *Improving Quality through Planned Experimentation* (New York: McGraw-Hill, 1991).

p. 194 For more on Frederick Taylor, see Charles D. Wrege and Ronald G. Greenwood, *Frederick W. Taylor: The Father of Scientific Management; Myth and Reality* (New York: Richard D. Irwin, 1991).

p. 196 See Kaoru Ishikawa, *Introduction to Quality Control* (Tokyo: 3A Corporation, 1990) Chapter 5.

p. 198 The eyelash learning curve sketch was drawn by Dr. Gipsie Ranney.

p. 200 Reengineering is the central theme of Michael Hammer and James Champy, *Reengineering the Corporation: A Manifesto for Business Revolution* (New York: HarperBusiness, 1993).

p. 207 In Japan, there are numerous variations of what we call the "7 Step Method." Some of these variations have 7 steps, others have 6, 8, or even 14 steps. Each tends to emphasize some particular aspect of the methodology more than others, such as solution development or understanding the current situation.

But they all follow the same basic flow. We began development of the Joiner 7 Step Method before we were aware of these other versions, but the version we use has been greatly improved by what we've learned from studying Japanese experiences with this methodology. Published versions of some type of detailed improvement or control strategy appear in Hitoshi Kume's *Statistical Methods for Quality Improvement* (Tokyo: The Association for Overseas Technical Scholarship, 1985). See also Kaoru Ishikawa, *Introduction to Quality Control* (Tokyo: 3A Corporation, 1990), pp. 71–72; Masaaki Imai, *Kaizen: The Key to Japan's Competitive Success* (New York: McGraw-Hill, 1986); Paul Lillrank and Noriaki Kano, *Continuous Improvement: Quality Control Circles in Japanese Industry* (Ann Arbor, MI: Center for Japanese Studies, University of Michigan, 1989), and *The Joiner 7 Step Method* (Madison, WI: Joiner Associates Inc., 1990).

PART FIVE

p. 225   For more information on how teams fit into a quality improvement environment, see Peter R. Scholtes, *The Team Handbook: How to Use Teams to Improve Quality* (Madison, WI: Joiner Associates Inc., 1988).

p. 226   See Alfie Kohn, *No Contest: The Case against Competition* (Boston, MA: Houghton Mifflin, 1986).

p. 229   One of the first cases in which we saw a human resource policy based on a company's intent came from the Falk Corporation.

p. 233   See John O. Whitney, *The Trust Factor: Liberating Profits & Restoring Corporate Vitality* (New York: McGraw-Hill, 1993).

p. 236   See Peter R. Scholtes, "An Elaboration on Deming's Teachings on Performance Appraisal" (Madison, WI: Joiner Associates Inc., 1987) and "Total Quality or Performance Appraisal: Choose One" (Madison, WI: Joiner Associates Inc., 1993).

p. 244   The fact that compensation is more a hygiene factor (a "Must Be") than a motivator was pointed out years ago by Frederick Herzberg, "One More Time: How Do You Motivate Employees?," *Harvard Business Review*, January-February 1968, No. 68108.

BASIC RECOMMENDATIONS FOR FURTHER STUDY

Fundamental Statistical Process Control: Reference Manual (adopted by Ford, Chrysler and GM); Available through the Automotive Industry Action Group (313-358-3580). 1991.

Brassard, Michael. *The Memory Jogger Plus+: Featuring the Seven Management and Planning Tools.* Methuen, MA: GOAL/QPC, 1989.

Deming, W. Edwards. *The New Economics: for Industry, Government, Education.* Cambridge, MA: MIT Center for Advanced Engineering Study, 1993.

Deming, W. Edwards. *Out of the Crisis.* Cambridge, MA: MIT Center for Advanced Engineering Study, 1986.

Ishikawa, Kaoru. *Introduction to Quality Control.* Tokyo: 3A Corporation, 1990.

Ishikawa, Kaoru. *What is Total Quality Control? The Japanese Way.* Englewood Cliffs, NJ: Prentice-Hall, 1985.

Juran, Joseph M. *Juran on Leadership for Quality: An Executive Handbook.* New York: The Free Press (Macmillan, Inc.), 1989.

Kume, Hitoshi. *Statistical Methods for Quality Improvement.* Tokyo: The Association for Overseas Technical Scholarship, 1985.

Scherkenbach, William W. *The Deming Route to Quality and Productivity: Road Maps and Roadblocks.* Milwaukee: ASQC Quality Press and Washington: CEE Press, 1986.

Scherkenbach, William W. *Deming's Road to Continual Improvement.* Knoxville, TN: SPC Press Inc., 1991.

Scholtes, Peter R. and other Joiner Associates. *The Team Handbook.* Madison, WI: Joiner Associates Inc., 1988.

Walton, Mary. *The Deming Management Method.* New York: Putnam Publishing, 1986.

Womack, James P., Daniel T. Jones and Daniel Roos. *The Machine that Changed the World.* New York: Rawson Associaes, 1990.

Wheeler, Donald J. *Understanding Variation: The Key to Managing Chaos.* Knoxville, TN: SPC Press Inc., 1993.

Wheeler, Donald J and David S. Chambers. *Understanding Statistical Process Control.* Knoxville, TN: SPC Press Inc., 1986.

The preceding books are available through your local business bookstore, as well as through:

American Society for Quality Control, 30 W. Wells St., Milwaukee, WI

53203; 800-248-1946 or 414-272-8575
SPC Press Inc., 5908 Toole Drive, Suite C, Knoxville, TN 37919; 800-545-8602 or 615-584-5005

Video resources:
The *Deming Library* video series. Available from Films Incorporated: 800-323-4222, ext. 44
Fundamentals of Fourth Generation Management, an eight-module video-based instructional program developed by Joiner Associates Incorporated. Available from Joiner Associates (800-669-8326 or 608-238-8134) or Films Incorporated (800-323-4222, ext. 44.)

INDEX